The Future Is Upon Us

The Future Is Upon Us

ROY L. SMITH

ABINGDON PRESS—NEW YORK • NASHVILLE

With profound appreciation of

DOCTORS J. M. & MAVIS WILLSON

Whose enlightened dedication and Christian stewardship is reflected in the lives of thousands of students who have been inspired by the lectureships their generosity has provided

Introduction

I HAVE BEEN WARNED BY THE AUTHOR OF THIS BOOK THAT THE INTRO-
duction is not to be used for paying compliments. That admonition
will be heeded, but I must say that we have been friends for many
years and that Roy L. Smith's friendship is one of my most precious
possessions. Because I know this man, it is an honor and a privilege
to speak of what will most certainly be one of his most significant
contributions. From the time I first read the manuscript of *The
Future Is Upon Us* I was sure it would be an important book.

It is a strange thing that in the very time when we have more
facts than ever before thrown at us by the newspapers, radio, and
television, we are most confused. One would think that we should
all be well informed and thinking clearly. Facts without a frame-
work of meaning to set them in, however, are contradictory and
terrifying. Sometimes it seems to me that a moratorium on news
would be a good thing, for it would give the world's nerves a chance
to grow quiet. A constant bombardment of news, which is nearly
all bad, drives men to desperation which shows itself in hysteria or
dullness.

Men like C. P. Snow point out how wide is the gap between the
humanities and the sciences. We can hardly talk across the chasm,
and men on one side often regard the men on the other side with
distrust and suspicion. Yet we live in both worlds and our lives
are affected by both fields of experience. It is a startling thing to
realize that our lives are being shaped and directed by disciplines
whose vocabularies, to say nothing of their methods and goals, are
unknown to us. We cannot expect to be experts in more than one
small field of knowledge, but we know we must be aware of the

7

forces driving our civilization toward the future. And as Dr. Smith makes clear, that future is not something we can contemplate in any leisurely manner. It rushes upon us with the speed of light, and we find ourselves passing points of no return before we are sure we were right in taking off.

Now in the midst of all this miracle of change and progress the Church often finds itself talking to itself. Its words sound archaic and abstract. Its concepts seem more appropriate to a biblical scene than to the twentieth century. We need to ask ourselves if anybody is listening except those already committed to the Christian way. Of course there are people who think the Church has no business either listening or speaking to the world. They would regard the Church as a little group of people who have removed themselves from science, politics, economics, or business. They merely comfort themselves with the hope of an end to the whole affair and an expectation of their own salvation. Since Christians spoke in tongues in the first century we have had those who eye any attempt to speak to the world or become involved in the world as a loss of holiness.

Such as these, however, do not represent Christian orthodoxy. The Church in history has been at its best when it has regarded itself as an extension of the Incarnation and the Incarnation was God's witness of his concern and involvement in the whole life of man. The Church must withdraw at times only to gather its strength for a fresh assault on evil. To live in silence and safety is not its true destiny. The more complicated the life of man becomes, the more necessary it is for the Church to keep clear for itself and for its generation the true nature of God, of man, and of the meaning of human experience.

It is extremely important for churchmen to have a broad, overall view of their world. We need to be aware of the main stream of our culture and of the forces we have set loose. Yet many churchmen will shrink from accepting the responsibility because it seems impossible to fulfill. Who has time to read books in the many fields of science? How can a busy man educate himself about things which demand long years of study? Who can be aware of the main questions we must ask, to say nothing of finding the answers? Can we leave our business and family responsibilities to travel about the world and learn firsthand about the conditions in Asia, in Africa, in South America? The answers for most of us are negative.

We are in need of help, and I believe this book will be a guide for Christians who want to understand their time. You must not expect to find here an encyclopedia to answer all questions about all subjects. Here are broad outlines and at the end of each chapter is a bibliography to help the reader who wants to explore farther. It will be an excellent study book for church groups, and it will appeal to young and old. I found information which startled me and I was confronted with facts that amazed me. Altogether, something of the wonders and the dangers confronting this generation will be sure to find any person who takes the time to read and consider.

Dr. Smith has been a world traveler for many years. He once told me he had been in eighty-two countries besides his own. He has been a student of economics and history, besides being at home in the Bible and theological studies. As a writer and editor he has grown accustomed to research, and for five years he has been reading in preparation for writing this book. He is an honored churchman and a man who has won the confidence of Christians in many communions. Roy L. Smith could not write anything without making it clear that he has the perspective of the Christian faith and the viewpoint of a Christian preacher.

Personally, I hope that *The Future Is Upon Us* will stimulate study within the churches across the nation. Let the Church become a school again, and let church members commit themselves to adult education. Well-meaning but ignorant people will be no match for men who have knowledge. Once again it is necessary that Christians be those who can out-love their enemies—but out-think them.

GERALD H. KENNEDY
Bishop of the Los Angeles Area
The Methodist Church

Preface

DURING THE MONTH OF JULY, 1957, SEVERAL THOUSAND CHURCHMEN met on the campus of Purdue University, Lafayette, Indiana, to study the problems with which the Christian Church is confronted in this first generation of the Atomic Age. I had been invited to deliver the keynote address, it having been specified that I should describe the world as it might be expected to be in 1985.

In preparing the address I found it necessary to explore a wide range of problems, some of which were strange to one whose major field has been biblical research. Within the limits of a single address it was impossible to do more than identify the issues, and following that presentation it was suggested quite numerously that the theme deserved a more comprehensive presentation. Moreover, my interest had been taken captive, and during the years that have elapsed since the conference, every hour that could be taken from imperative duties has been dedicated to study of the main matters that compose the theme.

Because the scene shifts so rapidly, it is quite probable that some statements and statistics will be outdated by the time these pages reach the reader's eye. They are offered, however, as representative of the best balanced judgment I am able to achieve in the light of present knowledge.

I am under no delusions; I am well aware of the fact that I am not an authority in the technical fields into which I have ventured. I am, at most, only a journalist who has been present when experts have debated; I have sifted through great masses of material produced by scientific commissions; I have studied scores of government reports; I have read extensively in the literature of conflict;

11

and I have traveled widely in most of the lands intimately related to the tensions implicit in the years that lie ahead. It is inevitable that, having been engaged professionally in religious work for more than half a century, I should attempt to interpret the issues in terms of Christian convictions.

No book that ventures into such fields as are introduced in this volume could possibly be written by one individual. Editors, specialists, scientists, newspaper correspondents, government officials, librarians, and university professors have rendered great assistance. Special mention is made in the footnotes of various writings that have been of conspicuous aid.

In an effort to provide interested readers with information concerning additional sources of evidence, I have appended a brief bibliography to each chapter. No effort has been made to assess the respective merits of the various volumes, it being assumed that the reader is entirely competent to decide such matters for himself. It would be inevitable that much contradictory opinion is to be found in these writings, and this is a part of the value of the listing.

A special word of thanks is tendered herewith to Bishop Gerald H. Kennedy who has encouraged me since the project was first mentioned and who has contributed an illuminating introduction.

It is with a persistent hope that the Christian Church will find some way to bring a Christian conscience to bear on the contemporary scene, that this volume is offered as one man's effort to face the fact that *The Future Is Upon Us*.

Roy L. Smith

Contents

1

Defining the Issues

HARRY EMERSON FOSDICK, PREACHING ON THE TEXT "ONE DAY IS AS A thousand years," once said, "There is no democracy among days." A single event such as the publication of *Das Kapital*, the discovery of America, or the crucifixion of Jesus, may hold greater significance for the generations unborn than whole centuries in a stagnant period of history. It is of the utmost importance, especially to Christians, that we shall recognize the fact that we ourselves are living at such a time.

In the latter part of the eighteenth and the early part of the nineteenth century the life of England underwent a transformation which completely remodeled the nation. A new land philosophy developed; small towns became great manufacturing cities; the factory system made the English an industrialized people; and an accompanying series of social horrors appeared with which neither the government nor the people were prepared to cope. Congestion, health problems, child labor in its worst forms, and the exploitation of the laboring classes called for an entirely new treatment, including unprecedented legislation. The invention of the steam engine made abundant power available, and the tide of migration from the rural districts to the factory towns insured a numerous labor force for the new factories.

It had long been the custom on the English farms to put the children to work in the fields. Since England lacked anything like an adequate educational system to provide public schools illiteracy was a commonplace, and when the farmer's family moved to the factory town the father of the family saw little difference between his child's working in the field and the same child's working at a machine. Every child was viewed as an economic asset inside the family circle. Orphans were regarded as being only a little more than property. The resulting conditions constitute one of the shabbiest chapters in all the history of the "tight little isle."

This total upheaval in the nation's life has come to be known as the Industrial Revolution, and a revolution it was. England moved over from an agricultural to an industrial economy; agriculture was reorganized on an entirely new base; merchants and manufacturers came to dominate the life of the land; protective labor laws were enacted by a reluctant Parliament. There was no secret about it; nothing was kept under cover. The whole nation was groping its way toward the light, and public concerns were discussed freely. Germinative ideas were on the march, and England was swept up into a manner of life and experience for which the nation was quite unprepared either spiritually or economically. The change came about not as a result of a royal decree, nor was it forced upon the people by armed revolutionaries. Evolutionary forces were at work, and they could not be resisted.

Sir Charles Snow, the eminent author-scientist, has pointed out an extremely important fact in connection with the Industrial Revolution, in which there is both a hint and a warning for our times. He makes the damning statement that the intellectual leaders of England—authors, essayists, poets, philosophers, theologians—were quite unaware of the change that was coming over the land. The "civilized" segment of English society seems to have been oblivious to the fact that one culture was on its way out and another culture was on its way in. They lived out their days unmindful of the forces that were altering almost every aspect of life before their very eyes. The clergy were numbered among these.

Methodists have extolled the piety and the theology of John Wesley and have pointed with pride to his "concern for the poor." In this they have been well justified, for the famous preacher founded orphanages, schools, and other helpful agencies. He wrote vigorous letters to King George III pointing out the poverty of the people and protesting various parliamentary enactments. He went into the fields and preached to people who never darkened the door of the church. He seems, however, to have been as unaware of the operation of powerful social forces as were any of the other intellectuals. If one reads those of his sermons that have come down to us in print he gets no hint whatever that they were preached originally in the midst of a revolution. Nowhere does he indicate that he sensed the tragedy of the English factory child, nor does he seem to even know that thousands of English women

16

worked, near nude, with iron collars riveted about their necks in English coal mines, being allowed to come to the surface for air but once a week for a three-hour period.

Let none of the foregoing be interpreted as meaning that either Wesley or the intellectuals were unsympathetic with the poor of England. Their basic failure, and the failure of the time, was not callousness, but incomprehension. They simply did not understand the age of which they were a part.

The tragedies associated with the Industrial Revolution in England make crystal clear one of the major responsibilities of today's Christian citizens. Before we can render a redemptive service to our generation we must know its basic needs, and we must understand the forces and influences at work in society. We must judge between those that are destructive and those that are constructive. The sensitivity of Jesus must be applied to the problems of the people, and this means the people of the whole world. To make such an application is not an "elective" for our times. It is one of the "required courses" of the Atomic Age. The Sunday morning worship service in every church in the land ought to be an occasion, not when we achieve simple peace of mind, but when we come together to get our marching orders for the week. The service itself should be the most informing, disturbing, and instructive hour through which any of us sit during the week.

There is nothing more tragic in the life of a nation—or of an individual—than to assume we are on a joy ride when we are headed for an abyss. It is a part of the duty of the Church to interpret the times to the people, and this makes it necessary, on occasions, to pronounce doom. Even more, to interpret the future that is already upon us calls for a social and spiritual sensitivity the Church, generally, has not yet achieved. It remains to be seen whether or not this generation of Christians is able to summon minds and consciences in sufficient measure to make a continuing contribution to the solution of global problems with which we are faced. There could be no more tragic failure in all of human history than that we should allow the greatest revolution of all time to take place before our eyes without our recognizing or understanding the circumstances that underlie it.

There are those problems, of course, which must be described as being local, or at most, national, in their significance. Racial

17

segregation takes on a variety of forms, and in every case is an acute issue. The segregation problem which the people of the United States face, however, is very different from the doctrine of apartheid which is characteristic of South Africa. In each case the solution calls for a different approach, that approach being a local responsibility. Although the Algerian struggle is destined to have international repercussions, the solution of the problem lies with the French. More than 11,000,000 refugees constitute a problem for West Germany which is shared by no other nation in Europe or the Americas. On the other hand, the antiquated colonial policy of Portugal is a matter of world concern, although the Salazar government is doing everything in its power to defend it as a domestic question.

The chief characteristic of the future that is already upon us is the fact that our generation faces a series of problems which must be solved on a global basis or they will not be solved. Wendell Willkie returned from a world trip less than a generation ago, with the solemn warning to the American people that they had begun to live in "one world." The trends he had discovered in more than fifty world centers had convinced him that it was impossible for any nation to live apart from the rest of the world. There were threats in the overhanging skies that would be dissipated by worldwide action or they would not be dissolved at all.

In the situation in which the American people find themselves today there is a succession of domestic issues that can never be resolved until certain world issues have been settled. There can be no lowering of taxes, for example, until the threat of war has passed or until the economies of the underdeveloped areas have been turned upward. This means that if Christianity or the Church proposes to lead the way to redemption they must be prepared to move in on the world scene. There are those who would restrict the concerns of the Church to the issues of private lives and living, but this is to fail to sense the comprehensive character of the Christian message to the world.

R. A. Tawney, the British historian, tells the story of an English nobleman of a hundred years ago who became greatly irritated by the preaching to which he listened. "Things have come to a pretty pass," he said, "when religion is allowed to interfere with a man's private life." In similar vein there are those modern men who say,

"Things have come to a pretty pass if religion is going to move out into the fields of economics, politics, and international affairs." If redemption is needed in those fields, then those are good fields for good religion. To fail to extend the principle of redemption to those forces and influences which injure nations and peoples is to fail as certainly as if we failed in the matter of personal morals.

It becomes the duty of the Church and of Christian men to look frankly and fearlessly at four towering facts.

1. *The whole world is experiencing a population explosion which is capable of threatening the extinction of the human race.*

The demographers of the world are rather generally agreed that the population of the earth in the year 10,000 B.C., may have numbered as many as 1,000,000 persons. Estimates of the total population of the earth at the dawn of the Christian Era vary from 200,000,000 to 300,000,000. During the next 1650 years—until about the time of the founding of the Plymouth and Jamestown colonies in the New World—the global population doubled and in doing so achieved a total of 600,000,000. During the next three hundred years it quadrupled and by 1945 had reached a total of 2,600,000,000. Early in 1961 the population statisticians of the United Nations announced that the 3,000,000,000 mark had been passed and predicted that a 4,000,000,000 total will have been reached by 1975. If the trend of the last twenty-five years continues the earth will be peopled by 7,000,000,000 persons in the lifetime of individuals now living.

It calls for no crystal ball or scientific forecast to imagine some of the conditions which will prevail, in the United States, for example, when 2½ persons try to live, grow, maintain their health, get an education, and earn a living where one person is now trying to do those same things. This is only to suggest that the responsibility for providing education, medical care, housing, transportation, utility services, food, recreation, religious training, and government for 450,000,000 people in the United States where there are now 180,000,000 will transcend anything we are capable of imagining today.

Some few of the global aspects of this problem of an exploding population will be discussed in Chapters 2, 3, 4, and 5.

2. *Our world is experiencing a scientific breakthrough quite without precedent in all the history of the race.*

The dropping of the bomb on Hiroshima had the dramatic effect of catapulting the world into an awareness of the fact that we had suddenly moved over into the Atomic Age. Within the space of hours following the first announcement of the explosion of the bomb, one writer described it by saying, "An age has been born before our eyes."

No one man ever lived to see the beginning or the ending of the Ice Age, for the dawning and the setting of that period in the earth's history extended over many centuries. Neither did any man witness the beginning or the end of the Stone, the Bronze, or the Iron Age. But our generation moved into the Atomic Age between midnight and sunrise, and within a matter of hours that fact was recognized. If there is still confusion in the minds of plain people as to the precise meaning of the transition that should occasion no surprise. Actually, the wonder is that so large a portion of the world's population has accommodated itself to the new facts and forces so readily.

There is a potential revolution in the fact that we are now equipped with the scientific techniques, the economic and the industrial skills, and the paraphernalia of productivity which would enable us to banish hunger, disease, and illiteracy from the earth— if our resources could be liberated from military necessities and put at the disposal of architects of peace.

An exploration of the scientific breakthrough will be undertaken in Chapters 6, 7, and 8.

3. *Throughout the world, particularly in the so-called under-developed areas, there is in progress a mighty revolution of rising expectations.*

At least three factors have contributed to the deadly fatalism which has heretofore possessed many of the peoples of the so-called underdeveloped areas of the earth. (1) For nearly three hundred years hundreds of millions of the people of Asia and Africa have lived under a colonialism that has had the effect of stifling ambition and discouraging initiative. (2) For hundreds of years the spiritual leaders have taught the people that there was nothing they could do about their wretchedness. If misfortune overtook a man, rendering him helpless, it was explained as being "the will of the gods." Therefore, it was not to be resisted. (3) There has been no inspiring spiritual tradition to the effect that there is one divine authority whose will is the highest law of humanity and whose purpose is to lead men out of helplessness into magnificence.

Men who were hungry, diseased, ignorant, or wretched, without means of escape, have had an inclination to sink back into despair, consoling themselves meanwhile with the thought that their sufferings were a result of the will of the supernatural powers. Therefore, there was no hope except in submission. Social, economic, and political factors have made their own contributions to this fatalistic interpretation of life.

This widespread fatalism, however, is giving way to hope. Millions have become convinced that there *is* something they can do about their wretchedness, and they propose to do it. There is no general agreement as to what that something is, but at least this much is true. The peoples of the underdeveloped areas are breaking with their despair and are on the march—searching, questioning, weighing, and considering.

A study of this phenomenon will be presented in Chapters 9 and 10.

4. A desperate war is on in which two ideologies diametrically opposed in both method and objective are contending for possession of the world's minds.

There have been other periods in history when the balance of power has been achieved by establishing an equilibrium between two powerful alliances. The present cold war is of an entirely different sort, however. Its causes are new; its weaponry is novel; its strategy represents global planning; the ultimate objectives of the contending forces are completely different; and the outcome is packed with destiny for all men now living or yet to live.

There is a mistaken disposition on the part of the American public in particular to identify the present world struggles with certain individuals—Khrushchev, Mao Tse-tung, Marshal Tito, Fidel Castro, et cetera. But the roots go far deeper than the interests or opinions of any one individual, or even group of individuals. The world rightly judged Hitler to be a world menace. His ambitions were highly personal. The Central Committee of the Communist party is something entirely different, however. In spite of the fact that Communism has thus far been guided by certain powerful personalities, those individuals have been incidental. If, for example, Nikita Khrushchev were not in the driver's seat in

Moscow another Communist equally dedicated and equally difficult would be. The struggle will go on long after today's leaders of Communism are dead and buried. We are not at war with persons, but with ideas—with what the apostle Paul once called "principalities and powers." The struggle to which we are witnesses is a phenomenon entirely new among men and nations.

The current struggle between Communism and democracy—between "the East" and "the West"—calls for an entirely new approach. It is a war entirely different from any war ever fought between men. Not only is it true that every citizen of every contending nation is, or is to be, in the front lines, it is also true that every man's possessions, ideals, hopes, and convictions are involved in the struggle. In the strategy of the Communist leaders there are no permanent neutrals. The neutral of today is to be the object of attack tomorrow. According to Communist philosophy and design every nation and every race in the world is ultimately to be brought under Communist control. Any neutral nation is only one that has been allowed a breathing spell until the more immediate resistance has been liquidated, but liquidation is to be the eventual fate of every opposing political organization.

Because of the complexity of the Communist issue with which we are confronted and because such vast stakes are involved, it is necessary to extend the discussion of this subject through seven chapters—10, 11, 12, 13, 14, 15, and 16. Even so, this global problem can be presented only in its barest outlines.

Suggestions for Further Reading

"The Fabulous Fifteen Years Ahead." Reprint from *Changing Times*, THE KIPLINGER MAGAZINE (January, 1961).

Fischer, Louis. *Russia, America, and the World*. New York: Harper & Brothers, 1962.

Goals for Americans. Edited by the President's Commission on National Goals. Englewood Cliffs, N. J.: Prentice-Hall, Inc., 1960.

Manikam, Rajah B., editor. *Christianity and the Asian Revolution*. New York: Friendship Press, 1955.

Scott, John. *Democracy Is Not Enough*. New York: Harcourt, Brace & World, Inc., 1960.

Snow, Charles. *The Two Cultures and the Scientific Revolution*. New York: Cambridge University Press, 1959.

2

The Population Explosion

THERE IS SOMETHING IRONICAL ABOUT THE FACT THAT ONE OF THE most difficult problems with which we have to deal, with the incoming of the Atomic Age, is a direct result of one of our most conspicuous scientific successes. As we have lowered the death rates around the world we now find ourselves in the midst of a population explosion.

About the year 1930 a general decline appeared in the death rates everywhere, and since that time, in spite of wars, famines, and other calamities, it has continued its nose dive. The result is that the gap between death rates and birth rates has widened amazingly. With the close of World War 11 the use of antibiotics and insecticides boomed, and at the same time the death rate went into a further decline. The total effect has been a problem called people.

Karl Sax, the Harvard demographer, estimates the population growth of the world at about 40,000,000 per year. Other authorities put it as high as 50,000,000. There may be variations in estimates, but all population scientists agree that the upsurge is creating a crisis. Provision must be made for caring for perhaps as many as 1,500,000,000 additional human beings by 1985. This is equivalent to three times the population of both North and South America in 1960.

On January 1, 1960, the Population Reference Bureau estimated that the population of the United States in 1985 would exceed 275,000,000. The 4,000,000 added to the total every year is in excess of the population of any one of twenty-two states in the Union, or considerably more than four times the combined populations of Alaska and Hawaii at the times of their admissions. When our population has doubled by A.D. 2000, as we may expect it to do, we shall have more than half that of China in 1962.

The average American baby born in 1962 will live 21.5 years longer than his grandparents who were born in 1900. In December, 1959, the American Medical Association, meeting in Dallas, was warned that an average life expectancy of one hundred years was actually in sight. By the time 1985 has rolled around we shall be registering new births at the rate of 6,000,000 per year and witnessing the establishment of 2,000,000 new homes annually.

In Asia some populations are doubling each twenty-five years and within twenty years will be growing at a rate that will see them doubling in seventeen or eighteen years by A.D. 2000.

Some appreciation of the gravity of the global situation appears as we consider the circumstances which prevail in Japan.

From the 30,000,000 population at the time of Commodore Perry's arrival, Japan grew to 35,000,000 twenty years later in 1873; to some 40,000,000 by 1900; and to 55,000,000 in 1920 when the first census was taken. By the time of the attack on Pearl Harbor there were 73,000,000 Japanese in Japan and another 3,000,000 scattered around the Empire and the rest of the world.[1]

By 1960 the total had risen to over 93,000,000. Japan, therefore, has 11,000,000 more people to feed, clothe, and employ than at the time of the nation's surrender in 1945, the natural increase being 1,500,000 per year.[2] All this, it must be remembered, has come about in spite of the fact that the nation has been engaged in five major wars since 1895.

In 1948 the Japanese government became alarmed by the fact that 20 per cent of the nation's food supply had to be imported and by the additional fact that the adverse outcome of the war had deprived the empire of many of its natural markets. Therefore the government set out to bring the birth rate and the death rate into balance. That year the sale of contraceptives was authorized by the Diet, and health offices were set up throughout the nation to instruct the people in the matter of birth control. Abortions and sterilizations were legalized, and according to the press reports of August, 1958, legal abortions during the previous twelve months had numbered 1,300,000, with an additional 500,000 having been performed outside the "mother's health protection law." The overall effect has been a dramatic lowering of the birth rate from 34.3

[1] From *Too Many Asians* by John C. Robbins, p. 162. Copyright © 1959 by John C. Robbins. Reprinted by permission of Doubleday & Company, Inc.
[2] William Vogt, *People* (New York: William Morrow & Company, 1960), p. 162.

per thousand in 1947, to 17.2 by 1957. If the current trend is maintained a population gain may be expected to continue, though at a diminishing rate, until 1985, when there is some assurance of a leveling off, and stabilization may occur at the point of about 100,000,000.

The necessity of checking the upsurge of population in Japan is only little more immediate than in many another area of the world, though the Japanese situation has its own peculiar aspects. The total land area available for cultivation is approximately 17 per cent of the land area of California and cannot be increased by more than 5 per cent. Those acres now under cultivation are producing a higher caloric average than any other cultivated land in the world. The most scientific techniques are already in use, and the nation is supplementing its diet by the use of more seafood per capita than any other nation. The caloric intake of the average Japanese, though much higher than that of any other Asiatic, is only a little more than half that of the average American or Canadian. This is to say that in the present state of affairs in Japan we have a forecast of the situation to be faced by the best situated areas of the world in the year 2000. Nation after nation, on every continent, is face to face with the same conditions in greater or less degree, the effects of which demand immediate study.

Asia, with 1,552,000,000 people in 1957, can be expected to have a total of 3,870,000,000 in the year 2000 and may even cross the 4,000,000,000 mark. Africa with 240,000,000 will grow to 517,000,-000. Russia with 204,000,000 will increase to 379,000,000.[3] With the birth rates of almost all Asian nations exceeding 40 per thousand, the population explosion becomes a question of survival throughout the world.

The causes of the explosion are not hard to see. Throughout the earth the lowering of the death rate, to which reference has been made, has changed the aspect of every nation's life. During the decade from 1947 to 1957 the world death rate dropped from 22-25 per thousand to 18—according to statistics furnished by the United Nations Population Branch.[4] One major killer after another has been put to rout by the use of antibiotics and insecticides.

[3] Newsweek Magazine (April 27, 1959), p. 67.
[4] R. M. Fagley, The Population Explosion and Christian Responsibility (New York: Oxford University Press, 1960), p. 28.

The beginning of the victory over epidemics due to microbic infections accompanied the birth of biology. When Louis Pasteur paved the way for the vaccination for rabies and later supervised the vaccination of thousands of sheep he put into the hands of mankind one of its major weapons of defense against a long series of diseases. In a single year, 1884, the microbic bases of three infectious diseases were discovered: Loeffler found the bacterium of diphtheria, Nikolaier that of tetanus, and Frankle the cause of pneumonia. In 1894 the bacillus of the plague was found; in 1897 the cause of leprosy was identified; and in 1901 the Spirochaeta pallida was discovered to be the cause of syphilis.

From the identification of the causative bacillus to the compounding of the prophylactic is usually but a short step. In the case of malaria it was discovered that spraying with DDT had the effect of destroying the bacillus-carrying mosquito. Thereupon a global war was declared on the disease. The World Health Organization (WHO), operating under the United Nations, set up a pilot project in Ceylon which cut the death rate from twenty to ten per thousand. The results obtained in Greece were only a little less spectacular, and a similar campaign carried on in Bengal, Pakistan, was responsible for an increase of 15 per cent in the rice yields because of the increased ability of the workers to care for the growing crops.

In the war on malaria the saving of life is not the only gain. Whereas 65 per cent of the Ceylonese workers had not been able to work more than 60 per cent of the time because of malarial infection, the scientific approach to the problem improved the situation so that less than 5 per cent of the working time is now lost. A similar saving of time has been achieved in the case of yaws. Even endemic syphilis has been eliminated in many areas by the use of inexpensive penicillin.

Conspicuous in the prophylactic program has been the saving of life among young mothers and the newborn. Between the years 1880 and 1900 the death rate for all children in western Europe from all diseases was approximately 22 per cent; today it is between 3 and 5 per cent. According to a study made in 1855 the life expectancy of a child born in the United States was 40 years.[5] In 1960 the figure had risen to 70.8 years. In the years since World War I

[5] Heinz Wolterek, *A New Life in Your Later Years* (New York: The Dial Press, 1959), p. 33.

this index has increased 7 years in Australia and New Zealand, 8 in Denmark, 10 in Sweden, 12-13 in England, and 14 in the United States. In Ceylon, due to the spectacular success of the anti-malarial campaign, the expectancy has gone from 32.7 to 60.3 for men and from 30.7 to 59.4 for women.

While it is true that advances in medical sciences have been responsible for some of the most spectacular results in lowering death rates, there is another factor which must be taken into the account. Previous to 1940 the British, Dutch, and French governments made more or less serious efforts to protect the various Asian peoples for whom they were responsible in matters of health, infections, and epidemics. The color races are slow to admit that the colonial powers rendered them any service whatever, but the facts speak for themselves. Whatever criticism may be leveled at the occupying powers, it must be admitted that in many cases they left behind them some rather extraordinary results. Mass programs of sanitation, water supplies, vaccinations, and endemic controls of one sort and another were launched. Epidemics of various kinds were stamped out. The Christian missionary efforts were unusually effective, and with the exception of very rare instances, the standards of missionary medical institutions were high. In addition to the actual medical services rendered, such matters as flood control, highways, improved communications, and food inspections contributed to improved sanitary conditions, and these in turn made their contribution to public health. In addition there were the various research projects fostered by great philanthropic groups. Campaigns launched by private initiative blazed the trails for official action later.

With the conclusion of World War II and the sudden rise of new and independent governments interest in the question of public health mushroomed. Here was an area in which results could be obtained quickly. The new governments, anxious to rivet themselves in power, seized on offers of assistance from the United States and the United Nations and launched prophylactic programs of various kinds. Penicillin with which to treat yaws and syphilis became available in quantity. A million Javanese were freed from the terrors of the former within the space of months.

Any energetic health minister of a new government with sizeable funds at his disposal was in a position to work miracles almost overnight. Only rarely was he under the necessity of getting the permission of those who needed treatment. His own government was only mildly interested in the matter of expense, for the funds usually came from the outside. Spraying with DDT did not call for any expensive election or extended educational program. As the governments moved in the people became conditioned to expect that their problems would be solved for them. The party in power was credited for any improvements that resulted, and the colonial powers were blamed for all failures.

From all the foregoing it is evident that the population explosion is in very large part the result of a scientific breakthrough. The increased use of prophylactics, antibiotics, vaccinations, and public health measures has had the effect of lowering death rates everywhere. In the meantime the birth rate is ascending because of the better health of mothers during the childbearing period of their lives. In 1958 the Population Commission of the United Nations dealt realistically with the problem in a booklet entitled *The Future Growth of World Population.* "With the present rate of increase," the Commission said, "it can be calculated that in 600 years the number of human beings will be such that there will be only one square meter for each to live on."

Simple logic and common sense call for a forthright judgment. Some way must be found to halt this prodigious growth or the end will be be tragic disaster.

Suggestions for Further Reading

Brown, Harrison. *The Challenge of Man's Future.* New York: The Viking Press, 1956.

Fagley, R. M. *The Population Explosion and Christian Responsibility.* New York: Oxford University Press, 1960.

Robbins, John. *Too Many Asians.* Garden City, N.Y.: Doubleday & Company, 1959.

Sauvy, Alfred. *Fertility and Survival.* New York: Criterion Books, Inc., 1961.

Sax, Karl. *The Population Explosion.* New York: Foreign Policy Association, 1956.

Stuart, Alexander J. *Overpopulation: Twentieth Century Nemesis.* New York: The Exposition Press, 1958.

Vogt, William. *People: The Challenge to Survival.* New York: William Morrow & Company, 1960.

3

Give Us Tomorrow Our Daily Bread

THE MAJOR QUESTION EMERGING FROM OUR EXAMINATION OF THE population explosion is how an additional 1,400,000,000 human beings are to be fed, housed, clothed, educated, provided with employment and medical care, and trained for responsible citizenship in a scientific age. Even in a land which enjoys an advanced development, such as the United States, this problem is colossal.

We should realize that much more is involved in the population explosion than the threat of Communism, important as that is. The problem of population growth concerns the future of the human race. Each new starving belly among the millions of already hungry Asians adds to the sum total of human misery by an amount almost measureable. If humanity is to have a future, the unrestricted growth of population in already overcrowded lands must be brought to a halt.[1]

Even in the United States by the year 2000, which is not as far away as the beginning of World War I, the population will have doubled, and it is confidently expected that the food shortage will already have become a problem. As for Asiatic nations such as Ceylon, economists and demographers admit that there is no foreseeable possibility of the national production coming anywhere near matching the present rates of population increase. By what logic is it possible to assume that the world is better off because people have been saved from malaria, to die of hunger?

Life in a scientific age calls for skills and disciplines not required in a primitive age. It also depends upon the development of moral character, social responsibility, and political competence. As a practical matter, however, the problem of food moves up to the head of the line. We have passed the point where we can ignore the starvation which is endemic in the world today.

[1] Robbins, *Too Many Asians*, p. 18. Used by permission.

The terrible truth is that the people in many lands have less to eat than they had fifty years ago. On a worldwide basis mankind has been losing the race between food and population since the turn of the century.[2]

The cruel discrepancy between per capita food production in the developed and in the underdeveloped countries has widened instead of narrowed. Whereas in Europe the prewar level in per capita food production has been regained, and in the United States and Canada it has been exceeded, in the Far East (the figures include India and Pakistan, but not communist China) it has dropped off almost 15 per cent.[3]

In 1951 the Food and Agricultural Organization of the United Nations reported: "Most of those who were hungry in the five prewar years are now hungrier. . . . Production in most of the undernourished areas is failing to keep pace with the population growth." [4] There is no more grim fact anywhere on the horizon than this—that the gap between food and population is widening, in spite of (or perhaps because of) industrialization. Day by day the food deficit grows. There are other areas of course which face desperately serious problems in this regard, but because the 440,000,000 of India constitute so large a percentage of the total population of the earth, and because the birth rate is gaining rapidly over the death rate, this creating an acute crisis, it seems fair to cite the concerns of the Indian government in this connection. In 1951 the Government of India Planning Commission, after a thorough and scientific study of the nation's resources and all probabilities of help from the outside, concluded that the population of the sub-continent was to be relatively less well fed every year for a considerable time to come. So far as they could see there was no light on the horizon.[5]

No more than 25 per cent of the world's population enjoys a

[2] "The high dietary standard enjoyed by those of us who live in the United States is shared only by . . . about 9 per cent of the world population." Harrison Brown, et al., *The Next Hundred Years* (New York: The Viking Press, 1957), p. 54.

[3] Jonathan Bingham, *Shirtsleeve Diplomacy* (New York: The John Day Company, 1954), p. 42.

[4] Harrison Brown, *The Challenge of Man's Future* (New York: The Viking Press, 1954), p. 60.

[5] *Ibid.*, pp. 58-61.

diet in excess of 2,750 calories. Another 20 per cent must subsist on one containing 2,250 to 2,750 calories, and the remaining 55 per cent must get along on less. Perhaps as many as 1,500,000,000 human beings are eking out an existence on a caloric intake of 1,400 calories per day, or even less, which is about the level of a concentration camp.

To measure the world's diets in terms of calories is to overlook one of the most important aspects of the food problem—*vitamins.* Mere bulk is not sufficient to sustain life. Actually, 58 per cent of the people of the world are living on a diet that contains less than 5 per cent animal protein, and literally millions get no more than 1 or 2 per cent. Tens of millions do not taste meat six times a year. If the vitamin content of such diets were to be taken as the index we should have to say that no more than 17 per cent of the world's population is adequately fed. It is not just a matter of poverty. If every person in the world should suddenly come into possession of $100 and undertake to buy food, it would be impossible for all to get one complete meal, for the food does not exist. Neither can it be produced under contemporary conditions.

If the inhabitants of this earth are to be fed in any adequate degree at least five major alterations must be made in the present pattern of food production: (1) More acres must be brought under cultivation. (2) All acres now cultivated must be compelled to produce more. (3) New foods of greater nutritional value must be introduced into the world's diet. (4) Greater use must be made of marine materials which have nutritional values. (5) A start must be made in industrializing the underdeveloped nations.

1. Can the world's acreage be expanded?

The total land area of the earth amounts to approximately 36,000,000,000 acres, of which amount 10 per cent is covered perpetually with snow and ice. Another 4 per cent is in such areas as Alaska and Siberia where the growing season is limited to about ten weeks. Desert regions account for another 20 per cent. Then there are eroded lands and depleted soils upon which no dependence can be placed. Mountainous regions which offer no hope of food production represent a further subtraction, leaving about 2,500,-000,000 acres, which is an average of less than one acre per person for the present population. Of this acreage a substantial part is cultivated for the purpose of producing fibers, grazing sheep and other small animals, and producing food for horses, camels, donkeys, oxen, water buffalo, et cetera. Conservative scientists have estimated that 2.5 acres are needed to produce the food for an adequate diet for one person. This means that we already face a land deficit, and the problem is by no means academic.

Approximately 200,000,000 acres of the world's lands are now under irrigation, and it is estimated that an additional 1,000,000,000 acres of humid or sub-humid land could benefit from supplemental irrigation. Such irrigation of land now being cultivated and complete irrigation of an additional 200,000,000 acres of desert land could be expected to double present world food production.[6]

Irrigating arid land, however, is not the simple task it appears to be. Producing cabbages and carrots is a delicate operation which calls for an understanding of soil chemistry, crop rotation, some elements of agronomy, and a dozen other technical matters. The soil must contain a balanced ration of salts of various kinds; the water must be applied at precise periods of growth; and artificial fertilizer must be added to make up for any mineral deficiencies in the soil.

Water that falls upon the soil in the form of rain is said to be "soft" for the reason that it contains no mineral salts. Applied to the land it does not alter the mineral balance. Irrigation water is another matter, however. Water taken from surface streams has flowed over a succession of mineral deposits in the process of coming down from the mountains, and when this impregnated water is spread out over the land it carries these accumulated salts down to the roots of the plants where, under some circumstances, they may act like a vegetable poison. In the great Imperial Valley of California, which is irrigated with water from the Colorado River, the growers find it necessary to leach the soil at regular intervals to cleanse it of the excess salts. This is an expensive process that calls for great skill.

In certain sections of Texas, on the other hand, irrigation depends upon water drawn up from deep wells. All water obtained above the four-hundred-foot level is so saline that it destroys the vegetation. It becomes necessary, therefore, to go down to 1,200 to 1,800 feet to tap waters free from mineral contaminants. In another section it is necessary to tap surface waters and avoid

[6] *Ibid.*, pp. 137-38.

the deep flowing streams. The overall problems are as varied as the tracts to be irrigated.

Simple tube-well irrigation has brought about crop increases of 45 to 100 per cent in India. Without irrigation optimum use of water is impossible. Irrigation itself, however, creates complications. It requires, for example, that there be adequate drainage to avoid waterlogging of soils and excessive concentration of salts in the irrigated farmlands. It is said that 3,000,000 acres have gone out of cultivation in the Punjab alone from this cause.[7]

Additional difficulties are encountered in the Punjab, however, due to the fact that the capillary action of the water draws up strong alkalis from the subsoil which destroy its fertility.

The archaeological ruins of the great southwest section of the United States indicate that as long ago as a thousand years a lush civilization flourished throughout what is now the states of Arizona, New Mexico, and parts of Utah and Colorado. Then about five hundred years ago the Indians abandoned their cliff dwellings and disappeared. The reason remained a mystery for many years, but scientists are now convinced that the soil of such valleys as the Salt River and the lower Colorado became impregnated with minerals washed down from the heights and as a consequence failed to produce the necessary food supplies. The remains of an extensive irrigation system are to be seen over a wide area today in the vicinity of Phoenix, but because those primitive farmers did not understand the delicate chemistry of the soil, they unwittingly mineralized the good earth and thereby sealed their doom. The ancient canals were a model of engineering skill and worked perfectly up to the day they were abandoned. The soil revolted, however, and four hundred years of idleness has been required to sweeten it again.

For many years scientists have wrestled with the problem of desalinizing sea water. Actually, it is now possible to distill pure water from ocean water at about the cost of bottled water, but if it is ever to be of practical use to the desert farmer the cost must be reduced to something less than $10 per acre-foot. At that price the agriculturalist is under the necessity of spending about $30

[7] Vogt, *People*, p. 136.

per acre per year for each acre farmed. Comparable costs in India and Pakistan, for example, would be prohibitive. The complicated problem of fertilizing and leaching irrigated soil is such that only skilled farmers are capable of handling the situation. The alternative is a vast state project, socialistic by nature, in which a few experts take over the management in behalf of the unskilled tillers of the soil.

In the United States the irrigating farmer usually has an investment in 160 acres approximately equal to that of the department-store operator in the county seat. Any such investment on the part of the Indian or Pakistan farmer is out of the question. The only possible solution is a government project with large-scale credit to the individual farmer. The strain on the economy of any of the Asian governments would be extremely dangerous, and the management would of necessity be socialistic in character.

It is true, of course, that irrigation may solve a local problem, but on a nationwide basis there is another, and extremely serious, problem to be faced. *There is not enough fresh water on the earth's surface to cultivate the acres now under cultivation.* To bring more acres under the plow is a little like bringing more babies into the world to starve.

Approximately 11 per cent of the cultivated areas of the world today are watered by irrigation. If all the rivers in the world could be brought under control and their waters equitably applied to the soil, this total could be increased to as much as 14 per cent, or under extremely favorable circumstances to 20 per cent. To achieve the latter figure it would be necessary to negotiate difficult treaties between suspicious and jealous governments and to satisfy the demands of half a hundred flaming nationalisms. Special groups that have long enjoyed special privileges would have to be appeased. In the case of many of the eighty-two major rivers that empty their waters into the oceans the streams flow through two, three, or even four countries, each of which claims certain "historic rights." Rarely can a river be treated as a single unit, as in the case of the Tennessee.

The world's supply of water is diminishing at the very moment that the population is exploding. The total amount of moisture on the surface of the earth is fixed, just as are the weight and the chemical composition of the globe. There never will be any more water than there is at this moment, for no water reaches the earth from outer space and no chemical process is in operation which changes elements into water. The salinity of the sea is gradually increasing. The pressure on the scientists and engineers to find some way to "convert" sea water by an inexpensive method is growing by the year.

The geography textbooks have it that the United States is favored above all nations with natural resources. But there is one natural resource in which the United States, compared to Western Europe, has always been badly supplied. It is a basic one: water. Not only is rainfall over large parts of the country deficient, and abundant rainfall limited to small areas in the Northwest and Southeast; but because of geography, geology, or soil structure far too much of the rainfall we get seems to be lost in the run-off rather than stored up in the subterranean water table for future use.[8]

Since about 1940 indications have multiplied that we in the United States are exhausting our water capital. In West Texas, for example, in a vast area that has been made rich by what seemed to be inexhaustible water supplies, the water tables have been dropping year by year for almost two decades. In some localities they have been lowered as much as four hundred feet. Other losses have occurred in the San Joaquin Valley in California, where the fruit growers depend heavily upon irrigation. The prolonged conflict between Arizona and California over the use of Colorado River water grows more serious as the limit to which this source of water can be depended upon is rapidly nearing. Depletion of the underground waters is reported in almost every section of the nation.

It is extremely unfortunate that the average citizen of the United States goes on year after year blissfully unaware of the seriousness of the water problem with which he is intimately involved. It has been estimated, for example, that by 1985 the nation may be compelled to ration water on a national scale. Records of the U. S. Geological Survey indicate that even in 1961 more than one thousand cities and areas suffered so serious a scarcity of water that ration was enforced, and that as a result fifteen out of every one

[8] Peter Drucker, *America's Next Twenty Years* (New York: Harper & Brothers, 1957), p. 94.

hundred Americans were required to cut their water consumption. In 1961 the United States Senate Select Committee on National Resources warned the nation in no uncertain terms: "We face a water crisis that threatens to limit economic growth, undermine living standards, endanger health, and jeopardize national security. We live on the edge of water bankruptcy—so close to the edge that in the recent period of subnormal precipitation, one fourth of the nation was rationed for water."

The threat of a water famine, serious as it may be in the case of agriculture, is even more serious in the case of industry. The water requirements of an agrarian economy are vastly less than those of an industrial economy. Every ton of steel we fabricate, every heavy machine we put into operation, every chemical plant we build, must be supplied with water in abundance. By 1985 American industry will be consuming as much water as the agricultural and urban life of 1960 combined.

Meanwhile the sewage produced by 30,000,000 people is being dumped every day into the streams of the nation, making it necessary to purify hundreds of millions of gallons of water before it can be used for domestic purposes. The Missouri River has been called "a thousand mile sewer," but it is only one of hundreds of polluted streams. Thirty thousand municipal and industrial sewers empty directly into waters that are used to supply treatment plants. Fifty million pounds of solid sewage go into the water every day. In 1956 testimony was offered to the Congress to the effect that industry was dumping untreated wastes into the nation's water supply equal to the sewage produced by 110,000,000 people.

A Baltimore steel plant found itself a few years ago in need of water the city could not supply, whereupon an enormous plant was designed to extract the water from the city's sewage. In more than a score of great American cities studies are in progress, each searching for some method by which such water can be reclaimed. It frequently happens, however, that one industry impregnates the water with chemicals that act as "poison" in another industry.

The foregoing indicates that enormous amounts of water will be required as the world proceeds with its programs for industrializing. There is no industrialized nation on earth today that does not face some kind of water problem in a critical form. The extension of industrialism will only make the situation more acute.

2. Waste acres must be enlisted.

Considerable areas around the world now only partially employed can be converted to productivity. In Australia, for example, there is an extensive area of farmland lying between Melbourne and Adelaide which is presently supporting several hundred thousand people. Only a few years ago it was a waste upon which nothing grew. Then a large insurance company became interested, engaged a team of scientists to study the problem, and upon their recommendation the land was impregnated with cobalt and one or two other minerals. Within the space of days the valley was covered with a growth of grass which soon became lush. Today, thousands of homes dot the landscape. Other portions of the earth's surface might respond in a similar fashion to somewhat similar treatment.

A second project, also in Australia, is known as the Snowy Mountain Scheme. The Commonwealth government is spending millions of dollars to dig tunnels through the mountains to divert surplus rainfall on one side of the range to the arid acres on the other side. It is estimated that the land that will be brought under cultivation will support 2,000,000 people. It is quite possible that some scientific scheme can be worked out eventually to redeem "the dead heart of the continent," and if that should happen homes could be provided for 100,000,000 people—about two year's increase of the global population.

Brazil's vast Amazon Valley lies largely untouched, except by scattered tribes of aborigines. To bring it to productivity would call for a massive attack on the jungle and scientific sterilization of the soil to rid it of tropical diseases. When that had been done it would be necessary to undertake an enormous program of fertilization before the red soil could be induced to grow cereals.

In Ethiopia an estimated 160,000,000 acres of reasonably fertile soil await development, and the island of Mindanao in the Philippine group could be made to accommodate another 4,000,000 people. The central highlands of South Vietnam could provide for perhaps as many as 2,000,000. When all such suggestions have been totaled, however, they represent no more than tiny drops in a very large bucket.

The total arable land in India amounts to approximately 300,-000,000 acres, and if it were all cultivated with skill equal to that applied to Japan's soil the subcontinent might be made to produce

200 per cent more grain. Colin Clark, a British economist, is of the opinion that if Indians had the agricultural skills of the Dutch they might be able to support a population of 28,000,000,000 at the diet level of western Europe, but this would call for a water supply that simply does not and never will exist.

Travelers in the tropics and in South America and Africa are apt to get the impression that those continents contain huge areas of fertility that have never been tapped, but a cruel deception lies just under the surface. The red soils of the southern hemispheric continents are by no means the equivalent of the black loam of the northern hemisphere. They lack the mineral content and balance. There is not to be found on either continent an agricultural area that can compare with Illinois or Iowa.

Most tropical soils are infertile. The lush green jungles are deceptive. The equatorial heat and rain strip the earth of its richness, and high temperatures, bacteria, and tropical insects work havoc with the organic humus that makes the soil rich in other sections of the earth. The hot rains leach away the soluble elements of the soil, leaving it poorly adapted to agricultural purposes. In addition, oddly enough, the southern seas produce no comparable supply of marine life to that which is to be found in the lakes, streams, and oceans of the north. The consumption of fish, as food, south of the equator is no more than 2 per cent per capita that of the northern continents.[9]

All the foregoing is to say that an industrial economy as a substitute for the present agricultural economy is the world's one hope. But that revolution must await the accumulation of an almost incredible stock of capital, the wide diffusion of mechanical skills, and the training of billions of workers in scientific techniques, as well as political conciliations that are not in sight for the foreseeable future.

3. All acres must work harder.

Any program of industrialization will be, of necessity, a slow process. In the meantime, babies are being born at the rate of one every three seconds around the clock. If they are not to starve the acres now under cultivation must be compelled to produce more food. Denmark, Switzerland, and Holland—to name but

---

[9] Consult Robbins, *Too Many Asians,* pp. 144-47, for an excellent discussion of this question of the relative productivity of soils.

three small countries—have demonstrated the advantages of scientific methods which could be introduced into the fields of China, India, Pakistan, Vietnam, and other Asian and African countries. Compost, chemical fertilizer, fallowing, contour plowing, and crop rotation will produce much the same beneficial effects on one continent as upon another.

In Japan, where the land is cultivated very largely by hand, an average acre produces 13,000 calories, whereas the Western European farmer produces 8,000. At the same time the American farmer with his power machinery and wasteful methods produces 4,000 calories in competition with the Indian's 3,000. It must be remembered that mechanization does not put any fertility into the soil, nor does it add any dimensions to the acres. It only reduces the demand on muscles. It would be possible, however, to increase the land's yield if seed were selected with more care and if insecticides were used more generally.

The situation in India is one with which all southeast Asia must assist. It is of the utmost importance to the world that a nation of 440,000,000 people has deliberately chosen the democratic way of life, having thus far rejected the Communist way. If Indian democracy is not able to provide as much food for her millions, however, as Communist China is able to provide for her hordes then the battle will be lost in the grain fields no matter what happens in the legislative halls.

4. New foods of greater nutritional value must be produced.

A diet that is scientifically balanced will include a certain proportion of protein. This, it is generally assumed, means meat. Animal protein, however, is an expensive luxury. If we graze the land to produce it we will get about 43 pounds per acre per year. The same acre planted to soy beans will produce 450 pounds, and if it happens to lie in an irrigated field in western United States and is planted to alfalfa it will produce 1,500 pounds. If it be objected that human beings cannot be induced to eat soybeans and alfalfa it is only necessary to cite the experience of the Seventh Day Adventists, whose hospital kitchens around the world have devised, with remarkable acceptability, many ways of using vegetable protein and substituting it for animal protein. The famous charity "Meals for Millions" has done much pioneering in this same field.

Foods differ widely in their food values. Wheat, for example, yields less food per acre than rice, potatoes, or sugar beets. A crop that stands for a longer time green in the field may be expected to contain a larger quantity and higher quality of food material. The larger the fruit in comparison with the plant, the higher its caloric content may be expected to be.

It is reasonable to expect scientific agriculture armed with such knowledge to devise ways for augmenting the caloric production during the next quarter of a century. This will depend upon the ability of hundreds of millions of people to do two extremely difficult things: (1) They must accustom themselves to new dietary habits. (2) They must be prepared to break with agricultural procedures that are centuries old. *Those who cannot adjust cannot survive.*

Among the adjustments that will be required will be the use of foods that come directly from the fields to the dining tables. Whole-wheat bread, for example, provides a much higher degree of nourishment than the emasculated white bread even when it has been "enriched." Vegetables ripened artificially are far inferior nutritionally speaking. Fruits and melons are divested of their nutrient qualities by modern harvesting methods. If it is true, as the New Testament declares, that our bodies are "temples of the Holy Spirit" it would seem to be good religion for the churches to dispense scientific information on the subject of scientific feeding.

"In 1916 the Germans, desperate for protein, started a project in a swimming pool like a culture bath. They would dump in a ton of seed yeast and produce over-night eighty-three tons of food yeast." [10] In the United States refuse water that has served in producing paper is being used for growing yeast for human consumption, at 10 per cent of the cost of meat or eggs. Under the pressure of necessity we can expect the scientific laboratories to produce many new and acceptable foods by 1985. The miracles that have been worked by pharmaceutical firms can be matched in the field of foods.

5. *The seas must be farmed.*

All over the earth every hour of every day a process is going on to which the scientists have given the name "photosynthesis." It

[10] Quoted from an address by H. J. Rand of the Rand Development Co., March 5, 1957, delivered before the Wharton School of Commerce and Finance of the University of Pennsylvania.

is that activity by which plants extract carbon dioxide from the air and produce carbohydrates. Much mystery surrounds the operation, but all food production depends upon it.

It is known that 90 per cent of photosynthesis occurs in the oceans, and yet mankind has, for the most part, ignored the stores of vegetation produced by the seas. It does not lie outside the range of possibility that the grocers' shelves in 1985 will be stocked with marine delicacies of a highly nutritional value totally unknown today.

Along six hundred miles of the California coast, running down along Baja California, there grows a plant known to the scientists as "macrocyatia pyrifera" and to the fishermen as kelp. Already three commercial companies are harvesting this vitamin rich vegetable and processing it as food. Its versatility is such that it can be used profitably in the manufacture of paint, linoleum, ink, beauty cream, and even ice cream. When it is dried it is found to contain no less than twenty-five minerals. Studies now under way may lead to a program of kelp reforestation on a large scale. Other marine growths can be pressed into service as food suppliers, for the vegetables that grow in sea water are almost as numerous and varied as those that grow on land.

In 1949 the United Nations Conference on the Conservation and Utilization of Resources pointed out that 98 per cent of the fisheries of the world are concentrated in the northern hemisphere, and it was estimated that the expansion of fishing operations might increase the total of the world's catch by as much as 20 per cent. This, again, would call for a marked change in the dietary habits of the South American and African nations which consume relatively small quantities of fish.

6. *We must recognize the relationship between food production and industrialization.*

It is significant that the most highly industrialized nation on earth is troubled about the problem of overproduction. In spite of cutbacks, soil banks, and a sharp reduction in the number of agricultural workers, the American people are confronted with an embarrasing and expensive food surplus. Meanwhile the dimensions of farm machinery continue to expand until it is now possible for one farmhand equipped with American machinery to produce as much food as two hundred Pakistani working with primitive agricultural implements. There are areas in India, for example, where the production of the land could be doubled if the soil could be plowed to a depth of eight inches instead of being scratched to a depth of three inches by the ancient plows in use. But even a simple steel plow would cost as much as an Indian family earns in two years. I photographed a farmer in Thailand who, with his team of oxen and an old wooden plow, worked from sunrise to sunset to plow one acre three inches deep.

In America one farmer, working with his tractor and his intricate machinery, can produce enough food to support himself and his family, and 16 to 18 city dwellers besides. In Asia it takes two farmers, sweating and laboring with their oxen, their simple plows, and their own hands, to produce enough of a surplus of food to support one city-dweller.[11]

In Red China at least 80 per cent of the population is required to farm the land and produce food for the nation. This means that no more than 20 per cent are released for nonagricultural labors.

The ignorance of the Asiatic villager is the most formidable barrier to his economic independence. It is possible to eradicate the disease-carrying mosquito with an application of DDT, but there is no spray that will transform an ignorant farmer into a scientific agriculturalist. Nothing less than a massive educational program will ever do that.

No small part of the problem of feeding 4,000,000,000 persons in this modern world is encountered in the field of transportation. In China, for example, the record-breaking famine of 1960-62 was a result, in part, of the fact that food could not be moved from abundant areas to starving sections. Even if the 440,000,000 people of India were able to solve the problem on the village level an enormous investment would be required for the construction of highways which would permit the shipment of food from one section to another.

Added to all the problems of the underdeveloped nations is this: The capital that would permit an adequate program of industrialization to get under way is not available.

The facts presented in this chapter suggest that the missionary programs of the Protestant churches are in serious need of revision.

[11] Robbins, *Too Many Asians*, p. 85. Used by permission.

All too long the missionary has been sent out to save brands from the burning. The time has come to put out some of the fires.

As a small boy in a little Kansas Sunday school I was importuned by my teacher and by the pastor of the church to save up pennies and give dollars to the missionary cause and as an inducement I was promised that for every heathen saved there would be a star in my crown when I finally arrived in heaven. It was a crude appeal but it worked, and in large areas of Protestantism it continues to work to this day. There continues in my mind a vivid memory of the reaction of one "leading layman" to a report given of an agricultural mission in Cuba. He said, "I thought we sent missionaries to the heathen to save souls. I did not know we were supposed to teach them how to grow sugar beets." He thought he was expressing a high spiritual purpose when he made his remark.

Neither will I forget the painful question put to me by the pastor of a great Indian church, a man with three earned degrees from American universities: "What can we do to assist the Indian farmer to achieve a status of economic independence? It will be forever impossible to redeem this land until we can have a church that is self-supporting. We have not preached a full salvation until we have offered these people some hope of a successful escape from poverty, disease, hunger, and ignorance."

The problem with which the Indian pastor was in such close contact is one with which the missionary is confronted every day, and he cannot be Christian and ignore it—nor can the Church!

Beginnings have been made here and there in agricultural missions, trade schools, and domestic training. I have spent time with the agricultural missionary in Okinawa and have seen firsthand the difference he is making in the economic status of the farmers of his area. I have visited trade schools in India where boys have been trained in Christian institutions for churchmanship and economic independence.

To pray "give us tomorrow our daily bread" involves the Church in the necessity of launching a great adventure in which the services of every known science shall be requisitioned in behalf of a better life for the underprivileged of the world. And time is running out!

It is additionally interesting to know that no charges of waste and corruption have ever been leveled at Christian missionaries, and none of them have earned the damning title of "the ugly

American." Aside from occasional expressions of religious prejudice, there is no more trusted and honored group in any nation in Asia or Africa than the Christian missionary who serves unselfishly, intelligently, and usually with foresight and vision. Thousands of government agents who have gone abroad to administer foreign aid have found the Church there, awaiting them, with a world of experience and a prepared constituency.

Suggestions for Further Reading

Bingham, Jonathan. *Shirt-Sleeve Diplomacy.* New York: The John Day Company, 1954.

Bowles, Chester. *Ambassador's Report.* New York: Harper & Brothers, 1954.

————. *Ideas, People, Peace.* New York: Harper & Brothers, 1958.

Brown, Harrison. *The Challenge of Man's Future.* New York: The Viking Press, 1956.

Brown, Harrison, et al. *The Next Hundred Years.* New York: Tne Viking Press, 1957.

Cook, J. Gordon. *We Live by the Sun.* New York: The Dial Press, 1957.

Drucker, Peter. *America's Next Twenty Years.* New York: Harper & Brothers, 1957.

Faris, Donald K. *To Plow With Hope.* New York: Harper & Brothers, 1958.

Osborn, Fairfield. *The Limits of the Earth.* Boston: Little, Brown and Company, 1953.

————. *Our Plundered Planet.* Boston: Little, Brown and Company, 1948.

Pearson, Frank A. and Harper, Floyd A. *The World's Hunger.* Ithaca, N.Y.: Cornell University Press.

Peterson, Elmer. *Big Dam Foolishness.* New York: The Devin-Adair Company, 1954.

Robbins, John. *Too Many Asians.* Garden City, N.Y.: Doubleday & Company, 1959.

Stuart, Alexander. *Overpopulation: Twentieth Century Nemesis.* New York: The Exposition Press, 1958.

Thompson, Warren S. *Population Problems.* 4th edition. New York: McGraw-Hill Book Company, 1953.

United Nations Demographic Yearbook. Population Division, Department of Social Affairs, United Nations.

Vogt, William. *People: The Challenge to Survival.* New York: William Morrow & Company, 1960.

4

The Rape of the Good Earth

THE PROBLEM OF FOOD LEADS DIRECTLY INTO THE QUESTION OF CON-
serving the good earth which produces food. All human life depends
today upon that thin skin of topsoil, the average thickness of
which around the earth is only a little more than eight inches.
Every mouthful of food consumed by any human being, with the
exception of the relatively small percentage of marine foods, is
derived from that delicate covering.

According to a generally accepted opinion among scientists,
our earth took form about 5,000,000,000 years ago—some say
10,000,000,000. Living things are said to have appeared along the
edges of oceans, backwaters, and lakes about 2,000,000,000 years
ago, but because there was no soil to provide them hospitality they
left no trace.

About 350,000,000 years ago the Silurian Period began, with
primitive plants and animals establishing themselves on dry land.
Through many millennia primeval storms had loosed particles of
rocks, infinitesimally small, from parent ledges and had deposited them in crevices at the edges of bodies of water. By im-
perceptible stages such material accumulated at favored spots, and
about the same time living things began to come up out of the
water in search of congenial residences. With the passing of the
centuries highly specialized forms made their way up the slopes
and became independent of the seas.

In all such instances soil capable of furnishing food became the
prerequisite of life. As single-celled creatures died, leaving their
remains in the inorganic soil, they enriched the earth and prepared
it for higher forms of life to come later. As time went on vegetation
developed, plant roots mingled with and became a part of the soil,
and thus the skin of the earth thickened. Throughout all these
primal periods a simple law operated. *If any creature destroyed the
soil it destroyed itself, because it destroyed its food supply.*

When man put in his appearance he immediately began to display a characteristic that set him apart from every other creature. If his environment did not suit him he changed it. To protect himself against the storms he cut down trees to make a shelter. He moved rocks to build a wall. He carried plants from one location to another. He dug in the earth. "His intelligence and versatility made it possible for him to do something no other animal had ever been able to do—alter his environment, survive, and multiply." [1]

Anthropologists generally are of the opinion that the first "man" to put in his appearance on this earth arrived about 10,000 years ago, and at that point the first serious destruction of the topsoil began. Tools contrived to lighten labors became more and more destructive, and today gigantic machines are destroying at a prodigious rate. Some conservationists have declared that there has been more man-induced erosion of the earth since 1900 than during any previous 1,000 years of history.

Having domesticated the goat, the sheep, the ox, and the ass, to say nothing of the camel and the horse, man has grazed them on the grasslands until the soil was laid bare, exposed to storms and floods. In need of fuel with which to cook his food and warm his body, man has cut down trees, with the result that a single night's deluge may carry away topsoil that has been a million years maturing.

It has been the history of civilization from the beginning that man has destroyed the soil upon which he and his children have depended for their very lives.

Historical records for the last 6,000 years show that civilized man has never been able to continue a progressive civilization in one locality for more than thirty to seventy generations (800 to 2,000 years). There are, however, three notable exceptions: The Nile Valley, Mesopotamia, and the Indus Valley. . . . Aside from these cradles of civilization, however, civilized man's dominance over his environment lasted only a few generations. After a few centuries of growth and progress in a favorable environment, his civilization declined, he perished, or he was forced to move to new land. The average life-span was forty to sixty generations.

[1] Vernon G. Carter and Tom Dale, *Topsoil and Civilization* (Norman, Okla.: University of Oklahoma Press, 1955), p. 6. Used by permission.

In most cases, the more brilliant the civilization, the shorter was its progressive existence. These civilizations declined in the same geographical areas that had matured them, mainly because man despoiled or ruined the environment that helped him develop his civilization.[2]

The majority of the weak and poor nations of the world once lived in the midst of plenty. In every case the impoverishment began with the depletion of the soil. As the land was squandered, the civilization that had grown up on it sickened and died.

Following Columbus' discovery of the New World in 1492 a considerable period of time elapsed before any serious effort was made to colonize either of the Americas. Life in Europe was comfortable, and the soil was responsive. About the time the farmlands began to show signs of weariness, however, the eyes of the Old World turned toward the New World, and the tide of immigration started. As the pressure was relieved in one part of the earth, however, the wastage of the soil began in another.

Travelers in North Africa cannot have failed to be impressed by the monumental ruins which dot the landscape from the region of Gibraltar to the delta of the Nile. Most of the grain that fed the city of Rome in Jesus' day came from Egypt, Libya, Algiers, Morocco, or Tunisia. The ship upon which the apostle Paul was carried to Rome for trial was, almost certainly, loaded with wheat from Africa. The population of that section of Africa in Nero's time was somewhat in excess of 20,000,000 people, which is 2½ times today's population of 8,000,000. The destruction of the soil is the reason for the decrease.

At the beginning of the Christian Era Italy was already unable to provide sufficient food to feed the population, and imports from India, China, and North Africa drained the treasuries of the Caesars for two hundred years. On more than one occasion the Roman Empire was on the verge of bankruptcy because of the insistence of its oriental creditors.[3]

During the 1930's the Mussolini government spent nearly $500,-000,000 in an effort to restore exhausted areas to productivity, and more than 100,000 acres were redeemed from the Pontine Marshes. With Italy's defeat in World War II, however, this program came

[2] *Ibid.*, pp. 7-8.
[3] Barbara Ward, *Interplay of East and West* (New York: W. W. Norton & Company, 1957), pp. 15 ff.

to an end, probably not to be resumed in this century. Meanwhile Western Europe faces its own problems. Holland, Switzerland, and Sweden have accomplished near miracles in soil preservation, but the British Isles are compelled to import at least 25 per cent of the food required by the population, and the rest of Europe must be listed in the deficit column.

During the middle of the nineteenth century a potato famine in Ireland resulted in the death of tens of thousands. Because tubers are ravenous consumers of the soil the decades of potato farming had exhausted the land. This is at least a partial explanation of the fact that the Emerald Isle is populated today by less than half the number of people who lived there one hundred years ago.

The civilization of China is at least a thousand years older than that of Western Europe, and the impoverishment of the land has gone on that much longer. The result is that at least 80 per cent of the population must toil in the field to produce the scanty rations on which the nation exists. It is a fact that the Red regime has undertaken great public works aimed at restoring huge areas to productivity and has been remarkably successful in some sections, but the land is woefully incapable of providing for 700,000,000 people, and the problem will mushroom with the population explosion. For at least two hundred years there has been a general exodus of Chinese to Malaya, Indonesia, the Philippines, Burma, and Thailand, as well as to South America, Mexico, and Cuba. The invasions of Vietnam, Laos, Cambodia, and Annam are but a modern version of the movement that has been going on for three centuries.

The largest tracts of raw land are held by the Russians, and Stalin, followed by Khrushchev, engineered a gigantic effort to convert hundreds of thousands of acres to cultivation in western Siberia. The effort thus far has been only partially successful because of the reluctance of Russian youth to face the hardships and handicaps of pioneering. The Soviet government is, however, acutely alert to the problem of soil depletion and has assigned a team of scientists to the task of protecting Russian soil. A totalitarian government enjoys this advantage; it is not compelled to wait indefinitely on the voluntary efforts of the farmers. It can command them, and it is not necessary to wait for a majority vote before introducing remedial measures.

Hunger has always been an active ally of revolution. An ignorant man who is also hungry can hardly be expected to be reasonable, and there is always a danger that the depletion of the land may be followed by an undermining of the political convictions of the masses. The impoverished are tempted to surrender their liberties to those who promise food without stopping to count the costs. Perhaps it is not amiss in this connection to remind ourselves that the founding fathers of the young American republic were usually men of means. Three of the signers of the Declaration of Independence—Washington, Hancock, and Franklin—were esteemed to be the richest men in America. The Declaration of Independence and the Constitution of the United States were framed by men who in another generation might have been called "economic royalists."

Today's powerful position of the United States is due in part to the fact that the American continent was settled at a time when the resources of Europe were running dangerously low. For three hundred years the fertility of the New World was shipped to the Old World in the form of agricultural products, and nothing was done to replenish the loss. It was assumed that the natural resources of America were inexhaustible. It has been estimated that since the settlement of Jamestown, in Virginia (1607), and Plymouth, in New England (1620), at least one third of the productive topsoil of the North American continent has been exported, wasted, or eroded away. Of the nearly nine inches of fertility that once covered the New World north of the Panama Canal no more than six inches remain. Wasteful methods of agriculture are to blame.

The Soil Conservation Service of the United States Government estimated in 1955 that the nation was losing the equivalent in productivity of 500,000 acres of good farmland every year.[4] The Department of Agriculture has estimated that 280,000,000 acres of crop and range land has been destroyed since the day Columbus first set foot on the little island of San Salvador and that an additional 100,000,000 acres have been so badly damaged by erosion that they cannot be restored by any known method. Geologic and biologic processes are extremely slow, and no artificial substitute

[4] *Ibid.*, p. 250.

has ever been found. Elmer T. Peterson, one of the nation's conservation authorities, writing in the *Saturday Evening Post*, estimated that another 1,000,000 acres of cropland have gone into airports, parks, reservoirs, cities, highways, and other non-food-producing uses, and such land is always the most productive land.[5]

The United States Soil Conservation Service estimates further that each year 5,400,000,000 tons of topsoil are eroded from the nation's acres. Of this total 3,000,000,000 tons are skimmed off the surface of the lands devoted to agriculture. The volume of silt that goes down the Mississippi into the Gulf of Mexico amounts to 1,306,000 cubic feet *every minute!* This is a layer eight inches thick from off forty acres. The silt annually deposited in Lake Meade by the Colorado River above Hoover Dam amounts to an area of 100,000 acres one foot deep.

Even a thick layer of earth is of little use if it does not contain life-giving elements. To speak in simple terms, the soil under our feet is a vast laboratory in which occur innumerable chemical reactions and biological changes. There is an infinite number of submicroscopic organisms—living things upon which food production depends. "Nature consists of a chain of interrelated and interlocked life cycles. Remove any one factor and you will find she cannot work efficiently." [6] An epidemic among the earthworms, for example, can be as serious in terms of human life as an epidemic of measles among children.

When a bushel of grain, a gallon of milk, or a pig is shipped to market a certain amount of the soil's minerals has been deported. If no replacement is made the soil is impoverished exactly as a savings account is depleted if no deposits are made.

Food shipped to the cities represents a loss to the land, for the waste from food consumed is carried away as sewage. It is, therefore, a permanent loss. In 1950 U. S. Surgeon General Thomas Parran estimated that 3,000 American communities that year dumped 2,500,000,000 tons of raw sewage into the streams of the nation every day, each pound representing a loss of fertility from the land. "The economic pressure brought by the mechanization and consequent industrialization of our people has compelled

[5] Editorial in *The Saturday Evening Post* (July 19, 1958), p. 8.
[6] Jerome I. Rodale, *Pay Dirt* (New York: The Devin-Adair Company, 1945), p. 11.

our farmers to mine their land, not manage it. Thus for several generations farm income has come from the sale of fertility, and not from the real wealth manufactured on its fields." [7]

Lord John Boyd-Orr of England, one time Director General of the Food and Agricultural Organization of the United Nations, has pointed up the problem in a single sentence: "In a hungry world people will be more attracted to the country which has the biggest supply of food than to the one with the biggest supply of atomic bombs." [8] Two out of three people now living are destined to suffer premature death unless the problem of productivity can be solved. The supreme issue in this modern world is whether or not the earth can be managed so that it will supply the food that is to be required by the excess of population. The relation between people, politics, and productivity is the problem of our times. "It is not without significance that in the Lord's Prayer, the petition for our daily bread has priority even over the petition for the forgiveness of sins, a fact worthy of consideration by the Churches." [9]

Milton Eisenhower has described the situation: "It is probable that since the dawn of history . . . man has destroyed as many productive areas as now exist in the world, and this destruction has contributed mightily to the decline and fall of civilizations." [10] Sir Boyd-Orr added, further:

There are 12,000 million acres of desert, probably the greater part of which was man-made. . . . The march of civilization has, for the greater part of the earth's surface, been a march of destruction as regards the fertility of the soil upon which its existence depends. If the process were to continue unchecked, the now barren lands which once supported flourishing States and empires and now support only a sparse population in poverty, could be taken as a warning of the decay of our own civilization.[11]

An additional hazard connected with the depletion of the soil relates to the matter of health. In 1936 a massive study was made of

[7] Lionel J. Picton, *Nutrition and the Soil* (New York: The Devin-Adair Company, 1949), p. 14.
[8] *The White Man's Dilemma* (London: Allen & Unwin, Ltd., 1953), p. 76. Used by permission.
[9] *Ibid.*, p. 29.
[10] *Ibid.*, p. 69.
[11] *Ibid.*, pp. 69-70.

3,463,948 English school children, 2,424,299 of whom were found to be in need of dental care. An investigation of their diets indicated that a vast majority of them suffered from a serious lack of essential minerals. Between the diseased teeth and the mineral shortages there was a direct connection. A study made by Harvard scientists among the skeletal remains found in the Pecos Valley in the Southwest showed there had been a noticeable diminution in stature among the prehistoric Indians and an increase in deformities due to arthritis and in dental caries which could be traced to soil depletion.[12]

Sixty bushels of corn taken off an acre of Iowa land means that from twenty-five to twenty-eight pounds of phosophorus have been taken out of the soil—and an even larger amount of calcium. If no chemical refund is made the loss is permanent. There is something very significant in the fact that the most minerals are being taken out of the soil at the very moment that the nation's medical bills are skyrocketing. As of 1960 the American people were paying half as much for medical care as for all food supplies.

The Christian Church has long proclaimed it to be its mission to preserve the "faith once delivered to the saints." The time has come to expand its concern to include "the soil once delivered to the saints." I have attended great church assemblies for forty years, both in the United States and abroad, and cannot remember ever having heard as much as one voice raised in condemnation of those who are raping the good earth. It was a fundamental doctrine of the ancient Hebrew religion that "the earth is the Lord's." If this were a theological treatise an extremely interesting case could be made out for the conflicting doctrines of the land, as between the Hebrews and their pagan neighbors. To be a good steward of the land is to assume one of the basic responsibilities of the religious life. The church that does not take an interest in the crime against the land will stand under judgment before generations unborn.

Churchmen generally are concerned about the world that is to come as well as the world in which we live, but we are indifferent toward the world that is getting away from us. If it is religious to provide help for famine victims it is also religious to stand guard over the soil from which our great-great-grandchildren must derive

[12] Cf. W. A. Price, *Nutrition and Physical Degeneration* (New York: Harper & Brothers, 1939), p. 383.

their sustenance. Just as surely as the Church is commissioned to do something about juvenile delinquency, so also it ought to be saying something about and to those who are contributing to the delinquency of the croplands.

Suggestions for Further Reading

Boyd-Orr, John. *The White Man's Dilemma.* London: Allen and Unwin, Ltd., 1953.

Carhart, Arthur H. *Water—or Your Life.* Philadelphia: J. B. Lippincott Company, 1951.

Carter, Vernon G., and Dale, Tom. *Topsoil and Civilization.* Norman, Okla.: University of Oklahoma Press, 1955.

Peterson, Elmer. *Big Dam Foolishness.* New York: The Devin-Adair Company, 1954.

Picton, Lionel J. *Nutrition and the Soil.* New York: The Devin-Adair Company, 1949.

Price, W. A. *Nutrition and Physical Degeneration.* New York: Harper & Brothers, 1939.

Rodale, Jerome I. *Pay Dirt.* New York: The Devin-Adair Company, 1945.

Ward, Barbara. *The Interplay of East and West.* New York: W. W. Norton & Company, 1957.

5

Hunger, Politics, and Birth Control

A BODY OF GOOD SOLID FACTS HAS BEEN ASSEMBLED IN THE FOREGOING chapters, and we are now ready to consider one of the thorniest questions with which civilization must deal during the next twenty-five years. Unless some solution can be found for the problem of birth control the race will find itself face to face with disaster. We have introduced death control to the underdeveloped areas of the world without offering any help in the matter of birth control. The result is a population growth that has become a global threat. Some acceptable means of contraception has become of immediate concern to every nation on earth.

There are more hungry, illiterate, dissatisfied, bitter, desperate, ignorant, and helpless people in the world as these lines are being written than ever before in human history, and their numbers are increasing by the hour. There is no rug under which they can be swept. Literally millions of children are being damned into the world. "That the present explosive world situation is basically due to widespread hunger and misery naturally resulting from too many children is beyond reasonable doubt." [1] The Communist strength is being recruited throughout the world by tens of millions of births every year.

Archaeologists have pointed out the fact that no less than fifteen civilizations have risen to magnificence on the earth within the period of recorded history and then suffered collapse. Paleontologists have identified a long list of species that have come into existence, thrived, and disappeared. In all cases their disappearance has resulted from an exhaustion of their food supplies. By what logic, therefore, do we dare hope our civilization will enjoy a kinder

[1] Alexander Stuart, *Overpopulation: Twentieth Century Nemesis* (New York: The Exposition Press, 1958), p. 235.

fate? [2] We owe it to ourselves and to the generations that come after us to understand the laws that regulate population growth and take such measures as lie within our reach to preserve our gains.

Somewhat more than 150 years ago an English clergyman, the Rev. Thomas Robert Malthus, introduced a proposition into the world's thinking that caused a furore which has not subsided to this day. He said that it is an inescapable law of life that population grows faster than do the means of subsistence. Whereas food materials increase in an arithmetical ratio, population increases by a geometrical ratio. [3] In other words, unless something is done to check the growth of population or to expand the world's food production racial starvation is inevitable. The longer the condition persists the wider the gap grows between food and population. The fact that the race has survived up to this time, the clergyman explained, is because it has suffered a series of population checks—wars, famines, plagues, and pestilences. [4] In the absence of such calamities it is necessary to invent preventive checks which might be expected to have the same result. As an orthodox clergyman of the Established Church he could not condone abortions, and he could, therefore, see no way out of the dilemma. Wars and other horrors, he confessed, must continue.

As the Rev. Mr. Malthus argued the matter, and as today's population explosion makes critically plain, the situation reduces itself to a simple mathematical formula. Every million additional people on the earth consume additional millions of pounds of food, fibers, medical supplies, and other materials every day. [5] Unless new sources of supply can be developed there can be but one result. Those already living below normal standards must share with the newcomers, which will mean a further lowering of standards for all. There is no magic by which the facts can be changed. To add to the seriousness of the total situation there is the burgeoning of the

[2] Cf. Julian Huxley, "Man's Challenge: The Use of the Earth," *Horizon* I, No. 1 (September, 1958), pp. 48-55.

[3] For a condensation of the various editions of Malthus' *Essay on the Principles of Population*, see Macmillan edition, 1929.

[4] For a study of the laws of reproduction see Stuart, *Overpopulation: Twentieth Century Nemesis*, Chapter VIII.

[5] Dupont economists have figured that 4,000,000 American babies born in 1960 will consume in their lifetime 1,000,000,000 pairs of shoes, 200,000,000 tons of steel, 1,000,000 new houses, 25,000,000,000 pounds of beef, and 63,000,-000 suits and dresses.

world's cities, whose population are consumers and not producers of food. In 1910 there were but ten cities in all the world with a population of 1,000,000 or more. In 1961 there were sixty-five, each one of which must requisition food supplies from the diminishing productive acres. As for the "checks" upon which the clergyman relied, they have never proved sufficient. It has often happened that a nation's population has increased during the very years that it was suffering disastrous losses.[6]

Even at the risk of repeating the argument, let us take a look at the situation with which Egypt is confronted. When the first census was taken at the close of the nineteenth century the population was less than 10,000,000. By 1947 it had increased to 19,000,-000, and by 1964 it will be nearing the 30,000,000 mark. Nasser's grand scheme for the Aswan Dam is an attempt to provide more productive acres. The nation's fertility rate is the highest in the world—and almost 50 births per 1,000 population, with the death rate having declined to 20.5 per 1,000.

There is but one alternative: A growing population must expand its productivity, or it must lower its standard of living.

The present state of world affairs permits no soft words about hard facts. The people are outbreeding their school systems, their production of food and clothing, their means of communication, their supply of teachers and doctors, their hospitals and housing, and their capital resources upon which they must depend for the provision of the necessities of life.

There is a danger that we may be deceived by statistics. It is reported, for example, that illiteracy was reduced in Brazil from 65.3 per cent in 1900, to 50.6 per cent in 1950, but that percentage does not make it clear that the total number of illiterates increased from 6,300,000 to 15,300,000 in the same period. All over the world hunger is breeding unrest which plays directly into the hands of the Communists. The October revolution of 1917 in Russia proved that 5,000 determined and single-minded men can exercise a power

[6] At the time of the outbreak of the Sino-Japanese war in 1937 the population of Japan was approximately 73,000,000. On the day the Emperor surrendered to General MacArthur this total had increased to something in excess of 80,000,000 in spite of the fact that there had been no interruption of hostilities. In spite of almost continuous warfare inside China since 1926, and her engagement in World War II, when her casualties mounted into the millions, her population has increased by tens of millions.

completely out of proportion to their numbers. If each of these 5,000 were hungry, and if they appeared on the streets of any capital in the world, they would make themselves heard and felt no matter how large or how small the country.

This becomes a very personal problem. A death rate can be changed by a decree of the government, but the lowering of the birth rate depends upon millions of personal decisions made under primitive pressures.

A wide variety of meanings have been attached to the term "birth control," with the result that we usually discuss the matter emotionally rather than logically. It becomes necessary, therefore, to define our terms, and in doing so we find that the proposal can take any one of seven forms.

1. *Coitus interruptus*—an interruption of the sex act for the purpose of preventing the male cell from coming in contact with the female ovum.

2. Any *mechanical means* which prevents contact between the sex cells.

3. *Sterilization*—a surgical operation which renders an individual incapable of exposing a life cell to impregnation.

4. *Continence*—a complete abstinence from the sex act.

5. *Abortion*—removal of the impregnated ovum from the womb.

6. *Rhythmical intercourse*—engaging in intercourse only during the period of female sterility.

7. *Chemical control*—the administration of a drug designed to render the female incapable of conception.

It sometimes becomes necessary to identify the method one condemns or approves. The Roman Catholic Church, for example, rejects the charge that it is opposed to birth control on the grounds that it favors rhythmical intercourse, while birth-control advocates indignantly deny that they favor abortions.

In spite of the fact that I strongly favor birth control when practiced under the direction of the family physician, simple honesty requires me to concede that the opposition of the Roman Catholic Church stems from a moral conviction. If the basic principle upon which that opposition rests is to be granted the arguments derived therefrom are logical. The position is, therefore, to be respected even when it is rejected.

"Basic to everything which the Roman Catholic Church says

57

on birth control is the conviction that the procreative end is primary in marriage or, put somewhat more inclusively in the words of Thomas Aquinas, marriage is chiefly for the 'procreation and education of children.' " [7] That is the base of the church's teaching.

Relatively little has been said about the matter until recently, when popular discussion of the population explosion has brought the matter to the fore. In the year 1930, however, Pius XI issued an encyclical known as the *Casti Canubii,* in which the canon law was quoted as saying that "the primary end of marriage is the procreation and education of children." In an allocution issued by Pius XII in 1942 the statement was amplified slightly, and in 1944 the *Roman Rota* enlarged the scope of the question still further, but the concept of the procreative purpose of marriage remains primary in Roman Catholic theology.

The Rev. William J. Gibbons, a member of the faculty of Fordham University, has stated the position of the Catholic Church in precise terms:

Q. What method of regulating the number of offspring does the church sanction?
A. The Church's teaching on the matter of regulating number of offspring could be reduced to three heads.

The first is what we called delayed marriage, especially beyond the very productive years—in the late teens and early twenties.

The second is continence within marriage for a protracted period, which some people practice—in fact, even in non-Christian areas—in order to space children more effectively.

And the third is periodic continence or use of the sterile period during the woman's monthly cycle. Where there are legitimate reasons present, it is perfectly all right morally to use this latter method. Modern science has progressively made it more effective, and we can hope for further advances in the foreseeable future. [8]

In 1951 Pius XII rendered a specific judgment in the matter of the rhythm method and gave it his approval.

As might be expected, the Protestant position until recent years has varied with denominations. The prevailing voice of 1962, how-

[7] John von Rohr, "Christianity and Birth Control, I. The Roman Catholic View," *The Christian Century* (September 28, 1960), p. 1115.
[8] From a copyrighted interview in *U.S. News & World Report* (December 21, 1959), p. 59.

ever, is almost unanimously sympathetic with the position taken by advocates of birth control, although that has not always been true. In 1913 a committee of the bishops of the Established Church of England published a condemnation of all mechanical and chemical means of contraception, and this position was supported by the Lambeth Conference of 1920. In both instances this example was followed by the Protestant Episcopal Church of the United States. Then in the summer of 1958 the Lambeth Conference, which consists of the archbishops and the bishops of the Anglican Communion, made a unanimous declaration in favor of contraception, and this was followed by a similar action on the part of the American bishops in 1961. In 1931 the Federal Council of Churches, in a restrained report, looked with some favor on the proposals of the birth-control advocates, which caused a storm of controversy. In more recent years occasional Protestant periodicals and extreme fundamentalist groups have contended for a position near to that of the Roman Catholic Church, but the preponderant Protestant opinion generally supports the birth-control advocates.

By way of contrast it should be said that there is nothing in the tenets of any Oriental religion that interposes any serious objection to birth-control measures, except abortion. The Shinto religion, for example, does not recognize the child as a living person until it has seen the light of day. As a consequence the position of the Japanese government in encouraging abortions does not raise the moral issue that would be raised in the case of a European people. Moreover, the offer of the Indian government to pay the expenses of sterilization for any man desiring to limit his family does not encounter objections from the religious authorities of that land. Generally, the non-Christian religions raise no objection to the dissemination of birth-control literature or information.

Confronted by the fact that 100,000 individuals are added to the world's population every twenty-four hours and that three out of four of them are doomed to live a lifetime unfed, the world faces a simple moral question: *Is it any more immoral to resort to some method of artificial birth control than it is to bring children into this world knowing they will go hungry from the first day of their arrival until the day of their death?*

The problem posed by the Roman Catholic Church's opposition to artificial methods of birth control must be faced frankly.

That the Catholic Church has a perfect right to interpret morals in the light of its own convictions goes without saying, and it has a perfect right to require conformity on the part of its members. *Roman Catholic authority ends at the membership boundaries of that communion, however. Beyond that line Catholicism has no right to impose judgment—either moral or political—upon others.*

Yet that is precisely what is being done. Two American states— Massachusetts and Connecticut—have laws which forbid physicians to give birth-control information to their patients, even if it is, in their judgment, done to save life.[9] Neither of the great political parties of the United States has been willing to take any position on the subject of disseminating information in other countries, even to those who ask for it. Inside the United Nations World Health Organization the opposition of predominantly Catholic countries has prevented any contributions of information or techniques related to birth control.

There is, however, another barrier which must be surmounted. Most Asian women have been reared from childhood to believe their highest function in life is to rear children. Any proposal in the direction of birth control is held under suspicion because it sounds "Western." It is commonly believed that an expanding population is an evidence of national virility and desirable from a military standpoint. This argument loses much of its weight in the light of nuclear weaponry, but it continues to be a patriotic and nationalistic appeal. Also, and in addition, every oriental family looks upon each child as an economic asset because he can work in the field.

There is an additional aspect of the case which further complicates the problem. Most oriental women do not have a predictable menstrual rhythm because their scanty diets do not sustain a standard of health that will assure the hungry woman of a regular fertility cycle. Even the slighest shock is capable of disorganizing the entire menstrual pattern.

To deal intelligently with the situation it is necessary to inquire as to whether or not there is any artificial birth-control method that has proved to be reliable, and the honest answer is "no." Any method to be practical in the underdeveloped areas of the world must be sufficiently inexpensive to permit its use by those families

It should be said that the Connecticut law was originally passed by a legislature that was predominantly Protestant.

whose total income does not amount to more than $100 per year. This means that expensive aids used in such countries as the United States are prohibitively priced.

In the second place, any method depends upon a minimum of education and information. There is the case of the Indian women who were unable to count the days of their fertile period and to whom any recourse to the rhythm method was, therefore, an impossibility. Then there was another case of women who were given strings of twenty-eight beads, each seventh being of a different color, and the women took them orally. The task of teaching 150,000,000 women the rudiments required for successful co-operation would be enormous. Training 438,000,000 in even the simplest procedures is a staggering task.

Any artificial method, to be successful, depends upon at least a minimum of sanitary protection. When one considers the conditions under which 1,000,000,000 people live—without even clean water—the problem is baffling indeed.

It is necessary to consider the isolation in the midst of which millions live. In India no less than 845 languages are used, many of which have never been reduced to writing. Hundreds of millions in both Asia and Africa have no access to radio, read no newspapers, attend no public lectures, and are completely shut away from the currents of modern life. To educate such people requires that the teachers go directly into the villages and teach from door to door.

The ideal solution, of course, would be a medicament that could be taken orally and which would render the individual sterile for a predictable period of time. Most of the scientific quest has gone into this field, and a beginning has been made. Once such a product is available, however, the problem of distribution must be faced.

The story of the search for "the pill' is a long one, which includes many a serious hint and not a few fantasies.[10] One government agent worked among the Shoshone Indians and found them using a weed, *Lithosperum ruderals*. Then there is the East Indian field pea, *Pisum Satvium*. Each has yielded some encouraging results but nothing substantial has been developed.

Late in the year 1960 the United States Food and Drug Adminis-

[10] For a reliable account of the search of a medicament the the reader is referred to Norman Himes, *Medical History of Contraception* (Baltimore, Md.: Williams Wood & Company, 1936).

tration certified for marketing a synthetic hormone product which had been given the name "Enovid." This does not mean that it was guaranteed for birth-control purposes, but that it was safe when administered according to a physician's orders.[11] The production of the pill followed the logic of an extremely interesting theory. Biologists, endoctrinologists, and gynecologists have been searching for years for an explanation of various weak links in the human productive chain. They knew, for example, that a number of conditions existed which made conception temporarily impossible. If it were possible to control one of these links it would be possible to control the whole process of reproduction.

Extensive experiments proved that as soon as a fertilized ovum begins to grow in the womb a drug called progesterone begins to appear in increased amount in the bloodstream, a condition that causes the ovaries to cease releasing ova. Therefore it was assumed that if properly administered, the drug would prevent pregnancy by preventing the release of ova. Therefore the hunt began for a drug that would do what progesterone did. After two years of research the scientists came up with 17-alpha-ethinyl-estraenolone— Enovid. A somewhat similar medicament, called Norlutin (19-NOR-17 alpha ethinyl testerone) is reported to have much the same effect. Still others are nearing the market.

Extensive tests in which thousands of women have participated have proved that induced sterility does not become permanent. As soon as a woman ceases taking the pills she again becomes capable of conceiving. Indeed, such women are apt to exhibit an accelerated percentage of pregnancies with no ill effects. The discouraging aspect of the matter is the cost—ten dollars per month for protection. The manufacturers feel this can be reduced in time, however.

Research directed at the possibility of suppressing the development of sperm in men is going on. Other researchers are studying drugs that would prevent the ova from clinging to the walls of the womb. The possibility of a vaccine that would temporarily sterilize either males or females continues to encourage some researchers.[12]

[11] Since the writing of this chapter both the Food and Drug Administration and the medical associations have called for serious re-examination of Enovid and other oral contraceptives.

[12] Albert Q. Maisel, "Where Do We Stand with the Birth-Control Pill?" *Reader's Digest* (February, 1961), pp. 60-64.

Rather oddly, one other source of opposition to birth control remains to be reckoned with, and it represents the opposite of Roman Catholicism. Theoretically the Communists hold steadily to the doctrine of Karl Marx and his "scientific principles of history" which leave no room for any such proposal as birth control. It is a Marxist dogma that labor produces wealth, and that an overflowing population ought to produce overflowing wealth. Malthus and Marx clash head on in China. Where Malthus looked on population growth as a disaster, Marx insisted that increasing a nation's population was tantamount to increasing its supply of capital. In the Marxist view there can be no such thing as overpopulation.[13] Marx attacked Malthusianism as a by-product of a decadent capitalism and declared that overpopulation was a direct consequence of the private ownership of production. In this he is followed, generally, by modern Communist theoreticians.

In the year 1957, however, the Red regime in China launched what promised to be an all-out and aggressive campaign in behalf of birth control. The walls of factories were covered with slogans that referred to the matter. Lectures were broadcast. And literally millions of pictures, models, and movies were spread across the nation. Nothing in the way of propaganda was omitted. Abortion and sterilization were legalized. Four factories manufacturing contraceptives were thrown into high gear. Then, just as suddenly and without any official explanation, the campaign was shut off. Today the official line is the classic Marxist line.

In the meantime, in 1957 the Soviets convened a congress of more than 1,000 physicians for the purpose of discussing the question of family planning. At that conference contraceptive devices were on display, and lengthy discussions were held relative to the question of distributing them and training the people to use them. It is currently known that the birthrate in Russia has declined from 47 per 1,000 in 1913 to 25.3 in 1958.[14]

In India some states are offering bounties to parents who agree to sterilization after the birth of the third or fourth child. In Japan official encouragement is offered to those who volunteer for sterilization according to prescribed conditions. On June 5, 1961, contra-

[13] Robbins, *Too Many Asians*, p. 42.
[14] Alan F. Guttmacher, *Babies by Choice or by Chance* (New York: Avon Book Division of the Hearst Corporation, 1961), p. 61.

ceptives went on sale at the state controlled Central Pharmacy in Tunis, preliminary to a general sale throughout Tunisia, this being the first step to be taken by that nation in the direction of birth control.

It needs to be repeated that the governments of the densely populated societies in Asia are more ready to be helped in this area than the west is to help. As anyone who follows governmental affairs knows the actual requests of recipient governments are adjusted to the kind of aid they are prepared to extend. There are no signs that any such intimations are coming. The only discernible reason is the fear lest religious controversy be engendered in the United States by any projects in the field of family limitation.[15]

Here is an issue upon which every Protestant denomination can take a strong position. Inasmuch as no help can be hoped for from political sources, Protestant Christian bodies must accept the challenge and assume the responsibility. Missionary doctors, hospitals, clinics, and nursing schools should be authorized and equipped to disseminate information to all who seek it. Pastors, evangelists, teachers—all mission workers should be trained to give at least elementary instruction in strict medical terms.

If it is a Christian service to provide care for orphans, then surely it is also Christian to prevent, if possible, the birth of those who are to be doomed to hunger. It is true, of course, that population controls will not solve all the problems, but there will be no permanent solution without them. Protestant pastors owe it to their congregations to instruct them on the subject of the population explosion and its relation to birth control, that they may understand the moral judgments involved.

Suggestions for Further Reading

Coale, Ansley A., and Hoover, Edgar M. *Population Growth and Economic Development in Low Income Countries.* Princeton, N.J.: Princeton University Press, 1958.

Cook, Robert. *Human Fertility: The Modern Dilemma.* New York: William Morrow & Company, 1951.

[15] Fagley, *Population Explosion and Christian Responsibility,* p. 64.

Darwin, Charles G. *The Next Million Years.* Garden City, N.Y.: Doubleday & Company, 1952.

De Castro, Josue. *The Geography of Hunger.* Boston: Little Brown & Company, 1952.

Dickinson, R. L. *Techniques of Conception Control.* Baltimore, Md.: The Williams & Wilkins Company, 1950.

Dickinson, R. L., and Gamble. *Family Planning, Sterility, and Population Growth.* Baltimore, Md.: The Williams & Wilkins Company, 1950.

Fletcher, Joseph. *Morals and Medicine.* Princeton, N.J.: Princeton University Press, 1954.

Himes, Norman E. *Medical History of Contraception.* Baltimore, Md.: William Wood & Company, 1936.

Kamat, Melba, and Kamat. *Diet and Fecundity in India.* London: Proceedings Sixth International Conference on Planned Parenthood. 1960.

Population Trends in Eastern Europe, The U.S.S.R. and Mainland China. Milbank Memorial Fund, 1960.

Sax, Karl. *Standing Room Only.* Boston: Beacon Press, 1955.

Stone, Abraham, and Himes, N. E. *Planned Parenthood: Birth Control Methods.* New York: The Viking Press, 1958.

Sulloway, Alvah. *Birth Control and Catholic Doctrine.* Boston: Beacon Press, 1959.

United Nations Statistical Yearbook. New York: Columbia University Press, 1958.

Vogt, William. *Road to Survival.* New York: William Morrow & Company, 1948.

Winfield, Gerald. *China: The Land and the People.* New York: William Morrow & Company, 1948.

World Population and Resources. London: Political and Economic Planning, 1955.

6

The Birth of an Age

ON THE EVENING OF AUGUST 6, 1945, THE END OF HOSTILITIES IN World War II seemed to be in sight. The damage that had been worked in the course of the war would have to be repaired, of course. New rights would have to be accorded to colonial peoples, and a new status would have to be granted to men of color, for they had won that concession at the hands of the white man by their war performances. But the troublemaking nations—Japan, Germany, and, in a measure, Italy—were exhausted. Russia had proved to be a valuable ally, and the United Nations held promise of becoming an organization capable of enforcing peace. The whole situation appeared to be very encouraging. The world of 1938 was to be restored, and everyone would begin life where he had left off six or seven years before.

It was not as simple as that, of course, and everyone knew that to be true. A long series of problems awaited the world and the governments of the world. Millions of displaced people would have to be returned to their homes; other millions of enslaved workers would have to be rehabilitated; tens of millions of workers would have to be transferred from munitions factories to peacetime industry; huge factories that had been turning out fleet-loads of war material would have to be adjusted to consumer production; social and economic dislocations would have to be patched up. To none of these were any great numbers of the people giving any attention, however. They were thinking only of the end of the war.

The immediate problem was that of providing food, clothing, shelter, and medical supplies for the destitute of two continents. Universities and governments would have to be restored. An entire generation of doctors, teachers, public-health officers, and other professional workers would have to be trained in terms of advanced techniques that had developed under war pressures. Churches, libraries, art galleries, hospitals, and schools would have to be raised from the dead. All this was going to require an outpouring of public and private philanthropy on an unprecedented scale. The American people were ready for all that, however.

Barely under the surface was the prospect of a desperate struggle for the world's markets, and the American manufacturer whose factory was unscathed occupied a highly advantageous position. Synthetics had been developed, and these chafed for a try at the world's markets. There was to be, of course, the problem of returning millions of women to their homes from the factories and offices. Men under arms would have to be absorbed into industry. Civilians would have to be downgraded in favor of the returning soldiers who had been told their jobs would be waiting for them when they returned from the war. The American spirit is essentially optimistic, and life, progress, productivity, and prosperity seemed to be inevitable.

About midnight on that historic August 6 the radio programs were interrupted to permit an announcement from the government in Washington that an entirely new type of bomb had been dropped on the Japanese city of Hiroshima, completely wiping it out. With the caution typical of such announcements, the statement was limited to the barest of facts, but the impression was left that the effect had been horrendous. Few there were who realized that the simple announcement was the herald of the birth of a new age. It is still difficult, however, even after almost two decades, for millions of people to realize that standards, theories, measurements, and analyses of the preatomic age are no longer valid and that politics, education, industry, statesmanship, and even religion, must begin to think in new terms.

For the brief period of four years incident to World War I the American people had been thrust out into world affairs, but with the signing of the Versailles peace pact they had retreated again into their isolationist shell and, except for the export of manufactured goods, they had washed their hands of the woes of the world. Their energies had been absorbed in developing a new continent. Foreign trade had been but little more than an interesting theory to be debated in college classrooms, and if anyone had mentioned a "cold war" in those same classrooms he would not have been understood, perhaps even by the young PhD who taught the course.

There are historians who say that in terms of historical significance the launching of the bomb is second only to the birth of

Christ. A thousand years from now—perhaps even a hundred—the record of what we thought, how we reacted, and what we decided in the wake of the bomb will be subjected to the most critical analysis. At least one element in the case is unmistakable, however. The United States stands involved at the center of the world, and we will never be able to retreat unless destroyed. Isolationists are as extinct as the triceretops.

Never since the first man came blinking out of the primeval has the race been compelled to deal with so many crises in one crisis. Never has it found itself under the necessity of revising so many estimates, calculating so many new values, or establishing so many outposts of policy. The issues are so tremendous, the process of redemption has so many ramifications, and the importance of the individual has become so crucial that triviality has become a luxury that no man or nation can afford. Blunders committed now can become catastrophies a few decades hence. Our generation is on trial before the centuries.

The future has never depended so heavily upon the good judgment, faith, and moral sensitivity of one generation. We are at the peak of the centuries. Tomorrow we will be blazing trails to Mars. What the future holds in the way of scientific advance sounds like fantasy! At such a point the atomic bomb strode upon the stage.

The bomb that hung in the bay of the "Enola Gay," to be dropped on Hiroshima that August morning, had been nicknamed "Little Boy," but it represented the combined labors of 539,000 persons. At one time or another 10,000 subcontractors had worked on various parts of the enterprise. Approximately $2,000,000,000 had been expended in producing the one hundred pounds of fissionable material that was ready for use the summer of 1945. President Truman told the platform committee of the 1956 Democratic Convention in Chicago that the bomb dropped on Hiroshima carried but thirteen pounds of the fissionable stuff. Fifteen thousand officers and men assembled at the take-off field to carry out the complicated operation of getting the first bomb-carrying plane on its way.

When the great ball of fire eighteen hundred feet in diameter and 100,000 degrees Fahrenheit at the center had cleared away, twenty-eight doctors were left alive to care for a city of a quarter of a million, at least half of the population being casualties. When Otto Hahn, the German scientist who had first split the atom in 1938, heard the news his depression was so profound that friends sat by him constantly for days lest he take his own life. Hansen Baldwin, the military specialist on the staff of the *New York Times*, wrote: "Now we have been the first to introduce a new weapon of unknowable effects which may bring us the victory but which will sow the seeds of hate more widely than ever. We may reap the whirlwind."

The scientists of all the world had good reason to be troubled. A mysterious force had been loosed, the extent of its power being only dimly realized even by those who had unloosed it. Everything it would touch would be changed.[1]

There had been a time when a poet had exclaimed, "Give me men to match my mountains." Now devout men would pray, "Give us men to match our atoms!"

A new age was born before our eyes, and no man understood it!

Suggestions for Further Reading

Amrine, Michael. *The Great Decision.* New York: G. P. Putnam's Sons, 1959.

Byrnes, James F. *All in One Lifetime.* New York: Harper & Brothers, 1958.

Compton, Arthur H. *Atomic Quest.* New York: Oxford University Press, 1956.

Feis, Herbert. *Japan Subdued.* Princeton, N.J.: Princeton University Press, 1961.

Groves, Leslie R. *Now It Can Be Told: The Story of the Manhatten Project.* New York: Harper & Brothers, 1962.

Knebel, Fletcher, and Bailey, Charles W. *No High Ground.* New York: Harper & Brothers, 1960.

McGuire, Paul. *Experiment in World Order.* New York: William Morrow & Company, 1948.

Mowrer, Edgar Ansel. *A Good Time to Be Alive.* New York: Duell, Sloan & Pearce, Inc., 1959.

Titterton, Ernest William. *Facing the Atomic Future.* New York: St. Martin's Press, 1956.

[1] Claude Eatherly, an Air Force major who piloted the "Straight Flush," which was the lead plane of the Hiroshima mission, scouted the city and the weather conditions and radioed to Major Tibbetts who flew the "Enola Gay," which carried the bomb: "Red done one. Advise bomb primary target." He became thereby the individual who actually directed the bombing of the city. As a consequence he has suffered from a guilt complex ever since, with the result that his life has been reduced to wreckage. He has been arrested seven times and committed to mental hospitals nine times. He has been treated with great consideration by the U. S. Government, but he continues as one of the most tragic casualties among all the American fighting forces. See "What Happens to a Man Who Kills 100,000 People," *Parade Magazine* (May 20, 1962).

7

Men, Molecules, and Machines

HOWEVER SHOCKING THE DROPPING OF THE BOMB ON HIROSHIMA may have been it must not be viewed as an isolated event. As a matter of fact, the splitting of the atom is but one in a series of spectaculars. Hundreds of scientific achievements within the space of a decade constitute a scientific breakthrough of unprecedented dimensions.

The beginnings of the scientific age can be traced to a few scattered events in the nineteenth century.

One of the first manifestations of science to make a vivid impression on public opinion was the discovery of anaesthesia, round about 1850. To abolish pain—even at the dentist's—was no small thing. Then came, with Pasteur, with the discovery of microbes which upset the whole of medicine; that of vaccination against infectious diseases; Lister's discovery of antisepsis, and then Terrier's asceptic treatment, following which surgery was able to begin its beneficent ascent. . . .

Then came, in 1894, the first injections of anti-diphtheria serum. Thanks to the joint efforts of Behring and Dr. Roux, croup was conquered, and the lives of thousands of children were saved. . . . Then came the discovery, by the Curies, of radium, the "fabulous metal" which seemed to upset all the laws of the conservation of energy. And meanwhile thousands of industrial applications of science were becoming visible: chemical synthesis, electric light, transformation of the means of communication and transport, etc.[1]

Historians of a hundred years from now will doubtless declare that the course of human affairs took off in an entirely new direction during the decades of 1940-60 as a result of the revolution induced by science.

Until recently there has been little awareness on the part of the plain citizen concerning the near miracles that were being worked

[1] Jean Rostand, Can Man Be Modified? tr. Jonathan Griffin (New York: Basic Books, Inc., 1959), pp. 41-42.

in the laboratories. Beginning with the dropping of the atomic bomb, however, followed by the detonation of the hydrogen bomb in the South Pacific, and still later by Russia's launching of a man into space, the public has been shocked into something just a little like appreciation of the wonders that are being worked every day.

We are at the point where we are in danger of becoming indifferent to miracles. They no longer astound us. Reports coming in from all over the world tell the story of brilliant victories over diseases. Yaws, beriberi, syphilis, tuberculosis, dysentery, smallpox, cholera, hookworm, and leprosy are being brought under control.

When we begin scanning the reports from the biological laboratories we find ourselves in the midst of breathtaking possibilities, some of which call for moral judgments of extreme delicacy. Tens of thousands of cows are artificially inseminated every year. In some sections of Canada it is the standard practice. Moreover, in the modern laboratory it is a commonplace to substitute a chemical agent for the paternal cell in certain types of life. The "miracle" has been worked numberless times in the case of sea urchins, frogs, and even rabbits, and the secretary of the French Academy of Sciences has suggested the possibility of a similar generation of human beings.

There have been numerous instances in recent years of Frenchwomen who have mailed announcements to their friends informing them that they have given birth to children conceived by artificial insemination, and American gynecologists have reported similar impregnations. Precise statistics are not available, but educated guesses inside medical circles put the number at several thousand per year. Some authorities are now insisting that the facts concerning insemination by outside donors should be brought out into the open and that mothers and children should be protected against unfavorable criticism.[2] In a number of cases children begotten by artificial insemination by the consent of both husband and wife have been adjudged to be legal births by American courts.

The subject is still farther complicated by the discovery that semen treated with glycerine can survive extremely low temperatures —as much as 80 degrees Fahrenheit below zero—without losing its

[2] Miller, "The Guidance of Human Evolution," *Perspectives in Biology and Medicine*, III, no. 1 (Autumn, 1959).

capacity to fertilize. Two highly reputable American physicians have reported births in which semen was used which had been frozen for several months in a medium containing glycerine, and the children are normal in every respect. Biological theorists are saying it is possible to freeze semen and preserve it for a hundred years, after which it will inseminate an ovum. If they are correct in their opinion it would mean that an individual could become a father a full century after his death. The legal complications that might result can easily be imagined. What might be the claims that could be lodged against an estate, for example?

Biologists have already succeeded in removing a fertilized egg from the body of one rabbit and transplanting it to the matrix of another, with a normal birth resulting. The same technique has been successful in the case of sows and mares. Illustrations of the extent to which biologists can play a kind of scientific game of biological chess with the reproductive processes could be multiplied through many pages, for the availability of the sex hormone in pure crystallized form has opened up incredible possibilities. By using pituitary hormones animals of gigantic size have been produced, and with the aid of thyroid hormones frogs no larger than flies have been generated.

At England's Cambridge University there is maintained an Animal Research Center, whereat a group of scientists headed by Dr. Cyril Adams has been getting results from hormone-treated highbred ewes that are positively fantastic. Ova have been harvested, fertilized with sperm from highbred rams, and then planted in lowbred ewes. By this method it has been possible to multiply valuable strains several times as fast as would have been possible by the natural process of breeding. In an effort to improve the breed of South African sheep a variation of the plan was used in which fertilized ova were planted in the wombs of rabbits which were then shipped by air. When they arrived four days later they were flushed out with sheep's blood serum and replanted in the wombs of ordinary ewes. In due time high bred English lambs were born. The possibilities involved in this technique appear to be almost limitless.

Not content with manipulating the generative processes, the biologists have succeeded in grafting organs of one animal onto or into the bodies of other animals. The eye of a salamander, for example, has been affixed to the body of a newt and made to function. Isolated organs such as testicles, ovaries, even hearts, lungs, wombs and glands, have been removed from living bodies and kept alive outside their original environment. In one case a cow's udder was kept alive and induced to produce milk in a test-tube situation.[3]

The scientific breakthrough is by no means limited to the physiological sciences. Electronics, hardly known to the world even by name twenty years ago, has been devolped to the point that the scientists are now building machines that "think." Electronic assemblies have been put together which are able to remember, consider, test, and accept or reject suggestions.

Checker-playing machines have been built which can defeat experts. The public is familiar with the ability of electronic brains to work out complicated mathematical problems but is not widely aware of their capacity to reflect, reason, and memorize. The calculating power of the machines now built exceeds the total effectiveness of the entire human race, and their careers have just begun.

Electronic devices are being used in calculating the most complex formulas, designing highways through mountain terrain, formulating plans for jet planes, working with critical speeds, fashioning trajectories, measuring the movements of ocean currents and also their speeds, determining the movements and speeds of ocean winds and meterological tides, proving complex logical propositions, establishing relationships between strange chemical formulas, and solving almost any problem that has a purely mathematical or logical base. It has even been predicted that by 1985 a machine will have been developed which will keep itself in perpetual repair, replacing worn or exhausted parts as the case may require.

Electronic tortoises have been put together which crawl, respond to light, attract or repel one another, and when they are tired—when their batteries run down—they have been "trained" to go to the source of their energy, hook themselves up by means of proper connections without manual guidance of any kind, and there restore their "faculties." An artificial duck has been built which waddles, swims, swallows pieces of bread, and evacuates them in what appears to be normal fashion. Other creatures have been

[3] I am deeply indebted to Jean Rostand and his various books including *Can Man Be Modified?* for information presented in this chapter.

manufactured which display all the characteristics of living organisms with conditioned reflexes.

Experimentation now going on aims to modify the brain of the human embryo by irrigating it with blood, adding hundreds of thousands of cells and otherwise improving it as an organ. It is believed that within the space of no more than two or three decades it will be possible to increase the differences between the weights of the two hemispheres of the brain, thereby increasing the intellectual ability of the individual. Already there are at the disposal of the embryologists hormones and chemical agents that hold promise of stimulating the brain, making it a better instrument of the mind. Henry Turkel, a Detroit physician, has worked something near a miracle in treating mongoloids and others suffering from cranial deformities with inexpensive medication increasing their intellectual receptivity, reducing their repulsive physical characteristics, and opening the way to useful citizenship. It is expected that his methods, if applied to the "slow learners" to be found in all schools, will enable them to accelerate and maintain the pace of the rest of the schoolroom.[4]

Considering the forecasts of the biologists, biochemists, nuclear scientists, mathematicians, astronomers, and astrophysicists, we are compelled to exclaim with the Old Testament psalmist:

> What is man that thou art mindful of him,
> and the son of man that thou dost care for him?
> Yet thou hast made him little less than God,
> and dost crown him with glory and honor.
> Thou hast given him dominion over the works of thy hands.
> (Ps. 8:4-6a R.S.V.)

Suggestions for Further Reading

Changing Times. The Kiplinger Magazine, 1729 H. Street, N.W., Washington 6, D.C.

Harrison, George R. *What Man May Be.* New York: William Morrow & Company, 1956.

Pfeiffer, John, *From Galaxies to Man.* New York: Random House, 1959.

Rostand, Jean. *Can Man Be Modified?* New York: Basic Books Inc., 1959.

[4] Reported in an address delivered at Chicago, December 26, 1959, before the American Association for the Advancement of Science and the Council for Exceptional Children.

Rostand, Jean, and Bodin, Paul. *Life, the Great Adventure.* New York: Charles Scribner's Sons, 1956.

Sinnott, Edmund W. *The Biology of the Spirit.* New York: The Viking Press, 1955.

——————. *Matter, Mind, and Man.* New York: Harper & Brothers, 1957.

Wallace, Bruce, and Dobzhansky, T. *Radiation, Genes and Man.* New York: Holt, Rinehart & Winston, Inc., 1959.

Webster, Gary. *Wonders of Man.* New York: Sheed and Ward, 1957.

8

Lifting the Ceiling of Civilization

THROUGHOUT UNCOUNTED CENTURIES THE CIRCUMSTANCES OF EVERY man's life were determined by his own unsupported powers or by the employment of his own wit. He could aspire to no more abundance than that which he was able to produce or protect by his own strength. When he exerted himself to the limit he was able to provide for the support of no more than one-half person other than himself. The whole of life was dependent upon the energy resident in muscle tissue. The cave man was never able to accumulate any surplus. He considered himself fortunate if he came through to the end of the day with his hunger satisfied. Each day was a problem complete in itself.

When the Neanderthal man—or one of his near of kin—discovered the principle of the lever, the use of the wheel, or the effectiveness of the fire pit, the immediate result was a lightening of the burden of life. Workers equipped with levers or wheels were able to produce more when they expended the same amount of energy. The new tools, however, did not create power; they only made it possible to apply it more effectively.

Then came the domestication of animals, and burdens were transferred from the backs of men to the backs of beasts. Still it was muscle power that provided the energy required in producing the necessities of life. Man had not yet learned to utilize the willing powers that lay ready at hand, unused. The simplest formula for civilization was sufficient. Varying levels of intelligence and occasional physical differences might tip the scales slightly in favor of first one and then of another tribe. All men were endowed approximately equally, however. For the most part issues were decided upon the basis of the effectiveness with which muscle power was applied.

Sometime during the year 1543 a Spanish sea captain displayed in the harbor of Barcelona a device he called a "steam engine," but it was never assigned to the task of lifting a load off any man's back. In the year 1769 a Scotchman named James Watt patented a condenser which made it possible to apply the power of steam to a piston enclosed in a tight chamber, and with this the first real engine became a possibility. When its flywheel had completed the first revolution under its own power, an ally of almost incredible value had been added to man's equipment. At last he was independent of muscle tissue.

Mankind possessed a machine by which all of life could be enlarged and revolutionized. Even a crude engine was capable of delivering the power that would enable a single worker to produce more and better goods than a score of handcrafters could fabricate with their unaided hands. The political aspects of the matter was staggering. Eight million Englishmen, equipped with power machines were more than a match for 40,000,000 French and Belgian handcrafters supplemented by 20,000,000 Germans.

Within a decade the economic balance of Europe was upset. The English, living only a few feet above generous supplies of coal, began to outstrip their continental rivals, and by the end of the century they were the undisputed masters of the commerce of the world.

The introduction of the steam engine, however, launched a revolution that became cataclysmic. Workers left the farms by the thousands to work in the factories. One factory worker equipped with a machine could supply the needs of ten farmers, with the result that manufacturers scouted the world in search of markets and developed an enlarged doctrine of colonialism.

Within a decade it became evident that England was expending her human resources in a way that threatened the nation's health, morals, and honor. By 1850 half the population of the British Isles were to be found in cities of 20,000 or more. In the middle of the sixteenth century London appears to have numbered less than 100,000 inhabitants, but by the middle of the nineteenth century it had mushroomed to 3,000,000. In the meantime more than twenty cities had grown up on the sites of what had been small towns, each one exhibiting the problems of poverty, congestion, and lack of sanitation.

It is outside the scope of such a study as this to go into the record of social decay that set in as an accompaniment to the Industrial

Revolution in England, but it should be mentioned that it was in the midst of this deplorable situation that Karl Marx arrived in London and began writing *Das Kapital*. It was inevitable that the German revolutionary, working and living in a London slum—than which there was nothing worse in the world—should have been profoundly impressed by the inequitable system of distribution that prevailed in English industry. Everywhere he saw British factories producing mountains of goods, and everywhere he saw the English people living in dire poverty. As a consequence, the economic philosophy he worked out in *Das Kapital* was concerned with the problem of distribution almost exclusively. As an economist he was almost completely blind to the problem of production. The *Communist Manifesto* he worked out, with the assistance of Friedrich Engels, a German factory manager in charge of an English mill, was drafted under a black cloud of coal smoke, before a social conscience had awakened in England.

Two basic features contributed to the development of the Industrial Revolution in England: (1) The invention of the steam engine and (2) the availability of inexhaustible (?) supplies of coal which supplied the energy that drove the engines. There would have been no revolution had there been no energy available for the engines.

The primitive fire pits were fueled with wood. Every mention of fire in the literature of the ancients refer to a wood fire. A single notation appearing in one ancient record suggests the possibility that coal may have been used in a religious ceremonial as early as A.D. 852, but it did not come into general use until 1,000 years later. The first American coal mining was done in Virginia in 1750, but again the "black rock" was ignored. The heat supplied to the Founding Fathers as they wrote the Constitution of the United States in Independence Hall came from burning wood. It is highly improbable that George Washington ever saw a coal fire, for coal did not come into general use until 1820. Even as late as 1850 no less than 90 per cent of the fuel consumed by the young nation consisted of wood, and all the fuels then in use provided the energy for no more than 12 per cent of the work output of the nation. Of the total consumption of mechanical energy throughout the world in 1960 less than 7 per cent is of wood origin.

There can be no relief of the burden of life in the underdeveloped areas of the world unless they can be at least in part industrialized. The man with the hoe cannot possibly complete with the man with the tractor. The moment we suggest worldwide industrialization, however, we run into the fact that the world's fuel supplies are nearing the point of exhaustion. The shortages of fuel is one of the world's critical problems, and the solution cannot be long postponed.

Already 80,000,000,000 tons of coal have been taken from the earth. At the current rate we are consuming 2,000,000,000 tons per year, in addition to 5,000,000,0000 barrels of crude petroleum. When a ton of coal or a barrel of oil has been consumed it can never be replaced. Already we are being warned that we are approaching the bottom of the barrel. The meaning of this is perfectly clear: there can be no worldwide program of industrialization until some new supply of energy has been found.

There are, of course, the Colorado shales, which can be treated to produce gasoline. Trillions of tons are available, and gasoline therefrom is already being marketed. Scientific opinion is divided on the subject of probable costs, but even if such gasoline can be produced at a reasonable price the solution would be no more than temporary, for the exploding population is skyrocketing the demand for fuel. The prospect of finding any major oil deposits is not encouraging.

The question of fossil fuels can be stated very easily. (1) Petroleum is the fuel base of the world's economy. (2) The supply is fixed. (3) The end of the supply is in sight. (4) A new source of energy must be found if the industrialization of the world is to be achieved.

In the year 1949 the United States Energy Commission requested Palmer Putnam, a consulting engineer, to prepare a study of the world's energy requirements over the next fifty to two hundred years. He settled upon 1,000,000,000,000,000,000 British thermal units as his standard of measurement, calling it the energy unit. Calculating in terms of 1950, he found that the total world consumption of energy amounted to one fifth of an energy unit annually. His studies led him to the conclusion that during the first 1860 years of the Christian Era the race had consumed between six and nine such units, that between 1860 and 1947 four more were consumed, and that by the year 2,000 the world would be consuming at the rate of *one unit per year.*

He further calculated that the known gas and oil reserves were capable of furnishing six units, but that no more than a fraction of these reserves could be recovered by any known method presently employed. His final judgment was that no more than three fifths of one energy unit could be depended upon for each year. In other words, *the end of industrial expansion was in sight!*[1] Just at that point uranium appeared on the scene.

At precisely fifteen minutes before four o'clock on the afternoon of December 2, 1942, Enrico Fermi, the Italian nuclear physicist, thrust control rods into a uranium pile which had been set up under the west stands of the football field at the University of Chicago and called the wierd assembly into life. Like some fantastic creation from another world it poured forth neutrons. *At that moment the gates of the Atomic Age swung back and a new act of creation took place!* The one limitless supply of energy in the universe was being tapped. If the fission reaction could be harnessed the energy requirements of all the race for all time would belong to mankind.

Atomic energy, like any other form of energy, is obtained from fuel. In a single pound of uranium there is as much resident energy as in 1,300 tons of coal, and the world's uranium reserves are said to represent 1,650 of Putnam's energy units. One other feature of the case opens up fantastic possibilities, however. In every gallon of ocean water there is to be found a certain amount of deuterium— heavy water—which is capable of supplying as much energy as two hundred gallons of gasoline. Reputable physicists believe the hydrogen atom can be "split" to produce energy for industrial use, and when this occurs we will be in possession of the basic energy by which the universe operates. There will be no limit to the power available to man for any purpose to which he sets his mind.

When the possibility of unlimited stores of energy is thrust into the contemporary scene it begins to appear fantastic. In spite of the cautious statements of the energy commissions of the world it is commonly known that we are on the brittle edge of discoveries of almost incredible magnitude. When the energy of raw hydrogen

[1] See Putnam, *Energy in the Future* (Princeton, N.J.: D Van Nostrand Company, 1953).

has been tapped there will be no task requiring power that will remain outside the field of man's aspiration. The industrialization of the whole world will become an immediate possibility.

Mankind has come to the most dramatic moment in human history. The horizons of life are being lifted everywhere.

Certain words of the New Testament have a very modern sound: "All things are yours!"

Suggestions for Further Reading

Brown, Harrison. *Challenge of Man's Future.* New York: The Viking Press, 1956.

Clark, Stanley. *The Oil Century.* Norman, Okla.: University of Oklahoma Press, 1958.

Putnam, Palmer. *Energy in the Future.* New York: D. Van Nostrand Company, 1953.

Rister, Carl Coke. *Oil! Titan of the Southwest.* Norman, Okla.: University of Oklahoma Press, 1949.

9

The Revolution of Rising Expectations

FROM ALMOST EVERY QUARTER OF THIS EARTH THERE COMES THE word that suddenly, and almost without the "developed" areas of the world knowing anything about it, the peoples of the underdeveloped lands are awakening and are in the grip of a vast new aspiration. They are beginning to expect of life what they have never expected, in all the thousands of years of their existence. It is not only that they are beginning to demand more comforts, necessities, and machines, but also that they are seeking cultural, spiritual, and intellectual privileges and benefits. In the best sense of the word, it must be said that they are dreaming of the "new life" and setting out in search of it.

Someone with a gift of pungent expression has given this new experience the name "the revolution of rising expectations." Our world and our generation present to the historians a spectacular never before conceived. Not only have we developed the power to achieve, but the will to achieve is developing along with it throughout the earth. There is something very thrilling in it all.

Strictly speaking, we are witnessing a development which is centering about two poles. (1) A social and political cataclysm is reorienting the political opinions, moral convictions, social practices, and spiritual incentives of all the world, and the effects inside the underdeveloped areas are unprecedented. (2) The scientific powers and techniques now ready at hand make it possible for us to change the entire structure of civilization so that the ancient fatalism is being questioned as never before.

Within the last two decades hundreds of millions of the people of the earth have come to the conclusion that their fate is not fixed at birth and that it is not unalterable, as some of their spiritual leaders have assured them it was. They have, therefore, decided *there is something they can do about their own wretchedness, and they have determined to do it.* At least they have determined to do something!

In their determination to do something hangs the secret of the hope of a large part of the future of the world. If, falsely led and cruelly deceived, they undertake to do the wrong thing the disaster will be catastrophic. If rightly and unselfishly led—they are guided and enabled to do the right thing—the results can be dazzling.

Many factors have contributed to this abrupt change in the mind of the underprivileged of the world, but at least some part of the awakening stems from seeds sown by the Christian missionaries who have gone to the ends of the earth teaching the revolutionary doctrine that all men are made in the image of God. This has had the effect of creating a self-respect, a sense of dignity, a new concept of the importance of the individual, and a "will to become" that is revolutionary.

Once any man begins to believe he is made in the image of God he becomes a difficult man to enslave. He develops a new concept of justice, responsibility, honor, and dignity. He becomes ambitious to emancipate himself from evils that have been long endured because they have been believed to be inevitable. He determines to free himself from pain, hunger, disease, and ignorance, in the belief that he and his children were destined not to be victims, but free children of God. He may be guilty of impatience, and he may be incapable at first of correctly measuring all the true values of life, but the determination to do something in his own behalf is the first fruit of his belief in his own value as one who has been made in the image of God.

The development of various media of communications during the last two decades has provided the people of the under-developed areas of the world with a chance to see how the peoples of the developed areas live. On a little teakwood table in a village silk shop in Thailand there lay an assortment of American women's magazines. They were somewhat outdated, and they bore abundant evidence of having been studied by perhaps scores of the village women. The demure little salesgirl explained it, saying, "All our women want to dress like American women." Her comment provides an opportunity for an abundance of jests, but it also makes necessary some very sober thinking. American slick magazines are read around the world by millions of women who do not even know the name of the United States Secretary of State. They circulate among the people who never see an administrator of American foreign aid.

Twenty-five years ago the lives of millions were tinctured by a strong spirit of fatalism. Hunger, pain, disease, poverty—such evils were believed to be inescapable if not actual visitations of the gods. Today those same millions are defying the old taboos, revolting against ancient enslavements, and setting off in search of the elemental satisfactions of life—food, clothing, shelter, health— and the cultural and spiritual values—ideals, convictions, education, individual worth, human dignity. If they are creating new woes to take the place of old bondage it must be explained by the fact that, lacking experience, they have misjudged values or they have been deceived. At least they are shaking off their chains, and once that men have learned that they can live free of chains they can never again be enslaved.

One of the striking aspects of the revolution of rising expectations is the new concern for health. No longer are men content to suffer pain because it is "the will of the gods." One of the first projects to be launched by any new government is apt to be a national hospital. More new institutions of healing have gone up in the last decade than were built in the previous century. It can almost be said that a health program for the people is designed as soon as a new government gets its currency printed. Certainly no government which does not dedicate its first efforts to the question of public health can stay long in power. There still remains throughout large areas of the earth a tragic burden of pain and a threat of disease, but nowhere are they officially ignored.

In this connection it should be noted, perhaps, that all such public-health programs are strongly flavored with something that is called "socialism" by many Americans. It is obviously impossible to erect modern hospitals, to train modern technicians, and to stock a country with modern pharmaceutical materials with funds raised by popular subscription among people who go to bed hungry every night. Private charity could correct many conditions if the relatively few extremely wealthy could be touched by man's in- firmities. As matters stand at the moment, however, governments are assuming the responsibility, partly for political reasons and partly because they can get assistance from abroad for a great humanitarian enterprise.

In similar fashion the governments of the world are under a tremendous pressure to organize national programs of education. In one national capital after another the tourist will be shown new and modern campuses, glittering like freshly mounted jewels. All are crowded with students. Not the least impressive feature of most of the new universities of the Old World is the fact that their doors are open to young women on the same terms as they are to young men. Girls in laboratory smocks work alongside young men, much to the academic embarrassment of those same young men. In science many girls are chalking up brilliant records.

Admittedly, the statistics coming out of Red China are subject to serious suspicion, but when all allowance has been made for official inflation it remains true that millions of people behind the bamboo curtain are becoming literate. There is an awareness everywhere that glowing economic expectations cannot be realized without an accompanying educational program.

The second pole of the revolution of rising expectations is in the broad field of science.

In the hundred-year period from 1840 to 1940 science made possible, directly and through technology, a total revolution not only in the circumstances of life, but also in our view of man's place in nature. In the twenty years since 1940 the change has been literally explosive. The mind of man has entered the nucleus of the atom and the nucleus of the cell, and man himself is now about to enter space.[1]

Within the last twenty years we have been equipped with reactors, transistors, and computers. In the fifteen years that have elapsed between the cessation of hostilities in 1945 and the launching of a man into space in 1961, we were introduced to cybernetics, chemotherapy, solid-state physics, micronuclear electronics, bionomics, astronautics, nuclear physics, thermonuclear research, ocean-bottom geography, and a considerable list of other science disciplines. For the first time in history a town has been lighted and powered with electricity generated by atomic energy. Anti-

[1] Warren Weaver, "A Great Age for Science," *Goals for Americans*, the Report of the President's Commission on National Goals, p. 103. © by The American Assembly 1960. Prentice-Hall, Inc., publisher.

biotics have come to the aid of medicine; machines have been invented which make it possible to lower the temperature of the human body to the point that heart surgery can be pursued almost indefinitely. Synthetic fibers have been woven into fine cloth; wood pulp has been spun into beautiful yarn; and fashion designers are now working with textiles made of paper. The International Geophysical Year provided information which makes it possible to bring ocean currents, cloud formations, and trade winds under control, thus giving man his first "dominion" over the weather. New elements have been put to use in agriculture, medicine, and manufacturing.

One of the most important facts in this connection is that *there are no scientific secrets.* Laws that come to light in one laboratory are usually known within a matter of hours or days in other laboratories around the world for the simple reason that electrons, neutrons, protons, deutrons, nuclei, and autoneutrinos recognize no color lines or national boundaries. They are the common property of all scientists, regardless of their political faith. Inasmuch as more than a score of nations have set up atomic energy commissions under the direction of skilled physicists, geochemists, astrophysicists, nuclear scientists, and mathematicians, and inasmuch as scientific instruments are available everywhere, Jesus' comment is very much to the point: "Nothing is covered up that will not be revealed." (Luke 12:2.)

As an illustration, there is the case of the first hydrogen bomb exploded by the United States in the South Pacific, March 1, 1954. The test was conducted under the strictest secrecy, but within less than three weeks the Japanese scientists had analyzed the radioactive dust from the deck of the "Lucky Dragon No. 5" and announced to the world the precise nature and power of the bomb that had been detonated.

It is difficult for most of us to sense the tremendous significance of the scientific breakthrough thas has occurred before our very eyes during the last quarter of a century.

For science is not technology, it is not gadgetry, it is not some mysterious cult, it is not a great mechanical monster. Science is an adventure of the human spirit. It is an essentially artistic enterprise, stimulated largely by curiosity, served largely by disciplined imagination, and based largely on faith in the reasonableness, order, and beauty of the universe of which man is a part.[2]

One of the dramatic aspects of this ultramodern world into which we are plunging is the shifting of the scientific scene from the tiny, impoverished laboratory manned by a single scientist working with clumsy equipment, to the vast organization, the elaborately housed and fantastically financed government installation whose operations reach out into limitless space. The National Science Foundation calculated in 1960 that the total funds expended by the United States in private and governmental research and development during the year 1955 amounted to $5,600,000,000 and that in the succeeding five years the total had increased to $12,400,000,000. Present-day calculations estimate that by 1975 this will have increased to $30,000,000,000.

Gone is the day of the isolated scientist who makes an accidental discovery while pursuing private research. In its place has dawned the day of mass attacks on the mysterious and the unknown, in which hundreds and even thousands of researchers, under the direction of impressive commissions and aided by electric computers, set out to analyze whole fields. The results include the elimination of diseases from entire continents, the increase of food supplies for millions, and a general improvement of the health of nations.

With the close of World War II tens of millions of Europeans lacked adequate food and many more millions were unemployed. More than half the great cities of the continent lay in ruins; somewhat in excess of 30,000,000 were listed as displaced persons. Hope had fled; transport was at a standstill; black markets were the common markets; morals were in eclipse; currencies were utterly unreliable; and rubble filled the streets of villages, towns, and cities. Hundreds of settlements had been completely destroyed; industrial installations were demolished; and hundreds of thousands—perhaps even millions—of human bodies lay buried under the debris. In spite of all this gloom and horror, however, there has been an amazing recovery. "Europe this side of the Soviet bloc is the most prosperous area of its size and population on the

[2] *Ibid.,* p. 105.

87

earth." [3] The recovery is an illustration of the competence with which mankind is equipped to meet the revolution of rising expectations.

The speed and competency with which Europe has rehabilitated itself since the close of World War II by means of techniques approved by the free enterprise system of social organization is the most difficult argument the Communists have to meet in their efforts to impose Marxism upon the world. We are witnessing an extremely convincing demonstration of the doctrine that there are no such producers known to civilization as free men. This demonstration of freemen's ability to achieve economic freedom and plenty at the same time is highly convincing behind any curtain.

Without taking time to explore the fantastic achievements which may be expected to be realized during the next twenty-five years, let it be said that we are equipped with the scientific techniques, the economic and industrial skills, and the paraphernalia of productivity, that would enable us to banish hunger, disease, and ignorance if our resources could be released from military demands and put at the disposal of engineers of peace. "The Marshall Plan primed the pump. But European ingenuity, organization, and experience are responsible for the high level of progress achieved and maintained." [4]

Suggestions for Further Reading

Adams, Richard N., et al. *Social Change in Latin America Today*. Published for the Council on Foreign Relations. New York: Harper & Brothers, 1960.

Fertig, Lawrence. *Prosperity Through Freedom*. Chicago: Henry Regnery Company, 1961.

Hempstone, Smith. *Africa: Angry Young Giant*. New York: Frederick A. Praeger, Inc., 1961.

Hughes, John. *The New Face of Africa*. New York: Longmans, Green & Company, 1961.

Millikan, Max F., and Blackmer, Donald L. M., editor. *The Emerging Nations: Their Growth and U.S. Policy*. Boston: Little Brown & Company, 1961.

Smith, Donald E. *Nehru and Democracy*. New York: Longmans, Green & Company, 1958.

See also bibliography for Chapter 1.

[3] Louis Fischer, *Russia, America, and the World* (New York: Harper & Brothers, 1961), p. 101.
[4] *Ibid.*

10

Of Nations in Commotion

NEARLY THIRTY NATIONS, WITH A POPULATION OF SOMEWHAT IN excess of 700,000,000 people, have become independent states since the close of World War II. Nothing comparable has ever happened in the history of mankind. Each one represents an underdeveloped area of the world, and each one has become a member of the United Nations, thus coming into possession of a forum from which to proclaim its purpose, announce its program, and lodge its protest. Whatever the failures of the United Nations may have been, it has at least offered a rostrum whereon any government on earth is permitted the enjoyment of free speech. This, too, is something new under the sun. Never in the history of mankind has it been possible for the small nations to lay their cases before the world for what they are worth.

Let there be no mistake about the matter. The small nations of the world take the United Nations seriously. In one national capital after another, in Central America, in Southeast Asia, and in South America, parks, libraries, community forums, and graceful monuments bear the name of the United Nations in some form— an eloquent tribute to the hope it has inspired in the hearts of the nations that have been so long inarticulate.

Until very recently the white man has enjoyed a preferred status everywhere around the earth. He has shared in privileges enjoyed by no other men; he has reaped profits in other men's homelands; he has exploited the natural resources that inhere in the earth upon which other men live; he has assumed rights because he was the master; he has enjoyed immunities from the laws of half the nations of the earth; he has in some cases demanded privileges he could not justify; he has allowed his superiority complex to blind him to the signs of the coming upheaval. In large part he has been oblivious to the signs of the revolution of rising expectations, and now that it has caught up with him he finds it difficult to understand.

One cannot travel long in the underdeveloped areas of the world without being made aware of the fact that the sun of colonialism has set. Fewer people are living today under alien rulers than at any time during the last five hundred years. In the brief space of two decades more than 1,500,000,000 men and women have been freed from, or have shaken off, alien domination—usually of the white man. One of the new commendable attitudes is the reluctance of "the man in the loincloth" to allow tourists to take his picture. His unwillingness to allow the white man with the camera to impose upon his privacy may seem trivial, but it is indicative of his rising self-respect and patriotism.

The foregoing is not to say that colonialism was all bad. Actually, it has made a very great contribution to the underdeveloped areas. Armies of civil servants have been trained in orderly, organized life. Expansive port facilities have been installed; railways have been built; highways have opened up remote areas; natural resources have been tapped; millions of individuals have been given some degree of training in agriculture; oil fields have been brought into productivity; mining operations have been improved; markets have been opened up for native handcrafts; a start has been made in organizing labor; capital has been accumulated; banking contacts have been improved; credit and capital have been spread about; schools, hospitals, radios, medical services, and mass communications have been multiplied. No infant government has found it necessary to start from scratch.

Arnold J. Toynbee, the famous British historian, in assessing the forces operating in the postwar world, has said, "Our age will be remembered not for its horrifying crimes or its outstanding inventions, but for the fact that mankind has dared to believe it practical to make the benefits of civilization available to the whole of the human race."

Every reason for the revolution of rising expectations goes back to one of four great trunk ideas.

1. The Christian missionaries are responsible.

Missionaries have been teaching millions of people in the underdeveloped areas of the world that they are made in the image of God—that they are endowed from their birth with "certain inalienable rights." An American educator who had spent thirty years in Korea once said to me, "If you give people that opinion of themselves they will never accept slavery willingly."

Literally thousands of Christian missionaries have gone to the ends of the earth with this doctrine. They have convinced the backward millions that, as human beings, they have rights and worth. Once the yeast of self-respect has been kneaded into the social dough a leavening is inevitable. Millions who have never accepted the Christian theology have accepted the Christian interpretation of human rights.

It is impossible to understand the vast upheaval in Asia today unless one sees it as a *social* revolution affecting every aspect of society— political, economic, cultural and religious. The struggle against Western imperialism is but one of its many aspects. It expresses itself in the growing industrialization of Asia, in the efforts to abolish feudal land systems, in the growth of large cities and the disintegration of village communities, in the removal of social inequalities, and in the growth of new convictions about the nature of the universe and the meaning of human life.

At the risk of over-simplification we may say that this social revolution has three major aims—political freedom, economic justice and social equality.[1]

2. *American idealism has spread around the world like a contagion.*

The one name known by more people of the world than any other, with exception of that of Jesus Christ, is Abraham Lincoln. His immortal Gettysburg Address is known, in whole or in part, and is quoted by more youth than any words that have ever fallen from human lips, with the exception of the Sermon on the Mount. Not far behind are the throbbing sentences of the Declaration of Independence, penned by Thomas Jefferson, and phrases from Washington's farewell address or his second inaugural address.

Later American spokesmen such as Woodrow Wilson and Franklin D. Roosevelt are quoted by schoolboys in Asia, Africa, and Latin America. For almost two centuries American publicists,

[1] Rajah B. Manikam (ed.), *Christianity and the Asian Revolution* (New York: Friendship Press, 1955), p .7. Used by permission.

orators, preachers, and educators—along with editors and states-men—have proclaimed the American doctrines of democracy, with the result that the underdeveloped nations of the earth have taken them seriously. Because they have believed we meant what we said, they have determined to translate those high ideals into their own languages and social structures. When the American govern-ment has not supported them in their aspirations, and when we have supported the wrong leaders and rulers, their disillusionment has been bitter and deep.

3. For the first time the world is living as one world.

Mass communications have made it possible for the editors of morning papers in Tokyo, Saigon, Bombay, Delhi, Capetown, Karachi, Teheran, Kabul, Ankara, Elisabethville, Manila, Khar-toum, Guatemala City, Buenos Aires, La Paz, and Bogota—and in a hundred other cities and ports—to comment editorially within three hours following the return of a jury that has refused to convict a gang of lynchers.

A bellicose speech by an American congressman who is under-taking to make hay with the voters back home may be read avidly by men of half a hundred nations on four continents. A hasty resolution by a church conference, adopted without thoughtful consideration of the issues involved, can start trouble for mission-aries in twenty lands within ten hours. Hollywood scandals are reported in the lands where Communist agents are engaged in fomenting unrest. American juvenile delinquency makes the front pages of every major city in the world, as do also the stories of student revels at Fort Lauderdale and Galveston. A riot in a Chicago housing development gets screaming headlines within hours.

4. Governments everywhere are under unprecedented pressures from the people.

For almost every disease that affects the bodies politic some political physician declares he has the remedy. Five-year plans are everywhere on the books. Many of the young governments are going out ahead of the people in search of cures for social sores. Because private capital does not exist in sufficient amount with which to bring in the millennium, 2,000,000,000 of the people of the world look to their governments for financial miracles.

In all this they are encouraged by the fact that there is a World

Import and Export Bank, even when they do not have the slightest idea as to what the function of such an institution may be. The fact that there are such organizations as UNESCO, World Health Organization, the Colombo Plan, American Point-Four Program, United Nations Fund for Economic Development, and thousands of national committees, bureaus, commissions and collectives has inspired the inexperienced people of the world to believe there is some social magic that can produce prosperity for all overnight. Some part of this is a holdover from the feudalism that has prevailed for centuries, and some part of it has been encouraged by the philosophy of statism that has been taking possession of the world during the last quarter of a century. The amazing thing is not that the world seems to be going socialistic, but that it is moving so slowly in that direction. Industry, commerce, finance, transportation, education, and capital have all assumed massive proportions. In the face of such the individual feels dwarfed, and it is inevitable that government should become massive. Never in the history of mankind have so many responsibilities been assigned to the politicians.

Historically speaking, the peoples of the underdeveloped areas are seeking for little more than the American colonists sought when they declared their independence in 1776. Just as the young government of the United States found itself harassed by a succession of dilemmas, so also the young governments of today find themselves imperiled by crises for which they have had little training. The moment a Nasser or a Castro comes into power he is confronted with problems for which his revolutionary training has not prepared him. It is relatively easy to start a jungle war and bring an unpopular government tumbling down. It is an altogether different matter to stabilize the life of a nation, establish the economic interests of the people on a dependable basis, educate them to assume the responsibilities democracy imposes, and purge the nation's life of injustices that have luxuriated for centuries.

The strong man on a horse is apt to be a terribly confused individual behind a presidential desk, and even the most brilliant rhetoric is a poor substitute for a smoothly functioning economic system. At least seventy of the member-states of the United Nations face twelve major problems, each of which constitutes a critical issue with which all must deal if they are to survive as successful democracies.

1. Truly democratic self-government must be established or the underdeveloped nations will go Communist.

The Western democracies must be prepared to support the infant democracies with all the powers at their command, even though the political dialect they speak may have a strange accent. All too many times the Western democracies have supported autocracies that were at war with democratic movements. Postwar France, for example, expended $2,000,000,000 in a futile effort to stem the tide of democracy in Vietnam, and this was almost the precise amount of money the nation received from the United States for postwar recovery. As a consequence it is difficult to convince the Asians that the American government is not an ally of autocracy. When the Communists offered to help the revolutionaries they were welcomed. Something of the same situation exists in the case of Indonesia, though toward the last of the struggle the United States did come to the aid of the democratic forces.

The struggle to establish a far greater degree of justice and equality in relationships among differing peoples has become a supreme issue in this new age. In the long view it is far more serious than the difference between the Western world and Russia. And there is not much time left for action. Quickly, lest a swollen stream of bitterness and hatred be released into history, the idea of racial equality must express itself in mental attitudes, social customs, and law.[2]

2. Food production must be stepped up.

The first responsibility of the new governments is so to order the economic affairs of their respective nations that the people need not go to bed hungry every night. As of today, the race between hunger and population is being lost everywhere around the world, except in western Europe, Australasia, Canada, the United States, and some few sections in South America.[3]

[2] Alan Walker, *A New Mind for a New Age* (Nashville: Abingdon Press, 1959), p. 75.

[3] If all the grain now stored in the United States were to be released to the substandard areas of the world, it would be consumed in less than twenty-four hours, and 1,500,000,000 people would be hungry before a week was out. In any event, the American surplus must be viewed as a temporary phenomenon.

As early as 1946 the United Nations Food and Agricultural Organization undertook an investigation of the food situation in a series of underdeveloped areas and estimated that in India alone it would be necessary to triple the production of fruits, vegetables, eggs, and fish; double the production of roots, tubers, fats, oils, pulses, and nuts; and increase the milk production by 40 per cent, in order to meet the minimum nutritional needs of the expanding population by 1960. In a 1955 review of the case it was shown that the overall situation had worsened instead of bettering. In March, 1961, the official census showed that the population had upped from an anticipated 400,000,000 to 438,000,000.

3. Agriculture must be revised.

Everywhere the problem is the same: More nutrition must be extracted from the soil. Japan has led the way with scientific seed selection, the use of chemical fertilizers, and new agricultural techniques. Simple iron plows, and occasionally small tractors, are appearing in scattered areas in Asia, taking the place of the ancient wooden implements. The additional depth of two inches in the furrows almost doubles the yield per acre. There is a limit, however, beyond which improved techniques and scientific skills cannot go in producing food, but there are millions of reluctant or weary acres that can be nursed back to productivity.

Perhaps more difficult than teaching new farming methods is the creation of a new psychology. In 1955 I visited an Indian village to which had been assigned a high-grade American bull. It had been hoped that a new blood strain might increase the milk yield of the local herds, but the pride of the village officials was wounded, and unwilling to concede any superiority to an imported animal, they ordered the bull butchered.

There is serious need for a program of education that will reach down to the 500,000 Indian villages and hundreds of thousands of hamlets scattered through Asia—outside of Red China—Africa, and South America. Millions of farmers must be taught the advantages of planting their crops in rows. More millions must be taught the advantages of good seed over poor seed. At least primitive principles of irrigation must be taught to a few community leaders who will guide their neighbors. Red China can compel farmers to change their ways, but a democracy must rely upon persuasion.

4. New land systems must be inaugurated.

Everywhere in the underdeveloped areas of the world the question of land ownership emerges as the major damper on food production. There can be no worldwide improvement until the land is in the hands of those who till it. The reforms that have been accomplished by the Formosan government in this regard are spectacular and set a pattern for all Asia. In the 1930's, 31 per cent of Japanese farmers owned no land at all and 42 per cent more owned so little that they were forced to rent additional land from someone else." [4] Rentals took more than half the crop, and in bad years the farmers ran into debt, being compelled to pay excessive interest rates to the money lenders. As tenants, hopelessly involved, they were voiceless in all matters of national politics. The first problem to which General MacArthur addressed himself was a distribution of the land. Almost 5,000,000 acres were purchased from the large owners who were compelled to sell, these being sold to 4,000,000 tenant and part-tenant farmers, none of whom were allowed to own more than 7½ acres. Within the space of months agricultural production began to climb, so that today the Japanese farmers are growing more food per acre than any other farmers on earth.[5]

There is no nation anywhere in the underdeveloped areas in which land ownership does not stand at the head of the list of economic problems to be solved. Unless acres can be divided by the democratic process, they will be appropriated by the Communist process.

5. A beginning must be made in industrialization.

The Neanderthal man, with his newly discovered lever, immediately became the equal of twenty of his neighbors who had no levers if a stone had to be moved. An American farmer on a tractor can plow more land than two hundred Indian farmers can turn over with their simple spades. Less than 12 per cent of the manpower of the United States, equipped with power machinery, is producing a surplus of food for a nation that enjoys the highest standard of living anywhere on this planet.

An altogether new element has entered the scene since 1938,

[4] Chester Bowles, *Ideas, People and Peace* (New York: Harper & Brothers, 1958), p. 42.
[5] *Ibid.*, pp. 42-43.

when the first nylon hose were offered for sale in a Wilmington, Delaware, department store. Since that time synthetic textiles have taken over, requiring Japan to overhaul its silk-based economy. Synthetic rubber, currently supplying 50 per cent of the market, has resulted in an agricultural revolution in half a dozen countries on two continents. Raw materials are everywhere in competition with chemically contrived substitutes. Heretofore the underdeveloped nations have depended for their living on the export of natural products. The industrial age is making it necessary to revamp national economies on a wholesale basis, and is achieving independence of natural substances.

6. *Capital must be accumulated.*

For centuries the feudal system trained the peasants to look to their overlords for their economic security. The landlord was the banker, the financial advisor, the agricultural dictator, and the political master. With the disappearance of the landlord class the people are turning to their governments. A democracy unable to establish conditions which make it possible for the people to provide for themselves is doomed. It is for this reason that the rivalry between India and Red China must be resolved in favor of the former. Unless a democracy can do a better job for the peasant and the poor, it will be rendered helpless in any contest with Communism.

The first essential of industrialization is some equivalent of money with which to provide machines. Capital can be accumulated in only two ways: (1) The people must consume less than they produce, or (2) they must attract risk capital from developed areas. Because the producers in the underdeveloped areas are now underfed, the first method has small chance of success.

In 1943 tens of thousands of the farmers of Bengal were drawn off the farms and paid generous wages for working on airfields, military roads, and camps needed by British and American troops. The farmers sold their scanty stocks of seed at high prices; the workers pocketed more money than they had ever handled in all their lives before. Within the space of weeks, however, the food pinch became severe, and a few months later hundreds of thousands were faced with starvation. Their money was not producing food.

Nowhere in Asia—with the exception of small areas in the Near East—Africa, or Latin America are there sufficient capital reserves to initiate any large-scale industrialization without producing a food shortage. Russia and China have achieved a considerable measure of success, but in both cases it has been at the expense of domestic budgets. Income needed for home consumption has been appropriated for heavy industry. The problem therefore reduces itself to simple dimensions. The provision of machines must await the accumulation of capital.

Let us cite India again as an illustration. The voluntary savings of 438,000,000 Indians, even including those of the wealthy, amount to no more than 3 per cent per year, in contrast to the 15 per cent that is saved by the people of the United States. By comparison this means the average American is able to save seventy times as much per year as the average Indian.

7. Education must be universalized.

For a long list of problems there can be no solutions until the people have been provided with the rudiments of an education. Communism can thrive among the ignorant if there is a small force of cadres capable of executing the orders that come down from above, but a democracy must train every citizen on the lowest level to make independent decisions.

8. Barriers must be erased.

It is difficult for citizens of an advanced democracy to realize how high the barriers are which must be surmounted in the under-developed areas. Because of the isolation of many sections those who use one tongue may be almost total strangers to those who use another. In one short drive in India I crossed through territory in which six different languages were in use. United Nations field workers have reported that there are literally millions of Indian peasants who do not even know the name of Nehru, to say nothing of understanding his political policies.

Religions, castes, mountain ranges, rivers, landlords, and even a few degrees difference in temperature have had the effect of isolating peasants from the main stream of a nation's life on at least three continents. During the last decade more millions of unprepared people have been thrust out into the maelstrom of national movements than has been the case in any hundred years of earlier human history.

9. Populations must be distributed.

At the very moment when 50,000,000 "excess babies" are being born into the world every year and when the population pressures are becoming unbearable, huge territories lie half occupied. If, for example, 20,000,000 Javans could be persuaded to remove to Sumatra the nation would gain a breathing spell and the migrants would enjoy an enlarged opportunity. If the oil-rich aristocracies of Iraq and Iran could be induced to accept their social responsibilities, and if they could be persuaded to use their petroleum millions to improve the lot of the peasants, the problem of the Middle East would approach a solution. Brazil could accommodate an additional 50,000,000 if the clearing of the jungles could be financed. Any effort, to achieve results, however, must proceed in the face of prejudice, superstition, ignorance, and national pride.

10. Population growth must be controlled.

It needs to be said again that the race between babies and food supplies represents Communism's opportunity. Any solution of the problem must be indigenous. The widespread suspicion that greets any proposal from the West makes the problem especially difficult. For centuries it has been assumed that an expanding population was a sign of national good health, and a defensive force. Man power has meant military power. Marx declared that labor produces all the wealth, and the more labor the more wealth. In this situation the Christian missionary occupies a key position. He lives in the midst of the people and usually has their confidence. This puts him into a position to interpret birth control and other economic matters as a constructive measure.

11. The refugee problem must be solved.

The refugee has been legally defined by the United Nations as "one who has been uprooted from his home, has crossed a frontier—official or traditional—and looks for protection and sustenance to a government or authority other than his former one." It has been said of the German refugees, for example, that they are "the most dangerous time bomb left behind by Hitler."

It is not too much to say that the refugee problem could unsettle the political and economic balance of western Europe. In West Germany alone there are 10,500,000 officially designated refugees out of a population of 49,550,000. They have their own political party and hold half a hundred seats in the Federal Council. One minister in the cabinet gives his entire time to refugee problems, and four other ministers have vital concerns in the subject. In West German schools 22.3 per cent of all children come from refugee families. If the United States were to be compelled to deal with an equal problem it would mean 35,000,000 people.

In Asia the problem is everywhere acute. In Korea there were 9,000,000 homeless in 1953. Late in 1959 it was reported that there were 2,500,000 in Hong Kong and scores of thousands more struggling to get in. In 1955 this writer drove through a "village" of refugees in South Vietnam which extended along the highway for forty-two miles. Following partition 8,500,000 Hindus and Sikhs fled from Pakistan to India, and 6,500,000 Moslems migrated from India to Pakistan. In Palestine nearly 1,000,000 Arabs live in refugee villages, of which number 200,000 are children who were born in such villages. Then, 400,000 Jews have been expelled from Yemen, Iraq, and North Africa. It is the refugees who compose the street mobs in Amman and who seek to shape the policies of Jordan. All over the continents of Asia and Africa people are still being uprooted, and until the refugee problem can be solved there will be no peace in the world.

Because of the population pressures in China an exodus began at least two hundred years ago which continues to this day, with millions congregated in half a dozen nations in Southeast Asia. More recently they have migrated to South and Central America. They are like the Hebrew exiles in ancient Babylon—forever remembering their motherland and continuing insoluble as citizens.

Until the last fifteen years they have walked in humiliation, because of the low estate into which their home government had fallen. They were imposed upon, despised, and denied numerous privileges. Instinctively proud and secretly contemptuous of the "inferiors" among whom they lived, they remained aloof, made money, and continued a people apart. With the upsurge of Red China they assumed an unaccustomed dignity and have become vocal. In Indonesia the government has discovered them as a problem, for in large numbers they are taking orders from Peking. Throughout Southeast Asia they are either deliberately or unintentionally creating issues. Now the problem is spreading to Africa and Latin America. Men who were immigrants, seeking a land in which they might make a living, only a few decades ago have become the most widely dispersed potential fifth column in the world. The problem of the unassimilated Chinese is one of the most baffling with which the young nations have to deal. This is, currently, the experience of at least fifty new governments.

12. Men must have something for which to live.

Throughout large areas of the earth the underdeveloped peoples have known nothing other than oppressive governments. Tyrants have come and tyrants have gone, but the tyranny has been much the same. Now come the Communists exalting the state and summoning the people to take pride in serving it. Religious passion and the dedication that ought to go into good religion has been taken captive by politics. The resources of the spirit are being inducted into the service of the state, as it is represented by the party.

There is a need in every country in the world for a faith that will capture the loyalty and the allegiance of the people—one that is grounded in the Christian principles of respect for human dignity, the worth of the individual, and individual moral responsibility. This is democracy's opportunity. The time has come when we should be emphasizing what we are for and not just what we are against.

This, then, is the supreme issue with which we are faced at the moment that the future is upon us: Shall the spirit of man rule or be ruled? In any attempt to answer the question we find ourselves face to face with Communism. To a consideration of this issue we now proceed.

Suggestions for Further Reading

Bowles, Chester. *The New Dimensions of Peace.* New York: Harper & Brothers, 1955.

Buckingham, Walter. *Automation, It's Impact on Business and People.* New York: Harper & Brothers, 1961.

Caldwell, John C. *Children of Calamity.* New York: The John Day Company, 1957.

Carter, Gwendolen M. *Independence for Africa.* New York: Frederick A. Praeger, Inc., 1960.

Cirtautas, K. C. *The Refugee.* Boston: Meador Publishing Co., 1957.

Crowley, Desmond. *The Background to Current Affairs.* New York: St. Martin's Press, 1958.

Drummond, Roscoe, and Coblentz, Gaston. *Duel at the Brink.* Garden City, N.Y.: Doubleday & Company, 1960.

Fromm, Erich. *May Man Prevail, An Inquiry into the Facts and Fictions of Foreign Policy.* Garden City, N.Y.: Doubleday & Company, 1961.

Hocking, William Ernest. *Strength of Men and Nations.* New York: Harper & Brothers, 1959.

Kenen, Peter B. *Giant Among Nations.* New York: Harcourt, Brace & World, Inc., 1960.

Kissinger, Henry A. *The Necessity for Choice.* New York: Harper & Brothers, 1961.

Loeber, Thomas S. *Foreign Aid; Our Tragic Experiment.* New York: W. W. Norton & Company, 1961.

McNeur, Ronald W. *Space-Time-God.* Philadelphia: The Westminster Press, 1961.

Medawar, P. B. *The Future of Man.* A Mentor Book. New York: New American Library of World Literature, Inc., 1959.

Meraes, Francis. *Yonder One World.* New York: The Macmillan Company, 1958.

Mills, C. Wright. *The Causes of World War III.* New York: Simon and Schuster, Inc., 1958.

Strausz-Hupé, Robert, *et al. A Forward Strategy for America.* A Foreign Policy Institute Research Book. New York: Harper & Brothers, 1961.

Sulzberger, C. L. *What's Wrong with U.S. Foreign Policy?* New York: Harcourt, Brace & World, Inc., 1959.

Warburg, James P. *Disarmament: the Challenge of the 1960's.* Garden City, N.Y.: Doubleday & Company, 1961.

Ward, Barbara. *India and the West.* New York: W. W. Norton & Company, 1961.

White, Lancelot Law. *The Next Development in Man.* A Mentor Book. New York: New American Library of World Literature, Inc., 1961.

11

The Dangerous Game of Playing God

What is man that thou art mindful of him,
and the son of man that thou dost care for him?
Yet thou has made him little less than God
and dost crown him with glory and honor.
—Psalm 8:4-5

ON THE EVENING OF NOVEMBER 8, 1895, KONRAD ROENTGEN, PRO-
fessor of physics at Julius Maximilian University, Würzberg, Germany, was experimenting with some gas he had imprisoned in a
pear-shaped tube. When he switched on the electric current he
noticed that some barium platinocyanide crystals which lay exposed on his desk glowed brilliantly. When he turned off the
current the glowing ceased. He finally came to the conclusion
that some invisible ray must be passing through the black paper
in which he had his glass tube encased, this ray causing the glowing. Because he did not know what it was he called it the X-ray,
"X" being the mathematical symbol for the unknown. Further
experimentation revealed the fact that the X ray registered a dramatic effect upon a photographic plate, and following up this
clue, Dr. Roentgen made a photograph of his wife's hand which
showed the skeleton in sharp outline. It was in this fashion that
the first gleam came through from the dazzling light of the Atomic
Age.

When the results of Roentgen's, and other experiments, became
known the medical profession seized upon the discovery as being
tailor-made for surgeons, and X-ray machines, hurriedly contrived,
were rushed onto the market. Then reports began coming in to
the effect that operators were suffering severe burns. One of
Thomas A. Edison's assistants died of injuries thus contracted,

and the great inventor ordered all experimentation to cease in his establishments. A general alarm spread through the medical world, and legislatures began banning the machines.

In the meantime Pierre and Marie Curie became greatly interested in the matter and discovered that certain unstable elements, particularly radium, emitted the magic rays and in identifying them said they were "radioactive." To the activity itself they gave the name "radiation." This led to the further discovery that electrically charged particles are discharged from atoms in the process of emitting rays. We now know that as these bombard the nuclei of atoms they strip away some of the planetary electrons, leaving the residue as an entirely new substance. Put in simple terms, this means that man has come as near to being a "creator" as he ever has in all his experience. He can make new elements!

In the course of time it was found that there are actually three different rays emitted—alpha, beta, and gamma—each of which is capable of damaging human tissue, though in differing degrees. Once that radioactive particles have been taken into the human body, either by being inhaled or as an accompaniment of food, they emit dangerous rays something like a machine gun firing bullets into a crowd. These subatomic missiles force their way through living tissue, mutilating and destroying as they go. Certain body cells, notably the sex and bone-marrow cells, are highly vulnerable to such attacks.

The chromosomes in the sex cells carry suspended along their length a series of infinitesimally minute bodies called genes. These are endowed with the power to regulate a long list of chemical reactions necessary to the maintenance of life. They are also closely related to the transmission of inherited characteristics. Any injury inflicted upon them or disturbance introduced among them can result in disaster several generations removed. In absorbing radiation we are gambling with the destiny of the unborn. Under attack from radioactive particles the chromosomes are torn loose from their moorings, the genes are scattered, and the total structure can be altered. This may result in the loss of the power to procreate. What geneticists call mutations occur, these being complete alterations of the physical and mental characteristics of the offspring.[1]

One of the most serious effects of radiation is the destruction of the red bone-marrow cells. These lie deep in the bony recesses of the body manufacturing red corpuscles for the blood. Under a sufficient exposure to radiation they cease to function entirely, the resulting illness being known as leukemia, fatal in almost every instance.

It is hardly necessary to remind the reader that in 1938 the world was teetering on the edge of catastrophe. Great scholars and scientists, including Albert Einstein, were casting uneasy glances in the direction of the United States, looking for a sanctuary in which they might pursue their researches in peace. By a fortunate circumstance four such, including Enrico Fermi of Italy, found their way to the Pupin Physics Laboratory on the campus of Columbia University. There news reached them concerning European experiments with the nuclei of atoms, and Dr. Fermi leaped to the conclusion that if the amazing powers already revealed could be controlled a source of energy would be exposed which would be unlike anything of which the world had ever dreamed.

Being informed about the researches going on at the Pupin laboratory, and sensing something of the military possibilities of the forces with which his fellow scientists were experimenting, Dr. Einstein wrote to President Roosevelt, hinting that they might be on the verge of discovering vast new powers and how to control them. The magnitude of Dr. Einstein's name could not be ignored, and after cautious inquiry the almost limitless resources of the United States government were put at the disposal of the little group of immigrant physicists.

On the afternoon of December 2, 1942, Enrico Fermi mounted a small platform in the laboratory at Chicago University and grasped a fateful switch. Herbert Anderson, an intimate friend, has told the story: "As Enrico Fermi stood before that silent monster he was its acknowledged master. Whatever he commanded it obeyed. When he called for it to come alive and put forth its

[1] Statistical evidence indicates that radiologists and others exposed to radioactive material in unusual amounts show a disproportionate incidence of sexual impotency.

neutrons, it responded with alacrity; and when at his command it quieted down again, it had become clear to all that Fermi had indeed unlocked the door to the Atomic Age." [2] It was precisely at this point that another word of the Old Testament psalmist took on startling significance: "Thou hast given him dominion over the works of thy hands."

The actual triggering of the atomic bomb occurred 1,840 feet above the Japanese city of Hiroshima. At first an awesome ball of fire formed and hovered low in the sky for a few seconds. Then it began ascending, boiling and churning as it arose, forming a gigantic suction which drew up into itself an enormous amount of dust, vaporized steel, vegetation, and debris. This was carried thousands of feet into the skies where the stratospheric winds spread it out over nearly half the earth like a vast lethal blanket, but no more than a few score of all persons then living were aware of the terrible hazards contained in that blanket.[3]

Inconceivable quantities of highly radioactive dust filled the upper sky, buoyed up by ascending currents of air that rose from the cloud masses below. As these particles spread out covering the earth gravity brought them back down to settle, quite imperceptibly, on vegetation or to float to some quiet eddy in a little stream that furnished drinking water for man and beast. Throughout the "lifetime" of those particles they will continue to fall to the earth, adding to its radiation. Some scientists estimate that a few of them may "live" for 500,000 years, always emitting radiation.

Radioactive particles produced by atomic explosions become extremely dangerous when taken into the human digestive tract, as has already been suggested. The effect of radioactivity is of special concern in the case of young children, however. Cattle, feeding on vegetation that has been showered by radioactive dust or drinking from contaminated streams, pass the hazard on in milk or steaks. The more tender the cell the greater the possible damage. The unborn and the very young, therefore, have a special stake in the question of bomb testing.

On March 1, 1954, the United States detonated a superbomb

[2] Cf. Ralph E. Lapp, *Atoms and People* (New York: Harper & Brothers, 1956).
[3] For the best detailed description of the development and launching of the atomic bomb see Fletcher Knebel and Charles W. Bailey, *No High Ground* (New York: Harper & Brothers, 1960).

above a tiny atoll in the Pacific. In terms of TNT the blast was equivalent to 15,000,000 tons, or thousands of times more horrendous than the bomb dropped over Hiroshima. In Russia's series of tests in 1961 it is believed that at least one, and perhaps more, may have been equivalent to 50,000,000 tons. There is almost no limit beyond which it is impossible to build such infernal machines.

Several hundred miles from the United States testing site a small Japanese fishing vessel—the "Lucky Dragon No. 5"—was caught in the fallout, which appeared as a fine whitish ash. The fishermen, unaware of the lethal character of the stuff that sifted down from the skies, soon began complaining of smarting eyes, painful lips, and inflamed nostrils. Then within a few hours some were seized with a dreadful nausea. Three days later others suffered from swelling and reddening of the face, neck, and hands. Within three weeks still other crewmen suffered a complete loss of hair, and within three months seventeen serious cases of jaundice developed among the crew of twenty-three. Upon arriving at their home port it was discovered that the fish they carried in their refrigerators were highly contaminated.[4] Other ships arriving from the same fishing grounds within the next few days were identified by the same conditions. Eventually hundreds of thousands of pounds of finny food had to be destroyed.

Meanwhile, on islands of the South Pacific the Micronesian populations suffered from more fallout. A total of 239 individuals were more or less seriously affected, including 28 Americans. The symptoms corresponded very closely to those reported by the "Lucky Dragon No. 5." Fertility does not seem to have been adversely affected, for ten apparently sound and healthy babies were born during the first few years following the misadventure.

As programs have developed looking toward the application of atomic power to peacetime uses, it has been discovered that the disposal of atomic ash represents an extremely difficult problem. Already this highly contaminated material has accumulated until the cost of disposal has become a matter of national concern. Because a single particle of ash may continue radioactive for five hundred years, it achieves something a little like chemical immortality. Bacterial infection can be washed away with iodine

---

[4] For a detailed, hour-by-hour report of the experience see Ralph E. Lapp, *The Voyage of the Lucky Dragon* (New York: Harper & Brothers, 1958).

water or eliminated with heat, but there is no known method by which food can be cleaned of radioactive infection. There is already agreement inside the medical profession that there is not, probably, any child anywhere in the northern hemisphere whose bones do not show traces of strontium 90, resulting from atomic testing. The Russian tests of 1961 have added to the radiation hazard of every square mile of earth's surface north of the equator as have also subsequent tests conducted by the government of the United States.

Modern scientists are able to strip the hydrogen atom of its single electron and appropriate the elemental force that holds the universe together. Power is now available to permit us to dream of the solution of any problem involving energy. We are creating elements. The psalmist's use of the word "dominion" is no longer a mere figure of speech. In whatever direction we look there is striking evidence indicating that the scientific breakthrough involves issues of which man has never before been aware.

Because the question of atomic fallout constitutes a problem of the utmost concern to every human being now living and billions unborn, we will proceed to inquire more closely into the matter in the next chapter.

Suggestions for Further Reading

Because this chapter and the next are so closely related the bibliography for both will be found at the end of Chapter 12.

12

In the Wake of the Split Atom

WHEN THE WORLD WAR II PLANES RETURNED FROM THEIR MISSIONS, having dropped blockbusters on Cologne, Berlin, Frankfurt, Tokyo, Kobe, or Yokohama, the immediate destruction was at an end. Fires had yet to be extinguished, and the wounded had to be given medical care, but those wounds began healing before the attackers were safely back at their bases. Except for memorials in such cities as Warsaw, Rotterdam, Berlin, and Frankfurt, almost all traces of war have been cleaned up or removed. Already teen-agers are listening to the stories of the war with a bit of impatience, saying, "All that happened before I was born."

When the "Enola Gay" and "Bock's Car" returned from dropping their respective bombs on Hiroshima and Nagasaki, however, that was not the end of the destruction. It was, in fact, only the beginning, and the end is not yet in sight. Water sources have been contaminated and may not be cleansed for fifty years. Vegetation has been impregnated with death and will continue to be capable of destroying bone marrow throughout at least a generation. Genes in the sex cells of uncounted thousands of persons have been thrown into confusion and may produce mutations a hundred years from now—some scientists say even longer. Radioactive destruction has been loosed in such a fashion that hundreds of thousands of individuals—perhaps even millions—have been exposed to dangerous effects, tens of thousands of whom have not yet been born.

It is one of the mysteries of nuclear science that the detonation of certain weapons has the effect of producing elements which have never existed anywhere in nature previous to the time of the explosions. Strontium 90, for example, has been called "the most toxic substance known to man." Cesium 137 and carbon 14 exhibit somewhat different characteristics under different circumstances, but the threats they pose to the health and survival of the race are only a little less terrible.

Human life is the rarest, most complex, and most precious of all the prizes in the universe. It is this prize that is now in the process of being diminished and rejected—by humans themselves. The humans are tampering with the vital fractions. They are rearranging the vital proportions in the soil. They are altering the radiation balance in the atmosphere. They are damaging their own germ cells, producing defective creatures and cancelling out hundreds of thousands of years of evolving development.[1]

The hideous dangers inherent in nuclear warfare arise from the fact that in exploding nuclear bombs produce substances that continue to be toxic through hundreds of years. It has been discovered, for example, that after twenty-eight years radioactive strontium 90 still retains one half of its energy—called the "half-life"—at the end of another twenty-eight years it retains one fourth, and at the end of the third period of twenty-eight years it retains one eighth of what it had in the beginning. In the case of cesium 137 the half-life is thirty years, and in the case of carbon 14, 5,600 years. This means that the fission products of an atomic bomb can work their dire effects through hundreds of years.

A second fact appears in this same connection. The human bone building process calls for calcium, but because strontium 90 bears a close resemblance to calcium, it is drawn into the bones and the blood stream, where it bombards everything within reach with high-energy particles producing bone cancer and leukemia. Cesium 137 seems to have an affinity for muscle tissue, where it is accepted instead of potassium. Because it is likely to be eliminated more readily than strontium 90, it does not hold quite the same threat. It does, however, emit gamma rays which injure the genes in the sex cells, and its evil results are more apt to appear in future generations.

The radioactive particles are pulled back to earth by gravity and fall on fields, forests, plains, and river courses. Cattle grazing in pastures that have been contaminated will take the dangerous

---

[1] From *In Place of Folly* by Norman Cousins. Copyright by Norman Cousins— 1960. Used by permission of Harper & Row, Publishers, Inc.

particles into their own bloodstreams and pass them on in the form of milk, steaks, and roasts. Vegetables growing in contaminated areas will carry the same dangers into the digestive tracts of human beings. Some part, of course, will be eliminated by natural processes, but a vicious residue will remain. It is commonly agreed among scientists that there are detectable quantities of strontium 90, cesium 137, and iodine 131 in all foodstuffs produced in the northern hemisphere. A further fact accepted by all reputable scientists is that every child in the United States—and probably in Europe—carries detectable traces of radioactive strontium in his bones. Inasmuch as this substance exists nowhere in nature there is but one possible explanation: *The strontium he carries in his bones is man-made!* It came from nuclear explosions, and with the exception of the bombs detonated at Hiroshima and Nagasaki, all these explosions have occurred in peace time. As a further result of nuclear testing, scientists are agreed that every quart of milk now being used inside American households—and again in Europe—contains measureable traces of radioactive strontium. Since milk contains potassium and since cesium 137 is often mistaken for potassium by the human body, American children are acquiring that poison as a part of their regular diet.

These two highly toxic substances are capable of altering the characteristics passed on in the germ plasm; they can produce stillbirths and malformations of various kinds. They heighten the susceptibility of a child to disease and have been known to produce a general debility.

Carbon 14, the third of the unholy trinity, acts in many ways similar to cesium 137, but the immediate danger is considerably less. Its half-life, however, is 5,600 years, which means that its long-term capacity for inflicting injury becomes very great in the aggregate.

One of the sinister aspects of the case is the peculiar fact that, once the radioactive elements have been deposited in the human body they cannot be completely eliminated. There is no way known by which we can immunize ourselves against them. Strontium 90 in the red bone marrow goes on bombarding its host with high energy particles day in and day out, every hour of the twenty-four. It is a fact, of course, that all of us are subjected to a certain amount of exposure to cosmic rays which reach us from outer space.

Likewise, every experience we have with flouroscopes, X rays, or similar medical devices leaves its radiation mark upon our body, these marks accumulating with the years. Under ordinary circumstances such exposures do little damage, but when the total is added to an exposure to nuclear-induced radiation it can very easily pass the point of toleration.[2]

There is no quarrel over the basic facts. The confusion results from disagreement over the significance of the facts.

There is no disagreement about the fact that radioactive strontium, radioactive cesium, and radioactive iodine do not exist in nature. These radioactive materials are man-made. Strontium 90, cesium 137, and iodine 131 are produced by nuclear explosions.

There is no disagreement about the fact that strontium 90 can produce bone cancer and leukemia in human beings.

There is no disagreement about the fact that iodine 131 can cause genetic damage.

There is no disagreement about the fact that, as a direct result of nuclear tests, detectable quantities of strontium 90 or cesium 137 or iodine 131 can now be found in virtually all foodstuffs. Among these milk is considered of exceptional importance, both because it is a prime source of nourishment for children and because it serves as a collection center for poisonous radioactive strontium.

There is no disagreement about the fact that detectable traces of radioactive strontium, radioactive cesium, and radioactive iodine have found their way into the bodies of human beings all over the world, the extent of the contamination being somewhat higher in the Northern Hemisphere than in the Southern Hemisphere.

There is no disagreement about the fact that poisonous radioactive strontium locates itself in the human bone, where it is stored; that poisonous cesium locates itself primarily in muscle tissue, and that poisonous radioactive iodine has an affinity for the thyroid gland.

There is no disagreement about the fact that the amount of radioactive materials in human bone and muscle has been increasing year by year. In the one year between 1958 and 1959, the deposition of strontium 90 and cesium 137 in human beings more than doubled.

There is no disagreement about the fact that whatever risks may have

---

[2] It is at this point that the debate becomes confusing. There is, as yet, no general agreement among scientists at to the exact point at which radiation is "safe." Suffice it to say that the level has been dropping year by year since the first bomb was dropped on Hiroshima. Estimates made then are altogether out of date. Even today's most conservative may prove tomorrow to be too high.

been involved in nuclear testing before 1960, the spread of nuclear testing to other nations would result, in the words of a U.S. Congressional subcommittee studying the effects of fallout, "in a serious radiation hazard to world health." [3]

One of the booby traps in any discussion of nuclear testing is the careless use of percentages. It has been estimated, for example, that such testing has resulted in no more than a 2 per cent increase in the world leukemia rate, but even so small a percentage means a total of tens of thousands of deaths per year. The statistics of a single twelve-month period can be very deceptive. Because of the long "life" of radioactive poisons the total cost can run into totals of even hundreds of thousands of casualties.

In any study of nuclear hazards three significant facts must be faced: (1) The presence of radio poisons is due directly to man's own activities. (2) Increased hazards will attend further development of nuclear operations. (3) It is possible to pinpoint the responsibility for any increase in the world health hazards and to do it precisely.

As of today, four nations are responsible for having injected radioactive poisons into the life of the planet—the United States, Russia, Great Britain, and France. There are recurrent reports to the effect that China is about to crowd into the brotherhood of atomic bombers, but as these lines are being typed that has not as yet occurred. In this connection it should be noted that, up to this date, the responsibility lies solely at the door of white men and of white nations. The "developed" nations have created the problem! [4]

In 1950 soil chemists at Earlham College, Richmond, Indiana, took a sample of top soil from one of the nearby farms, and having carefully insulated it against any further contamination, they set it aside for a period of nine years. In mid-1959 a second sample of soil was taken from the same location, and the radioactivity of the two samples was compared. The tests show that, while two inches below the surface both samples showed approximately the same rate of radioactivity, in the upper two inches the 1959 sample

[3] Cousins, op. cit., pp. 63-64. Used by permission of Harper & Row, Publishers.
[4] Although Russia is generally classified as a "white" nation, a very considerable proportion of the Russian population consists of peoples either oriental in their background or closely related therto.

showed a rate almost one hundred times greater. Careful tests made at the Los Alamos Scientific Laboratory show conclusively that the average individual is absorbing cesium 137, and other tests in other laboratories prove there is an increasing accumulation of radioactive materials in human skeletons. In every foodstuff exposed to the sun and rain there is a growing concentration of these materials, and in the waters of the Pacific Ocean there is a similar accumulation in the various forms of marine life.[5]

There is a disposition on the part of the average layman to assume that "the dust has settled" and that the problem has come to an end. In terms of conventional bombs this would be a reasonable conclusion, but there is nothing conventional about a nuclear weapon. There are actually two different types of fallout, each of which wreaks its own havoc.

The first fallout of debris from a nuclear explosion consists of a mixture of many kinds of radioactive material. Of the nearly 200 radioactive isotopes produced, perhaps as many as 150 have half-lives of less than twenty-four hours. While it is true that radiation during those first few hours is extremely intense, the destruction of the large majority of the fission particles is very rapid, and the danger recedes with equal rapidity as a consequence.

By far the more insidious and dangerous aspect of the fallout appears in the energy that is released from radioactive particles weeks, months, or even years after the explosion. In such cases the effects upon the human body are negligible until the particles are ingested with food, drink, or inhalation. Thereupon they become fixed in the bones or muscles and remain there, emitting destructive and disastrous rays, or streams, of energy for many years. In the case of bone cancer the victim may not be aware of any abnormal condition for as long as twenty-five years following exposure or contamination. Moreover, because of the fact that the wind of the stratosphere carries the radioactive particles on long journeys, the infection may occur half a world away months following the detonation of the guilty bomb.

In the case of growing children, where the increase in skeleton weight may be as much as 20 per cent per year, the accumulation of strontium 90 in the bones is very much more rapid than in the

---

[5] Cf. John M. Fowler (ed.), *Fallout* (New York: Basic Books, Inc., 1960), pp. 4-5.

case of an adult—even as much as four to seven times faster. Oddly enough, some bony sections of the body seem to be favorite parking places for the contaminants. Studies made by Swedish scientists have shown differentials of as much as six to sixty over the skeletal average.

A United Nations report on the effects of atomic radiation presents an estimate to the effect that 4 per cent of all human infants now have, or will have, serious hereditary defects as the result of pre-natal affectations. As far back as 1906 a team of French scientists proved that rapidly dividing cells are the most sensitive to radiation, and this holds great significance for the unborn. Any damage, however slight, to the developing fetus can mean damage which will result in deformities and abnormalities.

In all of the human body there are no more complicated and delicate structures than the chromosomes of the sex cells, nor are there any structures that have more to do with the character and the capabilities of the race than the genes which cling to the chromosomes. Every scientific study that has been made in these fields to this date shows that radiation is a wrecker which produces almost every type of aberration and distortion among the genes. The evidence is as conclusive as any the laboratories can produce.

In 1958 the three nations in possession of atomic stockpiles— Russia, the United States, and England—agreed to suspend the testing of nuclear weapons. Up to that time they had, counting all detonations, fired 174 megatons—92 fission explosions and 82 fusion. The radioactive material loosed upon the earth—all in the Northern Hemisphere—amounted to about 9,200 pounds. Much of this is still floating in the atmosphere at stratospheric levels and filtering down in a continous shower. Radioactivity in our food could be expected, therefore, to increase during the next twenty years even if there were no more nuclear firings. Careful calculations indicate that 1,300 pounds of radioactive carbon 14 has been added to the world's stock, just about doubling it. Inasmuch as this carbon has an affinity for the sex cells, the hazard of sex mutations has doubled.

In the face of such evidence the moral and spiritual issue becomes crystal clear. *Does any nation, even in its own defense, have the right to imperil the lives of all the people of the world—friends and foes alike—and jeopardize the lives of millions of the unborn?*

The overwhelming responsibility for safeguarding the future rests upon the citizens of those nations which have at least some control over their governments. No more difficult decision has ever had to be made by any generation, by any government, or by any people in all the long history of humankind. It is not alone a question of employing nuclear weapons in actual battle. The ash which rained down on the "Lucky Dragon No. 5" was a peacetime product.

Physical deformities and disfigurements, abnormal and still-births, and heightened susceptibility to disease among millions of "innocent bystanders" must be added to the billions of dollars the bombs have cost. The issue has ceased to be one for treasurers and has become one for humanitarians. It is not a question of finance but of conscience.

If the Christian Church is to establish any claim to moral and spiritual leadership during the next century the facts cited in the foregoing pages require that it shall organize for the purpose of informing and mobilizing public sentiment in the interest of effective action. Denominations, as well as local congregations, must assume responsibility for marshaling opinions behind facts. Every possible means must be employed to bring about an end to nuclear testing. In view of the fact that the situation will worsen with every testing, the demand must be made effective that the stratospheric storage of death must come to an end.

In view of the terrible implications of the whole question of nuclear testing—to say nothing of the other matters that raise the issue of race survival—the Church of Jesus Christ will be well advised if it suspends all petty theological bickering and declares a moratorium on sectarian strife in order to dedicate its combined efforts to the preaching of the Christian gospel to the whole world. We have come to the point in human affairs where we will be saved as a world or we will be destroyed as a world. There can be no fractionalism. The first issue of our age is the survival of the human race.

The Christian Church, and Christians, are on trial before the generations of the unborn. A hundred years from now enlightened men will be asking, "What was the Church thinking and saying while the air was being poisoned for all mankind? What kind of preaching did it demand of its preachers? With what kind was it satisfied? Why was it satisfied with 'peace of mind' while the future was in total jeopardy?"

The answer to such questions is being written at this moment, and we are the authors of that answer.

Suggestions for Further Reading

Amrine, Michael. *The Great Decision.* New York: G. P. Putnam's Sons, 1959.

Compton, Arthur H. *Atomic Quest.* New York: Oxford University Press, 1956.

Cousins, Norman. *In Place of Folly.* New York: Harper & Brothers, 1961.

Feis, Herbert. *Japan Subdued.* Princeton, N.J.: Princeton University Press, 1961.

Fowler, John M., editor. *Fallout.* New York: Basic Books, Inc., 1960.

Groves, Leslie R. *Now It Can be Told; the Story of the Manhattan Project.* New York: Harper & Brothers, 1962.

Jungk, Robert. *Brighter Than a Thousand Suns.* New York: Harcourt, Brace & World, Inc., 1958.

Knebel, Fletcher, and Bailey, Charles W. *No High Ground.* New York: Harper & Brothers, 1960.

Lapp, Ralph E. *Atoms and People.* New York: Harper & Brothers, 1956.

————. *The Voyage of the Lucky Dragon.* New York: Harper & Brothers, 1958.

Rostand, Jean. *The Substance of Man.* Garden City, N.Y.: Doubleday & Company, 1962.

Schubert, Jack, and Lapp, Ralph E. *Radiation: What It Is and How It Affects You.* New York: The Viking Press, 1957.

Schweitzer, Albert. *Peace or Atomic War?* New York: Holt, Rinehart & Winston, Inc., 1958.

Wallace, Bruce, and Dobzhanksy, T. *Radiation, Genes, and Man.* New York: Holt, Rinehart & Winston, Inc., 1959.

Wendt, Gerald. *You and the Atom.* New York: William Morrow & Company, 1956.

13

A Brief Intermission

A DELIGHTFUL OLD CHINESE SCHOLAR WHO WAS MY HOST IN PEKING many years ago took great pride in explaining a collection of ancient astronomical instruments. Pointing to one of them, he said, "Our compass was different from the one you of the West use. Whereas yours had four points—north, south, east, and west—ours had five—north, south, east, west, and where you are. You can never really set off in the right direction if you do not know where you are when you start." The geographers may not agree with the old scholar, but there is a profound lesson in his comment with which all sober-minded men will agree. No time is ever better spent than those brief periods we occasionally take out of our crowded days to discover our precise position.

Up to this point in our study we have been occupied chiefly with prosaic matters such as food, shelter, water, soil, health, energy, molecular manipulation, and physical survival. It now become necessary to face certain moral and spiritual issues as they appear in economics, politics, ideologies, social philosophy, religion, and global mind sweeping. To attempt any such study intelligently, it is imperative that we determine our present position in the revolution through which we are passing. In doing so we will be forced to face three uncompromising facts.

1. *The economic, political, and physical woes from which the world suffers today all developed under the system commonly called capitalism.*

As has been suggested in an earlier chapter, the colonialism which has characterized life in large areas of the world was not all bad. It is true that the sun has set upon the colonial system almost everywhere outside the Soviet sphere, but the inheritance left in the underdeveloped areas by the colonial powers include vast benefits bequeathed to the "liberated" peoples. To damn the sys-

118

tem without reservation is to shut one's eyes to obvious facts. It is also true, however, that the occupied lands have suffered evils and injustices galore at the hands of the occupying powers, these wrongs being the result in most cases of the operation of an unenlightened capitalism. It is impossible, for example, to estimate what the situation in Vietnam might have been if the French had administered this, one of the richest lands of southeast Asia, in the interests of the Vietnamese people rather than for the purpose of further enriching French capitalists.

Whatever the guilt or the innocence, the beneficence or the oppression, of the colonial powers may have been, the crucial fact is that poverty, disease, ignorance, and general wretchedness of hundreds upon hundreds of millions of the people of the earth has been endured by them under the system commonly known as capitalism. How far the system, and how far the peoples and nations themselves, have been responsible for these evils is a problem that belongs to another study than this. It is sufficient for our purposes to say that *capitalism and wretchedness have coexisted.* This fact is a well-stocked arsenal ready made for the Communist agitator.

One more fact must be noted with profound humility and an admission of guilt. Both World War I and World War II originated with capitalist nations. The scientific historian may protest that this point can be pressed too far—which is, of course, quite true—but the underfed men in loincloths can hardly be expected to be strictly logical, and in the Communist propaganda kit the capitalistic charge becomes an all-purpose tool. It is true, also, that Japan was engaged in hostilities with Nationalist China previous to Hitler's taking over Austria, but Japan was both a capitalistic and an industrialized nation long before it launched its vicious Manchurian adventure. As an additional damning fact, it must be admitted that all the great wars which have cursed the earth during the last hundred years have originated with capitalist nations which—with the exception of Japan—were also white.

2. *For the past two hundred years ours has been a white man's world.*

Again, a word of defense must be offered in behalf of the white man. His authority over the world has been exercised again and again in behalf of human welfare. He has maintained order, established markets, provided economic opportunity, and lifted the sights for all humanity. His missionaries have gone with healing in their hands to the most helpless and hopeless on all the face of the earth. His capitalists have opened doors, provided training, policed wild and savage areas, and otherwise befriended civilizing agencies and influences. But everywhere he has continued to be a white man who has, almost without exception, returned to his homeland at the close of his term of employment or service in the underdeveloped countries.

Though it cannot be discussed in this chapter for lack of space, one extremely critical circumstance must be mentioned as being one of the determinative facts of our world. The nuclear bombs thus far dropped in the course of direct military operations were dropped by a white nation on a people of color. It is a little difficult for the average citizen of the United States to sense the significance of this fact. It is not lost, however, upon the thinking of 1,500,000,000 of the people of the world who happen to live inside dark-pigmented skins.

By no possible logic can the white man be blamed for all the woes of the world, but neither can it be denied that these same woes either have grown up or have persisted while the white man was leader. He has been the master of the world while some of the most aggravated abuses have come to maturity. Against them he may have contended, and to cure them he may have given generously of his best efforts—but he suffers today exactly as any other "boss" must suffer in a situation where the conditions of life are under fire. Rightly or wrongly, he gets the blame. Again, it must be said that the Communists have exploited these facts and circumstances to the limit in the hope of discrediting capitalism. At the same time the Western powers—especially the United States—have been smeared as being "imperialistic." In other words, in the present war for the world's mind the white man suffers under a great handicap—*he is white!*

3. *Jesus of Nazareth is under attack everywhere in the color world because it is possible to make the underdeveloped people's of the world believe he is the capitalistic white man's God.*

Perhaps it should be admitted that in this matter the white man's churches and missionaries have been, in some part, to blame. I recall very vividly the first Christian church building I ever saw in a predominantly non-Christian land. In spite of the fact that the native architecture lent itself admirably to the requirements of a Christian house of worship, the little building gave the impression of being a typical New England church set down in the midst of a completely alien environment. It was impossible for any native of the land to enter the building without feeling he had been lifted up out of all his cultural experience and set down in a completely strange atmosphere. Moreover, any citizen of the land who might have been seen entering the church for worship could not have failed to be branded in the mind of onlookers as having been somehow alienated from his fellow citizens. That house of worship, chaste in all its lines and superbly beautiful in New England, announced to all passersby that the God worshiped in those holy halls was a spiritual import and a stranger in the land.

Also, the missionaries, almost without exception, have been slow to apply for citizenship in the lands to which they have gone to serve. Though some may have labored there for as many as fifty years, they have remained outside the political life of the land in which they have invested their lives. All this is understandable, of course, and there are good social, economic, and political justifications for their decisions. Because they have lived all their missionary lives as aliens, however, they have left the impression that their God was, also, no more than a temporary visitor—an importation from abroad.

Lin Yutang, one of the most brilliant of the modern Chinese scholars, writers, and philosophers, has put his finger on an extremely serious problem with which Christian missionary leaders have to deal. Born and reared in a Christian Chinese family which was rigidly loyal to the Christian Church, he charges that throughout his youth he was educated away from his racial heritage and culture, with the result that he became something like a man without a country. In that process he lost heavily. As a consequence he became, if not an actual atheist, at least an agnostic. Upon returning to the Christian faith he admitted his earlier mistake, but at the same time he calls to account the Church which uprooted him from the culture into which he was born. This, he declares, was entirely unnecessary. If Christianity had been translated into Chinese terms and had been permitted really to speak the language of the common Chinese people, he believes it might have taken

China captive. Instead of being absorbed by China, however, Christianity and the Christian missions have undertaken in all too many cases to subtract the Chinese converts from their history, racial identity, cultural aspirations, and ancestral hopes. Whatever the merit or demerit of the charge it suggests a question of grave concern to the Christian Church and Western survival.

Perhaps the greatest individual contribution to the Christian cause in Japan was the ministry of Toyohiko Kagawa, author, evangelist, social reformer, and oriental saint. He did more to attract the attention of the Japanese people to Christian ideals and principles than any missionary of his day. Because of his great literary skill and profound spiritual insights he succeeded in translating a Jewish redeemer named Jesus into Japanese terms. This, in the last analysis, is the major responsibility of the Christian mission to the world. We have been apt to forget that yellow, brown, and black men will always be yellow, brown, or black. If Christianity is to become redemptive in any land it must become indigenous.

It is exactly at this point that the so-called "younger churches" are making their greatest contribution. During the last two decades they have been producing leaders, scholars, thinkers, theologians, and teachers of their own, some of whom command worldwide attention. They are pouring their contribution to Christian thought and action into the mind and heart of the Christian Church through such agencies as the World Council of Churches and are commanding the respect of Christians everywhere. Little by little the color line is being blotted out, and more and more the importance of an integrated and united Church is becoming evident.

At least one more difficult problem encountered on the so-called "mission fields" must be considered. In the minds of millions of Americans there is much confusion as a result of the fact that leftists, radicals, revolutionaries, and Communists inside the underdeveloped areas are being recruited from the ranks of the educated youth of the respective lands. The reason is not far to be sought, however.

Because of the economic organization of the underdeveloped areas there are but two economic or social groups. At the top there is a small knot of rich, conservative, reactionary, and politically powerful individuals who believe the present system is good because it has been good to them. There is nothing in their culture or their religion that requires them to invest any of their concern in the poor, the exploited, the ignorant, or the wretched. Nor is there anything in the economic organization of life which calls for a vigorous and independent middle class. In nation after nation, including tens of millions—even hundreds of millions—of human beings, life is organized on the two-class basis. Each individual is apt to be either very rich or very poor. There is little middle ground, and there is, therefore, no strong middle class.

Every year the universities and colleges empty into the streams of the national lives a new graduating class. Young, without funds with which to launch their own economic enterprises and without the connections that will guarantee them a job, they become frustrated, bitter, and "leftish." I have met many of them around the world who feel they have been treated scurvily, unjustly, cynically, and even brutally. The high idealism preached to them by the missionaries has not resulted in better wages, better jobs, improved social status, or economic opportunity. It is not surprising, therefore, that Communism is able to exploit their disappointments and enlist their talents. In India alone, it is reported that tens of thousands of college graduates are finding it impossible to secure employment at the tasks for which their college training was supposed to prepare them. A hungry educated man can very easily become a dangerous man, socially, politically, and economically. Communism feeds on the frustration of such as these.

This, then, is at least a partial description of the world in which we must live. It is for possession of such a world that Communism is planning its strategy. As a humble woman said in the thirties, "It is too bad we have to have a depression just when we are in the midst of hard times," so also it is a matter of the utmost seriousness that we should have a war-to-the-death between Communism and democracy—between the East and the West, between the right and the left, between religion and atheism—just when we are in the midst of a cold war. That is exactly the situation in which we find ourselves, however, and our study requires us at this point to investigate the enemy and the forces arrayed against us. It is, therefore, to an intimate study of Communism that we must turn, and the turning is none too soon, for the future is already upon us, and Communism is riding high.

Suggestions for Further Reading

Anderson, Gerald H., editor. *The Theology of the Christian Mission*. New York: McGraw-Hill Book Company, 1961.

Bainton, Roland H. *Christian Attitudes Toward War and Peace*. Nashville: Abingdon Press, 1960.

Boyd-Orr, John, *The White Man's Dilemma*. London: Allen & Unwin, Ltd., 1953.

Buss, Claude A. *The Arc of Crisis*. Garden City, N.Y.: Doubleday & Company, 1961.

Butterfield, Herbert. *Christianity and History*. New York: Charles Scribner's Sons, 1950.

Frost, Raymond. *The Backward Society*. New York: St. Martin's Press, 1961.

Haselden, Kyle. *The Racial Problem in Christian Perspective*. New York: Harper & Brothers, 1959.

Hill, Norman, and Lund, Doniver A. *If the Churches Want World Peace*. New York: The Macmillan Company, 1958.

McGavran, Donald. *The Bridges of God*. New York: Friendship Press, 1955.

Maury, Philippe. *Politics and Evangelism*. Garden City, N.Y.: Doubleday & Company, 1959.

Muller, Herbert J. *The Uses of the Past, Profiles of Former Societies*. A Galaxy Book, 1957.

Perry, Richard L. and Cooper, John C. *Sources of Our Liberties*. American Bar Foundation, 1959.

Rādhākrishnan, S. *East and West in Religion*. London: Allen & Unwin, Ltd., 1958.

Smith, Eugene L. *God's Mission—and Ours*. Nashville: Abingdon Press, 1961.

Tetens, T. H. *The New Germany and the Old Nazis*. New York: Random House, 1961.

Thompson, Faith. *Magna Carta, It's Role in the Making of the English Constitution, 1300-1629*. Minneapolis: University of Minnesota, Press, 1948.

Trueblood, Elton. *Declaration of Freedom*. New York: Harper & Brothers, 1955.

14

The Men Who Split the World

IN 1914 WHEN THE ARCHDUKE FRANCIS FERDINAND AND HIS WIFE were assassinated on the street in Sarajevo, capital of the Serbian province of Bosnia, thus precipitating World War I, it could have been said that the world was more nearly living as one world than had ever been true in all the centuries of previous history. The white man was everywhere in control of the situation; a capitalist economy prevailed; the English pound sterling was the standard of exchange among the currencies of the world; the English language was fast becoming the common speech of all mankind; the laissez-faire philosophy of economics was almost everywhere accepted; the British navy policed the seas; European and American merchants and manufacturers were the world's suppliers of manufactured goods; Christian missionaries were going to the ends of the earth to "convert the heathen"; and Western dress was rapidly becoming the accepted attire of men of all colors. It is true, of course, that Kaiser Wilhelm of Germany was dreaming of a "place in the sun" for his country, but even if his ambition had been realized it would only have meant that one white man took the place of another. The basic structure of the world would not have been materially altered.

Then, just three years later, there occurred the October Revolution in Russia. As a result, Communism emerged as an economic and political philosophy destined to divide the world into three worlds—the East, the West, and the neutrals. As this page is being written a marked rift is appearing in the ranks of the leftists of the East which may or may not prove fatal to Communist designs. Should a split develop between Russia and China no one can foretell what it's effect upon the world might be. As of this date, however, the East—the Communists—must be accepted as a united front, opposed to everything democracy stands for. As a matter of self-preservation, the democracies must assume that their opponents cannot be divided.

There have been numerous communal experiments in the long course of the world's history, each one designed to provide some relatively small group with greater security, more of the good things of life, or a unanimity of effort in behalf of some cause. Without exception, however, all such experiments have been abandoned for one reason or another. This generation is witnessing a mammoth effort upon the part of governments which rule over more than 1,000,000,000 of the people of the world to establish the communal philosophy as the economic, social, political, and moral guide of all mankind. In all the history of the race there has never been put forth any effort even remotely comparable. So revolutionary are the proposals of Communism that it has become the solemn duty of every citizen of every free nation in the world to inform himself so far as is possible concerning the nature of Communism itself and concerning the alterations the Communists would make in the life of the race.

It has been said that "every institution is but the lengthened shadow of a man." To understand the institution one must know the man. In similar fashion it must be said that, to know modern Communism one must first know the character of the five men who have been its architects—Karl Marx, Nikolai Lenin, Joseph Stalin, Nikita Khrushchev, and Mao Tse-tung. It is of the utmost interest to discover that each was an atheist before he was a Communist, that each was a revolutionary as a youth, that each had been active in radical movements of one sort of another before joining any Communist organization, that each was a problem child inside his own family, and that each had been involved in numerous brushes with the law before he was identified as a Communist. One—Marx—was the son of a moderately successful professional man of conservative tendencies; another—Lenin—was the son of a minor nobleman; the three remaining—Stalin, Khrushchev, and Mao Tse-tung—were peasants. Only Marx could have been called an intellectual, even by a pronounced stretch of the imagination, although the others—except Khrushchev—had enjoyed the privilege of at least some university life before becoming a Communist.

126

Karl Marx was born in the city now known as Trier, Germany, May 5, 1818. His parents were Jews who had united with the Lutheran Church for reasons of expediency. From his earliest years he viewed his Hebrew ancestry with contempt and never allowed himself to forget that "he was born a Jew." His animosity toward his ancestry soon developed into a contempt for religion, and in his early youth he became an atheist. By the time he was twenty-five years of age he was almost a total stranger to all his family with the exception of his mother. When, in middle life, he came into possession of a small legacy as a result of the death of his father, it evoked from him no word of warmth—or even of respect—for the man whose name he bore.

Soon after his enrollment in the University of Bonn, his father became alarmed over the fact that he was displaying radical tendencies and for that reason transferred him to the University of Berlin. There he came under the influence of the philosopher Hegel and was soon admitted into a certain charmed circle of young intellectuals who had come to be known as the "Young Hegelians." Undertaking the study of philosophy as a young atheist, he found the Hegelian climate especially congenial and soon began to develop his own doctrine of materialism. In later years he described his mission in life to be that of "dethroning God." The essence of his belief was that everything in the universe could be described as the result of "matter in motion."

As a university student, both at Bonn and at Berlin, he associated with young social radicals, and upon his graduation from the latter school—with a PhD—he edited various extremist publications in Germany, Belgium, and France. In 1849 he arrived in London, with the Belgian police in hot pursuit, his offense having been an advocacy of radicalism. Thereafter for a period of a little more than sixteen years he haunted the library of the British Museum, reading every book he could lay his hands on that seemed to give any promise of adding to his knowledge of economic history.

No man ever divorces himself completely from his own generation, and Marx was no exception. Living in London's slums, he was surrounded from the first day of his arrival by the casualties of the newly born English factory system. No social conscience had as yet developed, and the lot of the factory workers was one of unrelieved misery. No labor laws had yet been enacted which were designed to restrain the rapacity of the factory owners and employers; nothing and no one protected the worker's children; no limit was placed on their exploitation or degradation. Everywhere on the continent something of the same conditions prevailed. In Germany and France a spirit of revolt was developing under the leadership of occasional intellectuals turned revolutionaries. In England, however, the atmosphere was uncongenial to radicalism.

The slums in which Marx and his family lived were crowded with the families of the factory workers. The poverty to which they were subjected is almost indescribable. The sufferings of the workers and the workers' children have been elaborated upon by countless authors during the last seventy-five years, but they were almost completely ignored at the time. The England Marx knew was enjoying an unparalled success as a producer of manufactured goods, but it was failing wretchedly in distributing the fruits of the factories among the producers. It is not surprising but it is highly significant that in all his writings Marx deals no more than cursorily with problems of production and devotes all his interest and energy to problems of distribution. Whatever his merits may have been as a student of history he never achieved a balanced understanding of economics. His prepossession with problems of distribution made that impossible.

While haunting the stacks of the library of the British Museum Marx became convinced that he had discovered the "scientific principles of history." Just as Charles Darwin believed he had found the explanation of biological development, Marx believed he had found the secret of history. In his huge work *Das Kapital* he undertook to establish the validity of that conviction.

Reduced to the simplest possible statement, Marx believed that certain inexorable, irrevocable, inescapable, and inevitable laws had been working throughout all history. Just as the Jew—and the Christian after him—believed that historical forces were working in behalf of some intelligible and foreordained end because of "the will of God," Marx believed his impersonal, scientific principles were also working to a predestined conclusion. That final end toward which they were working, irresistably, was worldwide Communism. When it has been established, Marx declared, the "state would wither away."

The doctrine of "the scientific principles of history" is the heart of Marxism. Having discovered and coded those principles Marx dismissed God and all thought of things "divine." In matter and motion he professed to find the explanation for everything, from primeval forces to the final triumph of Communism.

The subsequent influence of Marx's colossal work has become the most ominous fact on our horizon. At one point or another his philosophy impinges on every aspect of modern life. No college or university library is without its copies of his work, and almost every institution of higher learning in the world offers courses in Marxism—some sympathetic and some critical.

It is a mistaken idea commonly met in religious and political circles that Russianism and Communism are one and the same. Nothing could be further from the truth. If every Communist government in the world were to be overthrown before the year has come to an end the philosophy of Marx's scientific principles of history would remain to be dealt with. Moreover, it will continue to exercise an influence over the minds of men for hundreds of years to come. That huge bundle of manuscript Karl Marx carried across the English Channel and dumped on the desk of Otto Meissner, the Hamburg publisher, was an economic, social, political, and philosophical bomb designed and destined to split the world and upset a social order.

It is one of the anomalies of history that the man who proposed to reorder society was one who never managed his personal financial affairs with sufficient skill to provide his family with even the necessities of life. There was never a winter when he was able to wear his overcoat throughout the season. It was apt to be in the pawnbroker's for weeks at a time, so, too, were the children's coats and shoes. From Frau Marx's letters to her friends we learn of the unrelieved suffering which characterized the existence of the entire family. Except for the patient and persistent financial assistance of Friedrich Engels, the son of a German industrialist who was Marx's one unvarying friend, the family might have perished. Yet nowhere is there a recorded word of reproach or disloyalty. His wife and children were as completely convinced of his economic and political messiahship as he was himself. Whatever impression he may have made on his contemporaries, inside his family circle he was a loving father and a loyal husband.

As an individual Marx was irascible, arbitrary, intolerant, short-tempered, and uncompromising. These are qualities that may make a man effective as a crusader, but they do not make him popular as a person. This was true of Marx. When he left England in 1867 he was almost as much a stranger, after seventeen years of residence, as he had been the day he arrived. His most numerous acquaintances were pawnbrokers, debt collectors, and outraged creditors. Though he had lectured with some frequency to labor groups, he was almost without influence in the labor movement of Britain. On the occasion of his demise in 1883 his funeral was attended by less than a dozen people.

"My purpose was to aid in the liberation of the unhappy Russian people. Under a system which permits no freedom of expression, and crushes every attempt to work for their welfare and enlightenment by legal means, the only instrument that remains is terror. Terror is our own answer to the violence of the state. It is the only way to force a despotic regime to grant political freedom to the people." [1]

The speaker was Alexander Ulyanov, the twenty-year-old son of a Russian nobleman. He was charged with having conspired to assassinate Czar Alexander III. The scene was a courtroom in St. Petersburg, and the time was the early spring of 1887. It had been a daring scheme, half mad, doomed to failure from the beginning. The terrorists were reckless; the bomb was a fantastic affair; the police got wind of the plot and within the space of hours rounded up hundreds of youngsters, among them fifteen of the terrorists.

Alexander Ulyanov had inherited from his father a passionate devotion to the peasants, to which he had added a steeping in radical literature. In the process of reading he had repudiated religion—a common occurrence among Russian intellectuals at that time—and had turn to philosophic materialism. Standing before the court he had undertaken to shoulder the blame, hoping his confederates might be more successful the next time, but early in the morning of May 8, 1887, he and four of his companions were hanged in the courtyard of the Schlusselberg fortress.

When the newspaper which told the story fell into the hands of Alexander's younger brother, Vladimir—then nearing his seventeenth birthday—the young lad read it and, leaping to his feet,

[1] Quoted by David Shub in *Lenin* (New York: New American Library of World Literature, Inc., 1957), p. 11.

cried out, "I'll make them pay for this. I swear it." Therewith was born in him a hatred that was never to die. Out of that teen-ager, possessed by hate, there emerged Nikolai Lenin. The bitter speech of Alexander produced no result in the courtroom, but it seared the soul of his younger brother.

Vladimir Ulyanov was barely seventeen years old when his brother was finally executed. That fall he enrolled in the University of Kazan and immediately became immersed in student disorders. The school was a hotbed of discontent, and the writings of Fourier and Saint Simon, French radicals, were read avidly. As he later declared, he had "ceased to believe in God at the age of sixteen." A reading of Marx's *Das Kapital* did not initiate his atheism but confirmed him in it.

Expelled from the university because of his radicalism in December, 1887, he was finally permitted to enroll in the law school of the University of St. Petersburg as a result of the personal appeals of his mother. From that institution he graduated in 1891 and immediately opened a law office. When he began losing cases in the courts, however, he turned to promoting Marxist societies, and thereafter his whole life was given over to radical causes.

In 1892 a terrible famine struck in the province of Damara, accompanied by a scourge of cholera. Leo Tolstoi put forth prodigious efforts to organize relief, but Vladimir refused to have anything to do with the movement, declaring that the wholesale misery was due to a disordered society and that to try to relieve misery without reordering society was nothing more than a futile gesture. It was almost the voice of Karl Marx himself!

By the time he had graduated from law school Vladimir Ulyanov's personality had been thoroughly twisted by his hatreds. He no longer responded to ordinary situations in ordinary ways. He lived for but a single purpose—the establishment of a social order designed to Marxist specifications. All his faith was anchored to the doctrine of a carefully selected and thoroughly disciplined minority. In this he departed from Marx and struck off on his own.

Compassion, mercy, the dignity of the individual, the sanctity of personality—all appeals in the name of such fell on deaf ears, so far as Vladimir Ulyanov was concerned. Having abandoned all tender sentiments, he demanded of all who accepted his leadership that they should prove their loyalties with their hatreds. In this there is the explanation of much that has shocked the moral judgment of the world when it has come to fruitage in modern Communism. Karl Marx, himself, was no sentimentalist, but neither was he callous. He was capable of great bitterness, but he did not make a religion out of hate. In this Vladimir departed from his master.

In the fall of 1893 Vladimir Ulyanov abandoned his almost non-existent law practice and removed to St. Petersburg, where he became the leader of a group of revolutionaries known as "the Elders." Within the space of weeks he was sentenced to Siberia, and by the time he was released in 1900 he had become a shrewd, calculating, amoral, and conspiratorial revolutionist dedicated to a single purpose—the organization of a worldwide Communist party along Marxist lines.

It is not necessary to trace all the devious movements of Nikolai Lenin, as he came to call himself, through the seventeen years that elapsed between the time of his release from Siberia and his appearance in St. Petersburg in 1917 as the leader of the counterrevolutionary party. It is only important for our purpose that we understand the contribution this twisted personality made to the development of the modern Communist state. "Lenin brought about the revolution in Marx's name but not in Marx's way. The communist revolution was brought about in Russia in the name of totalitarian Marxism—Marxism as the religion of the proletariat, but it was a contradiction of almost everything Marx had said about the development of human society." [2]

To understand modern Communism it is necessary to distinguish between the ideas of Marx and those of Lenin. One was a scholastic and the other a man of action; one was a theorist and the other an organizer. Marxism was a philosophic system; Leninism was a blue print for a totalitarian state. The German was an intellectual; the Russian was a field general. The author of *Das Kapital* had been convinced that the state must wither away; the leader of the Bolsheviks was in dire need of the state if he was to achieve his dream of world conquest. He proposed to use it to spread his hatred across the earth. As a thinker he had almost no capacity for meditation. His knowledge of philosophy was skimpy. His inclination was to

[2] Nicholas Berdyaev, *The Origin of Russian Communism* (Ann Arbor, Mich.: University of Michigan Press, 1960), p. 106.

controversy. His grasp of economics was spotty and uncertain. "In the end he lost the immediate sense of difference between good and evil; he lost the direct relationship to living people; he permitted fraud, deceit, violence, cruelty." [3]

An indictment of Marx's infallibility as an historian appears in the fact that though he expected the revolution to begin in an industrialized nation, it actually was launched in a feudal nation. He anticipated a general uprising of the working masses, but the first victory was won by a relatively small body of desperate men who captured the machinery of government and in the process shot down thousands of their countrymen whose only purpose was to maintain law and order. The October Revolution was an imported disorder that took advantage of confusion to steal the machinery of state.

Having accepted Marxian economic theory—with such revisions as he deemed necessary—Lenin proposed to build a thoroughly disciplined party made up of individuals who were willing to take orders without asking questions. Force and violence were to be their weapons, the destruction of organized society their aim, and the "good of the Party" their moral code. The chaotic conditions existing in Russia during the autumn of 1917 provided the Communists with exactly the opportunity they needed. Power was seized in a series of lightning-like moves, and the revamping of the Russian state began.

Lenin was restrained by no moral scruples. Taking his cue from Bakunin, an early Marxist, he proceeded on the simple principle that everything that promotes the Party is moral, and everything that hinders it is immoral.

The nation was conditioned to the idea of a totalitarian state; it had never known anything else. Just as an American thinks in terms of freedom, the Russian assumed that any government would be totalitarian. Lenin, therefore, experienced little difficulty in building a new dictatorship on the traditions of old dictatorships. He could dismiss the question of "rights" with a gesture for no Russian government had ever recognized them. The value of the individual could be ignored. The supreme value to be established was an all-powerful state.

[3] *Ibid.*, p. 118.

In the process of building the Party Lenin found it necessary to "interpret" Marxism, to make it fit new circumstances, and this he did without apology or permission. The discipline he imposed on the Party left no room for dissent. Once the Party had accepted the principles of ruthlessness, force, violence, and dictatorship the way was cleared for Lenin to work his will.

The Lenin party shot, bludgeoned, bullied, and conspired its way to power. There were probably not more than 5,000 members in all Russia the day it took over authority, trampling over the corpses of hundreds of fellow Russians who had asked for nothing more than elemental human rights. One of the first official acts of the Party leader was the disbarment of thousands of Party members who had helped him win the victory, his reason being that the membership must be kept small for the sake of strict discipline.

It was inherent in Marx's theory that the revolution would involve the whole world. It was impossible to insulate any area from the inexorable "principles" just as it is impossible to emancipate any section of the earth from the operation of the law of gravity. Lenin therefore designed a Party that would encompass the earth, in which every member would vow undeviating loyalty to the high command of the Russian party.

The early organizations of the Communist party, devised by Marx and Engels, operated on more or less democratic principles, but the Third International, put together in 1919, saw Lenin securely in the saddle with all traces of democracy eliminated.

As the successful leader of the October Revolution of 1917, Lenin came into a position of power from which he could dictate the policy of the world organization. This he did with "firmness." No help was to be given to any movement designed to improve the lot of the oppressed, the hungry, or the exploited unless the objective was to hasten the world revolution. The youth who had refused to relieve distress in Samara was now the man who was determined to force upon the world a new order. *He was still unmoved by suffering; even the starving were to be sacrificed to the revolution if it became necessary.* A few years later he refused food from the United States to relieve the suffering of Russians caught in a famine, basing his decision on the same principle.

The second requirement was that members of the Party, wherever they might be, were to engage in treasonable activities against any government to which they might owe the ordinary obligations of citizenship. Lenin's words are very plain at this point; it is impossible to mistake their meaning. "Legal work must be combined with illegal," he said. "The Party that does not carry on systematic, all-sided, *illegal* work in spite of the laws of the bourgois parliaments is a party of traitors and scoundrels." [4]

In 1921 a list of twenty-one conditions were laid down for those parties outside Russia that might want to affiliate with the Comintern. One of these was a blunt demand that the Communists should sabotage every war effort if it was to the advantage of the Soviets that they should do so.

On June 22, 1941, Hitler launched his attack on Russia, which had the effect of making Russia one of the allies. The Soviets had to have help, and the only source from which such help could come was the factories of the United States. No one knew better than the Russians that such help would be given with reluctance as long as the Comintern continued as an arm of the Russian government. Therefore, it was dissolved in 1945 by an order from Joseph Stalin, Lenin's successor.

Karl Marx's theory is implemented today by a worldwide organization which is ingenius, amoral, and powerful. The Free World is confronted by an empire consisting of a long list of satellites which are, though pretending independence, actual colonies of Communism. According to Marx the state was destined to wither away; under Joseph Stalin it was riveted in place by economic, military, and ideological ties that make it one of the most powerful empires history has ever known. In those lands where Communism has come into control the state has saturated every aspect of life.

The creator of the Russian Communist monster was a peasant who has come to be known as Joseph Stalin. Iosif Dzhugashvili was born in a small country town near the Turkish border in the Russian state of Georgia, near the city of Tiflis, December 21, 1879. His father was the village shoemaker who squandered his earnings on liquor, but his mother was a profoundly devout woman who prayed earnestly that her son might become a priest of the church.

---

[4] Lenin, *Selected Works*, X, 45-46.

Social radicalism was in the air. Even the theological school at Tiflis had been caught up in the widespread spirit of revolt, many of the faculty being infected. Within a few weeks of his enrollment young Dzhugashvili, having been admitted as a result of the entreaties of his mother, was initiated into a secret society dedicated to the cause of the revolution. In the spring of 1899 his revolutionary interests were discovered and he was expelled, whereupon he became a professional Marxist revolutionary. Soon he ran afoul of the police and was shipped off to Siberia. He managed to escape and finally arrived in Finland, where he met Nikolai Lenin and soon became one of his trusted aides. Meanwhile he had become a thoroughgoing atheist.

In 1907 he returned to Tiflis and participated in a bold daylight robbery involving 341,000 rubles (about $170,000). Because the funds belonged to the government the international police were alerted, and a few days later one of Iosif's confederates was picked up in Paris when he attempted to exchange rubles for francs. The incident is of special interest to Americans for the reason that the confederate was none other than Maxim Litvinov who negotiated the recognition of Russia by the United States.

From 1907 until the outbreak of World War I, Iosif Dzhugashvili served under Lenin as an agitator, organizer, courier, and troublemaker. He was known to be bitter, hard, ruthless, and relentless. About the same time he gained a little fame as a journalist and changed his name to Stalin, meaning "steel." During the years between 1907 and 1917 he was arrested eight times, exiled seven times, and escaped six times. When the Russian revolution exploded he slipped back into St. Petersburg and put himself at Lenin's disposal.

Lenin knew him as a man of steel. He was altogether uninhibited, unscrupulous, and unafraid of any terrors. As an executor of official duties he became the personification of ruthlessness.

On Christmas day, 1923, Lenin lay dying. The Russian people, stricken by famine and Communist terrorism, wept beside the graves of millions who had died of starvation. Inside the Party a desperate struggle was going on, with fanatical leaders warring for power. In that situation the dying leader penned an appeal to the supreme governing council of the Party:

Stalin is too rude, and his fault, entirely supportable in relations among us Communists, becomes insupportable in the office of the General Secretary. Therefore I propose to the comrades to find a way to remove Stalin from that position and appoint to it another man who in all respects differs from Stalin . . . more patient, loyal, and more polite, and more attentive to comrades, less capricious, etc. . . . This circumstance may seem like an insignificant trifle, but I think from the point of view of the relation between Stalin and Trotsky . . . it is not a trifle, or it is such a trifle as may acquire decisive significance.[5]

By 1927 Stalin was firmly established and free to purge to his heart's content. His own words describe him better than either friend or foe have ever done. "To choose one's victim," he said, "to prepare one's plans minutely, to stake an implacable vengeance, and then go to bed . . . there is nothing sweeter in the world." [6] The casualties ran into the millions.

In 1935 the Communist leadership in Russia had all but decided to liquidate Stalin because of his utter ruthlessness, mass executions, and deportations. Nicolaus Baseches, his biographer, says that in a secret meeting of the Politburo a vote was taken which showed an almost unanimous opposition to his continuance in office. About that time Hitler's rise to power posed a dire threat to Russia, and also about that time the United States recognized the Communist government. These two events had the effect of soldering him securely in his place of power. Thereupon he inaugurated a purge that searched out even the most lowly who might be accused of disloyalty, and an estimated 5,000,000 were killed.

The war having been fought to a successful issue and the West lulled into amiability by an impressive performance on the part of the Russian forces, Stalin decided it was politic to resurrect the Comintern, and in September, 1947, the Cominform was brought into being to do the work that the Comintern had been designed to do. "Its actual purpose, to judge by what has happened since, was to provide the Soviet Union with a postwar instrument for making its own aims those of Communist Parties everywhere." [7]

[5] W. Cleon Skousen, *The Naked Communist* (10th ed.; Salt Lake City: Ensign Publishing Company, 1958), p. 121. Used by permission.
[6] *Ibid.*, p. 122.
[7] Harry A. and Benaro Overstreet, *What We Must Know About Communism* (New York: W. W. Norton & Company, 1958), p. 157.

With a compact and disciplined organization in every land available at any time for direct action and uninhibited by any conscience on the subject of treason, Stalin was in a position of power no ruler on earth could rival. Indeed, history has never known its counterpart. It is not necessary that Communists should constitute a majority anywhere. By manipulating minorities in fifty lands Stalin was able to appear as the head of a mighty world movement and create an empire.

As an illustration of the way the system works the reader is reminded of the "spontaneous demonstrations" in at least thirty countries at the time of the execution of Caryl Chessman, the California sex slayer. Communist youth, specially trained in Moscow in a "university" organized for that purpose, have created riots, whipped up frenzies, and made mountains out of mole hills and ranges out of solitary peaks. The humiliating experience of Vice-President Nixon in Venezuela and the "demonstrations in Japan" against the visit of President Eisenhower were additional incidents of the same general purpose and character.

Aided by disturbed world conditions between 1939 and 1953, Stalin started the Soviet chariot of conquest. He directly annexed a number of areas, such as eastern Poland, Esthonia, Latvia, Lithuania, part of Finland, eastern Czechoslovakia, part of Roumania. Then, using international communism as an ideological adhesive, Stalin created a Soviet orbit: Yugoslavia, China, Poland, Hungary, Bulgaria, North Korea, Czechoslovakia, Roumania, East Germany, Albania, Tibet, Outer Mongolia, and North Indochina (where bloody fighting was in progress at the time of his death).[8]

On March 5, 1953, the exalted son of the Georgian cobbler died. Following a brief period of confusion, during which Malenkov and Bulganin were in authority for brief periods of time, Nikita Khrushchev emerged as his successor. Then on the night of February 24-25, 1956, a speech was delivered which rocked the world—one that shook the Communist parties of the world to their foundations. In language almost unparalleled in Communist history, the new head of the Russian state denounced his predecessor as a liar, a murderer, and—worst of all—a perverter of Marxism-Leninism.

[8] J. Edgar Hoover, *Masters of Deceit* (New York: Holt Rinehart & Winston, Inc., 1958), p. 42. Used by permission.

The great god Stalin was torn down from his throne, and the world was under the necessity of taking the measure of another Communist dictator.

Lenin's death in 1924 resulted in a wild scramble for power inside the Communist hierarchy in Moscow. Ambitious individuals, mutually suspicious, each of whom aspired to wield the scepter that had fallen from the hand of the dead despot, began pulling the throttles on their machines. The contest went on for a period of years. Stalin eventually emerged as the victor, however, and in due time his competitors were liquidated in one way or another. When Stalin died in March, 1953, after a quarter of a century of undisputed brutality, he relinquished more power than had ever before resided in the hands of any human being. Again the struggle for power became desperate. This time, however, the issue was decided more speedily, and when the dust had settled a man almost unknown to the outside world was in the driver's seat.[9] Three years later, as has been mentioned, in a speech that lasted almost six hours he stripped the powerful Georgian of the last shred of respectability and portrayed "the greatest Russian of all time" as a liar, murderer, charlatan, deviationist, economic heretic, impostor and monster.

Who was this stranger who dared to draw the curtains apart, stride upon the stage, and deny Joseph Stalin his immortality?

Nikita Khrushchev was born on April 19, 1894, in the village of Kalinovka on the edge of Ukrania. His father is variously reported to have been a miner, a blacksmith, and a shepherd who was descended from a once famous Cossack. The family grew up in abject poverty, there being—so it is said—ten children, but concerning the other nine nothing is known.

Nikita's first employment was that of a shepherd boy. There are contradictory reports as to his education, some authorities saying he could not read or write until he was twenty-three years of age [10] and others saying he had a few terms in the village school.[11]

[9] It has often been said that Khrushchev is a Ukranian, but John Gunther, in *Inside Europe Today* (New York: Harper & Brothers, 1961), says he is a Russian (p. 308).
[10] See Edward Crankshaw, *Khrushchev's Russia* (Baltimore, Md.: Penguin Books, 1960), pp. 50 ff.
[11] Hearst, *et al., Khrushchev and the Russian Challenge* (New York: Avon Books Division of the Hearst Corporation, 1961).

Whatever the facts may be, he speaks Russian today with a marked accent, and his manner of speech is earthy, sometimes foul, and always that of a peasant. Before he was twenty he had earned a reputation for being an excessive drinker, but in recent years—because of the orders of his physician—he has become almost an abstainer. About the same age he took over in his father's blacksmith shop because of the older Khrushchev's heavy drinking.

As a result of the excesses of the local police, Nikita was showing evidences of radicalism by the time he was twenty, and because of that fact he was deferred from military service during World War I and assigned to a post where his mechanical ability made him useful. A girl cousin who had joined a Communist cell in Kharkov seems to have influenced him farther in the direction of the revolution, and in April, 1918, he applied for and was granted membership in the Bolshevik party. From that date to this he has been a loyal party man with an uncanny genius for attaching himself to the right coattails. In 1920 he was awarded a minor decoration by Trotsky "for services rendered the revolution" in the Ukraine, and shortly thereafter he was assigned to a school where he was expected to train for agricultural service. By the time he was twenty-six he was case hardened and bursting with energy.

Exact and detailed information concerning Nikita's early years is hard to come by. In 1924 he was a propagandist for the Communist party in the Ukraine, and it is said that he memorized long passages out of the writings of Marx and Lenin during this time. By various devices he managed to bring himself to the attention of Stalin, and in 1932 he executed one of the first purges in behalf of the ruthless Georgian—an activity which is said to have resulted in the suicide of Nadyezhda Aliluyeva, Stalin's wife. This seems to have reflected no discredit on Khrushchev for Joseph was thereby freed to legalize his relations with Rosa Kagonovich, the sister of Nikita's powerful sponsor.

As a young man Khrushchev distinguished himself at rural festivals with a certain rough and ready wit and with his unusual ability to dance the vigorous peasant dances, to sing the boisterous country songs—an activity he still relishes, and to eat prodigiously. All these accomplishments served him well when introduced to Soviet society in Moscow. The assistance rendered Rosa Kaganovitch opened the doors through which he passed into the presence of

Stalin himself. By 1932 he had become the second secretary of the Party and as such was completely obedient to his master. By 1937 he was assigned some of the dirtiest jobs and for faithful performance received several citations.

In 1937 he was assigned the job of cleaning out "unreliables" in the Ukraine, and by the time this assignment had been completed an estimated 400,000 were dead. Again, in 1943, when the Nazis had been driven out of the Ukraine by the Red Army, he was delegated the responsibility for punishing those who had collaborated with the Germans and another hideous bloodbath followed. The total number of those liquidated is not known, but informed estimates run into more hundreds of thousands. As a reward he was commissioned as a lieutenant general.

In 1953 Stalin died, having been senile for several years previous to his death. Georgi Malenkov and Nikita Khrushchev, the two individuals whom he seemed to trust, had subordinated everything—conscience, intelligence, dignity, self-respect, and the good opinion of friends—to his paranoiac judgments. Upon his death they were expected to ascend to power, Malenkov as Stalin's successor and Khrushchev as one of the powerful "secretaries." Within the matter of weeks, however, experienced observers began to detect evidence of a vicious battle going on under cover. On March 21, less than three weeks following Stalin's death, Malenkov "voluntarily" resigned from the secretaryship of the Party, to "concentrate on his responsibilities as premier." Therewith the campaign of attrition began, and by 1955 the duel between the two giants came to a climax when Georgi resigned all his authority, and accused himself of "incompetence." He was not liquidated, but was assigned to the management of a factory in a remote eastern section.

Since that day in 1955 the son of the Ukranian blacksmith has presided over the destinies of the far-flung Communist empire, wielding more power than has ever resided in the hands of any human being. It was his personal order that sent the Soviet tanks blazing through the streets of Budapest. It has been his authority that has held the Soviet colonies in line and his commands that have determined the character of Communist colonialism. It has been his raucous voice that has thrown the deliberations of the United Nations Assemblies into disorder, his boorishness that has

141

tried the souls of the statesmen of the world, his threats that have sent rumors through four continents, and his bullying that has made a travesty of all summitry. By deliberate falsifications of history he has appealed to the ignorant of the world. With double-talk he has used honorable words to conceal dishonest purposes. By an appeal to the newly independent peoples he has perverted plain meanings and distorted facts. He has manipulated economic crises for the purpose of concealing diabolical purposes. He has become a threat to everything politically honorable, morally defensible, and socially stable. Entirely lacking all the qualities of a theoretician, he has spread confusion, raised hopes for the purpose of enslaving men, and inflicted wounds on the world's life that will not heal in a hundred years. Wherever he has touched he has left a stain.

Such have been the men—Marx, Lenin, Stalin, Khrushchev—who have split the world.

Suggestions for Further Reading

Baldwin, Roger N., editor. *A New Slavery; Forced Labor: The Communist Betrayal of Human Rights.* New York: Oceana Publications, 1953.

Berlin, Isaiah. *Karl Marx: His Life and Environment.* New York: Oxford University Press, 1956.

Clarkson, Jesse D. *A History of Russia.* New York: Random House, 1961.

Crankshaw, Edward. *Khrushchev's Russia.* Baltimore, Md.: Penguin Books, 1960.

Daniels, Robert V. *A Documentary History of Communism.* New York: Random House, 1960.

Djilas, Milovan. *Conversations with Stalin.* New York: Harcourt, Brace & World, Inc., 1962.

Gibney, Frank. *The Khrushchev Pattern.* New York: Duell, Sloan & Pearce, Inc., 1960.

Gilbert, Rodney. *Competitive Coexistence.* New York: Book Mailer, Inc., 1956.

Hearst, et al. *Khrushchev and the Russian Challenge.* New York: Division of the Hearst Corporation, 1961.

Kellen, Konrad. *Khrushchev: a Political Portrait.* New York: Frederick A. Praeger, Inc., 1961.

Maclean, Fitzroy. *Tito: the Man Who Defied Hitler and Stalin.* New York: Ballentine Books, Inc., 1957.

Mehring, Franz. *Karl Marx: The Story of His Life.* London: Allen & Unwin, Ltd., 1936.

Pares, Bernard. *Russia.* New York: New American Library of World Literature, Inc., 1949.

Pistrak, Lazar. *The Grand Tactician: Khrushchev's Rise to Power.* New York: Frederick A. Praeger, Inc., 1961.

Roberts, Henry L. *Russia and America: Dangers and Prospects.* New York: New American Library of World Literature, Inc., 1956.

Salisbury, Harrison. *Moscow Journal.* Chicago: University of Chicago Press, 1961.

Schwartz, Harry. *The Red Phoenix: Russia Since World War II.* New York: Frederick A. Praeger, Inc., 1961.

Shub, David. *Lenin.* New York: New American Library of World Literature, Inc., 1957.

Stipp, John L. *Soviet Russia Today.* New York: Harper & Brothers, 1957.

Whitney, Thomas O. *Russia in My Life.* New York: Reynal & Company, Inc., 1962.

Wolfe, Bertram D. *Communist Totalitarianism.* Boston: Beacon Press, 1961.

—————. *Three Who Made a Revolution, Lenin, Trotsky, Stalin.* New York: The Dial Press, 1960.

15

The Meaning of Modern Marxism

AN EXTREMELY INTERESTING STORY TO WHICH MODERN STUDENTS of Communism could well give some serious thought is told about Karl Marx. Meeting with a group of European revolutionaries some years following the publication of *Das Kapital*, he listened as a series of speakers declared their loyalty to Marxism and then proceeded to interpert the scientific principles. Marx was never a patient man, nor was he apt to accept criticism cheerfully. These speakers were not critics, however; rather, they thought of themselves as friends of Marx and his opinions. In most cases they had persuaded themselves that they were actually speaking in support of Marxian theories. When he could hold his peace no longer the author of *Das Kapital* leaped to his feet and shouted, "If what I have been listening to is Marxism, *then I am no Marxist!*"

In view of the interpretations and revisions through which the original doctrines of Karl Marx have passed, it is quite necessary that we distinguish between the original faith set forth in *Das Kapital* and the modern Communist system with which our world is confronted. There is abundant reason why good Americans—and especially Christians—should abhor Communism, but that abhorrence should be intelligent if it is to be effective. Through almost one hundred years Marxism has undergone a process of erosion and has attracted to itself a variety of economic and political accretions. That with which we have to deal is an amalgam that cannot be explained by any simple analysis of Marx's huge volume of theory.

Modern Communism is a mighty stream into which many tributaries have emptied. Some part, of course, is pure Marxianism, but very much consists of an overlay of Leninism. Much of the practical precedent bears the imprint of Stalin, while the strictly modern policy of threats and retreats designed to keep the free world off balance is of Khrushchev and Mao Tse-tung. The Chinese leader has a great ambition to be recognized as a theoretician, but up to this time his chief contribution has been a very practical adaptation of Marxism, whereby he has been able to ride into power on the basis of peasant support. Whereas Marx was unable to see any possibility of establishing Communism as a world power except through a revolt of industrial workers, Mao Tse-tung—lacking industrial workers—achieved the same result with the aid of farmers and tillers of the soil.

Had Karl Marx lived long enough to see the October Revolution in Russia in 1917, or had he been a witness to the Red Chinese take-over in 1949, he would probably have rubbed his eyes in uncomprehending amazement. It had been one of his primary beliefs—one that neither he nor one of his contemporaries ever questioned—that the Communist uprising would enjoy its first success in an industrialized nation. Because of his experiences with the English workers and the western Europeans, his private opinion was that it would be German workers who would rise in revolt but whether it was to be them or their French radical allies made little difference. The revolution was to be a working-class uprising.

It never seems to have occurred to Marx that the first Communist successes would be registered in an agricultural land such as Russia was. Actually, and more or less privately, Marx despised the Russians as a race, and one of his bitterest early quarrels had been a private engagement with Bakunin, an extremely able Russian revolutionary. In 1867 China was a far-off land which figured in no way in European politics, industry, or history. "The world," in Marx's thinking, consisted of Europe, with only a little more than a passing thought for the United States.

The Russia of Marx's day was aloof, detached, unknown, and almost barbarous. It was to be treated with condescension and eliminated from the scene until the time came to take it over in a bloodless battle. There was practically no industrialism, which meant that there was no proletariat. As for the possibility of Communism's becoming a peasant movement, as it did in China under Mao Tse-tung, Marx would probably have esteemed this to be utterly impossible. In these two instances we have evidence of his fallibility as an interpreter of history. The class-conscious worker is almost nonexistent in lands where there is no industrialism.

145

Though Marx and Engels were in no way averse to violence, they did not expect the emergence of a dictator, a totalitarian Party, the liquidation of millions. Marx, in particular, had considerable confidence in the mass mind of workers, and at no time does it seem to have occurred to him that the revolution might be artificially induced by a small group of agitators who would seize power by force. This was a characteristic of Communism which was contributed by Lenin.

Surrounded by the miseries of the English factory workers and resenting the inequities of the English system of distributing wealth, Marx wrote *Das Kapital* as a study in distribution. Had he been able to see—or to anticipate—the American working man living under a democracy and occupying a home equipped with television, automatic refrigeration, economic protection, health and life insurance, political power, workmen's compensation laws, built-in rights, industrial pensions, medical care, legal rights, and social standing he might have given more attention to the question of production. The children of the factories of Marx's day in England had little or no opportunity for schooling, frequented no public libraries and looked forward to no university or trade-school education.

Nothing resembling the Protestant Reformation, with its emphasis on democratic procedures, had ever touched the Russian Orthodox Church. There are no such names as Zwingli, Melanchthon, Luther, Knox, Calvin, Wesley, "the Venerable Bede," or Cromwell in the Russian spiritual heritage. Orthodoxy has always been standard in religion and in politics. This made it easy for the people to move from one totalitarianism to another. The result is that Communism has become the orthodoxy that has supplanted the earlier orthodoxy of the church. It is quite impossible for a Russian to understand the two-party political system that prevails in America or the division of Christianity into Protestant and Catholic churches. There was a time when the church dictated the "correct" view. That function has now been taken over by the Party. To the view handed down by the Party all citizens are expected to subscribe. To dissent is to cut one's self off from social contacts, economic opportunity, legal privilege, and any spirit of free inquiry.

Because atheism was widespread in Russia, especially among the intellectuals, it was relatively easy for Communism to move into the vacuum. Religion ceased to be a private affair and became a matter of political and economic orthodoxy in which the government was greatly interested. The question of bread is a material concern for every man, but the question of bread for one's neighbor becomes a spiritual matter. Communism's concern in bread for the public has given it a religious coloration, at least in Russia. Modern Communism in Russia is a religion as well as an economic system.

It is difficult to evaluate modern Communism because of its many facets.

It has been at times a doctrine to explain history, to stimulate social revolution, to industrialize a primitive country, to justify the power of the ambitious leaders, and to advance Russian national interests in international politics. It has been a theory of society, of history, and of politics; a philosophy of values; a propaganda of revolution and nationalism; and a guide to revolutionary economic, political, and military strategy and administration. Functioning in such multifarious conditions and with such multifarious goals, consistency is not to be expected.[1]

Marx and Engels expected the world to be engulfed in what might have been called a "spontaneous uprising of the working class," and they therefore assisted, as they were able, any organization of working groups. It does not appear to have been any part of their strategy that a Communist government such as that which rules China today should move in to overthrow the government of a small country like Tibet and impose a dictatorial rule upon the people, liquidating millions in the process. The modern procedures, such as have been witnessed in North Korea, North Vietnam, Laos, East Germany, Cuba, and elsewhere were quite outside Marx's expectations.

When Lenin rose to power in Russia in 1917, after nearly two decades of agitating from outside Russia, an incipient labor movement was emerging in a few centers such as St. Petersburg, Moscow, Kiev, and Odessa. For the most part these workers were loyal to the old czarist government, but among them there were those who constituted the "public" to whom Lenin appealed and from among whom he recruited his confederates. The great majority,

[1] John L. Stipp, *Soviet Russia Today* (New York: Harper & Brothers, 1957), pp. IX-X.

however—the Mensheviks—were patriotic Russians who asked nothing more from the Czar than justice, fair play, decent working conditions, and some measure of civil rights. Lenin's followers— the Bolsheviks—were nothing more than a small minority who had delivered their very souls into the keeping of their master.

While in Siberia Lenin had worked out in his mind the organization of the revolution, building its whole structure about a minority Party which was to be the hard core. It was to be made up of individuals who could be depended upon to execute orders without asking questions. No man of an independent mind was to be admitted. Hatred was to be the common motive, and strict obedience the lifeblood of the movement. Making a pretense of preserving the appearance of democracy, Lenin surrounded himself with advisors, but he surrendered none of the dictatorial powers with which he invested himself from the beginning. Any man who raised disturbing questions could be liquidated, and many were. Karl Marx, with all his amorality, would probably have been stirred to vitriolic wrath had he lived to witness the October Revolution that claimed his name as its sponsor.

Lenin appealed to the principles of Marx as his authority, but only as he "interpreted" them. In doing so he worked out his doctrine of "the vanguard." This was to be a disciplined corps of revolutionaries pledged to undeviating support of the Soviet government and Communism or Marxism, as Lenin taught it. The important characteristic of this vanguard lay in the fact that every member, no matter what his citizenship might be, was to declare his first loyalty to the Communist party of Russia. In becoming a member of the Party he pledged himself and his loyalty even though the keeping of the pledge might require him to commit treason against the government under which he was a citizen.

It is, perhaps, at this point that an explanation of the position of Marshal Tito should be made. It is a fact, as the head of the Yugoslavian government has so often declared, that Marxism is the ruling philosophy of that landlocked country. For that condition Josip Broz, who came eventually to be known as Marshal Tito, is chiefly responsible. Because of a public humiliation at the hands of Stalin and an intense and patriotic devotion to his motherland, he refused to take orders from Moscow and was expelled from the Party. There is something mysterious about the fact that he was not crushed by Stalin's forces, but in surviving he has presented to the world an anomaly—a Communist country outside the world-wide Communist party. Whereas all card-carrying Communists around the world, outside Yugoslavia, are sworn to betray their native lands if necessary in order to forward the cause of the Russian party, no Yugoslavian Communist is so sworn. Whereas every Communist outside Tito's domain is a potential traitor, the Yugoslavian leader has never asked any man outside his little land to support him. It is a fact, of course, that the philosophy of the Yugoslavian government is Communistic, and is a further fact that Karl Marx is the final authority in Yugoslavia—subject again to Tito's interpretations—but at that point the resemblance to Russian Communism ends. Whereas Khrushchev is building his world-wide conspiracy with all the powers at his command, Marshal Tito is content for the time being to be the absolute dictator over the people of Yugoslavia.

Throughout the world, in every land, there are Communist parties dedicated to the cause of "the revolution." Every one of these parties is pledged to the support of the Russian Communist party and the Soviet government, even to the point of committing treason. The first international organization, known as the Comintern, was later dissolved because of the circumstances of World War II and still later revived under the name Cominform, under which it operates as of the present moment. This amounts to a worldwide conspiracy and is the justification for the fact that the United States Supreme Court has held that the Communist party of the United States is not a legitimate political group and is not, therefore, eligible to have its name and its candidates submitted to the American electorate. Thus, a clear distinction is drawn between an international conspiracy and a legitimate political party inside a democracy.

Karl Marx believed that he had provided the first scientific analysis of history ever presented to the world. He was convinced that he had laid bare the inexorable laws according to which society was destined to develop. It might be possible to delay the triumph of Communism, but it could not be permanently circumvented. In his six-hour-long address before the Communist Congress, held in Moscow, October 18, 1961, Khrushchev predicted that the force of the universal principles of history would have run their course by 1980 and that all the world would be Communist. It was the belief of Charles Darwin that there was a principle running through the process of evolution which had produced the living world as we know it—a principle that was both inexorable and inescapable. It was the belief of Karl Marx that there were principles running through history that were equally inexorable and equally inescapable, these principles working toward the achievement of pure Communism and the "withering away" of the state.

Marx made no appeal to any man's conscience, moral principles, or natural sympathies. The principles he enunciated were as impersonal and as inevitable as the law of gravity. He might be willing to employ force in speeding the victory of the revolution, but he was quite willing to await the appearance of the world upheaval, for he was convinced that it would arrive in time on its own power. He invested history with the power to determine every aspect of human life.

In the 1820's Georg Wilhelm Hegel made the philosophy department of the University of Berlin famous by his exposition of the philosophy of dialecticism. This theory undertook to explain all of life as a conflict between "thesis" and "antithesis," the outcome being "synthesis." Stripped of its technical phraseology this means that everything is a result of conflict between contradictory forces. As a student at the University of Berlin young Marx became greatly interested in the Hegelian philosophy. For several years previous he had been in revolt against religion—still bitter over the fact that he had been "born a Jew"—and Hegel, for him, offered to fill the vacuum. Through the years that he pored over the books in the British Museum Library he undertook to apply Hegelian principles to the world of social forces, political movements, and economic theory. Eventually he came out with his doctrine of dialectical materialism, sometimes called economic determinism.

Marx had come to the conclusion that everything could be explained in terms of matter. Inside it, as Hegel had said, there was going on the conflict of opposites. The product of this conflict was motion. Modern thinkers in some instances declare that time, force, and matter are a sufficient explanation of the universe. Marx was committed to the proposition that motion and matter were all the explanations needed. There might be various stages in the development of the historical setting, but the end was Communism.

Any man who declares his faith in Communism declares his acceptance of Marx's theory of dialectical materialism. He admits that he believes in no God and that that which we call the "soul" of a man is nothing more than the result of conflict in matter.

From Marx to Khrushchev there has been one undeviating agreement: *The classless state is to be launched via a revolution.* Marx, as has been said, had no scruples against the use of violence, but he did not presuppose it as a necessity. Lenin did, and on the basis of that presupposition he undertook to stir up violence throughout the earth. In one of his frank moments Lenin wrote:

Marxists have never forgotten that violence will be an inevitable accompaniment of the collapse of capitalism in its full scale and of the birth of a socialist society. And this violence will cover a historical period; a whole era of wars of various kinds . . . This is an era of tremendous collapses, of wholesale military decisions of a violent nature, and of crises.[2]

He concluded, "While the state exists, there is no freedom. When freedom exists there will be no state." [3]

Vyshinsky, a modern Russian spokesman, recites the same theme: "In our state, naturally, there is and there can be no place for freedom of speech, press, and so on for the foes of socialism. Every attempt on their part to utilize it to the detriment of the state—that is to say, the detriment of the toilers—these freedoms granted to the toilers, must be classified as counter-revolutionary crime." [4]

Joseph Stalin was repudiated by Khrushchev in a speech that shook the world, but the Georgian's philosophy and policies remain standard Communist procedure so far as the international situation is concerned. His official statements on the subject of the class war may, therefore, be accepted as authoritative and orthodox. "We have no freedom of the press for the Mensheviks and the Socialist Revolutionaries who represent the interests of the beaten

[2] Lenin, *Selected Works*, VIII, 315-16.
[3] *Ibid.*, p. 87.
[4] Vyshinsky, *Law of the Soviet State* (New York: The Macmillan Company, 1948), p. 617.

and overthrown bourgeoisie. But what is there surprising about that? We never pledged to give freedom to all classes and to make all classes happy." [5]

In the early years of the revolution Lenin outlined the Party's position with complete candor. "It is necessary, immediately, for all the legal Communist parties to form illegal organizations for the purpose of systematically carrying on illegal work, and of fully preparing for the moment when the bourgeoisie resort to persecution. Illegal work is particularly necessary in the army, navy, and police." [6] To all this Vyshinsky added, "The defense of the U.S.S.R., as the socialist motherland of the world's proletariat, is the holy duty of every honest man everywhere and not only of the U.S.S.R." [7] The careful student of *Das Kapital* will find treason nowhere advocated, but conspiratorial activity has become standard Communist practice everywhere in behalf of the world revolution.

Modern Communists have developed great skill in exploiting any wrongs which persist under capitalism. They can be trusted to agitate in behalf of any man jailed on a controversial issue or under circumstances which make a "crusade" possible. A "Committee for Defense" is organized, funds are solicited, and the sympathetic are exploited. No accounting of funds is ever made, and this makes it possible for a major share of the monies raised to be siphoned off into a Communist treasury. Demonstrations are arranged for the purpose of embarrassing the police and casting doubt on the constituted authorities. Attractive names are given to these "crusades" for the purpose of undermining confidence in the government and its law enforcement agencies.

One of the results of this type of activity is the deflection of honest and socially minded citizens from worthy causes. They do not want to run the risk of being branded as "fellow travelers." That there are occasions where injustice is done an accused person, and where injustice is worked on classes or groups cannot be denied. Good citizens want these conditions corrected, and are willing to assist in the correction, but they hesitate to become active lest they should discover that they have been imposed upon by individuals with Communist connections. The total result is confusion and an

[5] Stalin, *Leninism*, I, 404.
[6] Lenin, *Selected Works*, I, 17.
[7] *Ibid*, V. 152.

enfeeblement of the public opinion that is necessary in any reform.

In every land in which the Communist party is organized—legally or illegally—there are those Communist agents who have been trained as troublemakers. I was a witness to the demonstrations in Japan which protested the visit of President Eisenhower and saw the system working effectively. The mobs were under the direction of leaders who had been trained like a corps of college yell leaders. The denunciations were all mimeographed and in the hands of the leaders, as if they had been a movie script. The tens of thousands of demonstrators were clay in their hands. When the matter was sifted out by the police it was found that those responsible for the demonstrations were known Communists, numbering no more than a few score.

This type of activity is known, technically, among the Communists as "field work." Hundreds of young Communists from all over the world have been trained for this type of activity in a school in Moscow which is organized for that specific purpose. They have been trained in the diabolical art of creating confusion, arousing hatred, distorting facts, playing to prejudice, developing mob psychology, organizing riots, disturbing the peace, and encouraging conflict. Not the least important course in their training is the use of clubs, rocks, and other improvised armament. Upon returning to their homelands they become saboteurs, disturbers of the peace, inciters of mobs, and agitators deluxe. Among university students they have proved to be especially effective, siphoning off a legitimate idealism into illegitimate activity for subversive purposes. Impassioned and inflamed youngsters are encouraged to stone embassies, burn flags, harass visitors, destroy property, and submit demands. It is all carefully planned in secret meetings of a few trusted "graduates" and proves to be unusually effective.[8]

Because no other institution has more at stake in the outcome of the conflict between Communism and democracy than the Church, it is of the utmost importance that a distinction shall be drawn between Communist propaganda and legitimate social reform. One of the duties of the Church as a loyal friend of democracy is to defend the right of the honest thinker to do and to

[8] For a more extended description of this type of Communist activity, see Nathanial Weyl, *Red Star Over Cuba* (New York: Devin-Adair Company, 1960).

express his own thinking. To adopt Communist methods in defending democracy is to admit defeat.

Suggestions for Further Reading

Bennett, John C. *Christianity and Communism Today*. New York: Association Press, 1960.

Berdyaev, Nicolas. *The Origin of Russian Communism*. Ann Arbor, Mich.: University of Michigan Press, 1960.

Cronyn, George W. *A Primer on Communism*. New York: E. P. Dutton & Company, 1960.

Djilas, Milovan. *The New Class: An Analysis of the Communist System*. New York: Frederick A. Praeger, Inc., 1957.

Draper, Theodore. *The Roots of American Communism*. New York: The Viking Press, 1957.

Hayek, Frederick. *The Road to Serfdom*. Chicago: University of Chicago Press, 1944.

Iversen, Robert W. *The Communists and the Schools*. New York: Harcourt, Brace & World, Inc., 1959.

Lewis, John. *Marxism and the Open Mind*. London: Routledge and Kegan Paul, Ltd., 1957.

Medina, Harold R. *The Anatomy of Freedom*. New York: Holt, Rinehart & Winston, Inc., 1959.

Overstreet, Harry A., and Bonaro. *The War Called Peace*. New York: W. W. Norton & Company, 1961.

————. *What We Must Know About Communism*. New York: W.W. Norton & Company, 1958.

Plamenatz, John. *German Marxism and Russian Communism*. New York: Longmans, Green & Company, 1954.

Roy, Ralph Lord. *Communism and the Churches*. New York: Harcourt, Brace & World, Inc., 1960.

Skousen, W. Cleon. *The Naked Communist*. Salt Lake City: Ensign Publishing Company, 1958.

Solberg, Richard W. *God and Caesar in East Germany*. New York: The Macmillan Company, 1961.

Speier, Hans. *Divided Berlin, The Anatomy of Soviet Political Blackmail*. New York: Frederick A. Praeger, Inc., 1961.

West, Charles C. *Communism and the Theologians*. Philadelphia: The Westminster Press, 1958.

Yugoslav Communism; A Critical Study. Printed for the use of the Committee on the Judiciary of the United States Senate, 1961.

16

The Sun That Is Rising in the West

AN INTERESTING STORY IS TOLD OF THE LATE THEODORE ROOSEVELT, who was entertaining a personal guest on the grounds of the White House. The two were discussing some matter of public concern while a little house dog of which Roosevelt was very fond was sniffing about in search of entertainment. Suddenly the President's pooch sighted a mongrel trotting down the street just outside the high iron fence. With a wild cry Roosevelt's dog set off in hot pursuit. After a brief engagement in the street, punctuated with a series of yelps and snarls, the little dog came scampering back whining and bleeding from half a dozen wounds.

"Teddy," the guest said with ill-concealed amusement, "I don't think your dog is much of a fighter."

"Oh, yes, he is," the president replied; "he's a wonderful fighter. But he's an awfully poor judge of dogs."

The diplomatic reverses of the last few years, the successes of the Communists along half a hundred fronts, the growing popularity of the Red Chinese regime, and a variety of adventures which have resulted disastrously for the United States raise some serious questions as to our ability to judge dogs. At least in the case of Red China we are in danger of making a disastrous mistake. On all levels we are underestimating the nation with which we have to deal.

It is unfortunate that the average American—including the tourist who has traveled in the Orient—has had so few opportunities to know the educated, cultured, and highly intelligent Chinese. Acquaintanceship has been limited, for the most part, to occasional exchanges with the laundryman down the street or with young and inexperienced Chinese students who have no more than a limited understanding of the English language and who are apt to hide their real thinking under obsequious courtesy. Even the more

155

fortunate of us have had no more than occasional opportunities to meet the shrewd Chinese trader, the learned scholar, or the infinitely patient scientist. As a consequence we have grossly underestimated the capacity of the 700,000,000 people called Chinese with whom we suddenly find it necessary to deal.

It is a further unfortunate fact that as a people we have almost no knowledge of Chinese literature, philosophy, history, or social idealism. There are not, perhaps, five hundred students of the Chinese language in all the colleges and universities of the nation. There are not more than half a dozen universities that offer courses in Chinese art, history, philosophy, or literature. The great Chinese dramatists, poets, and literati are quite unknown. The Taping Rebellion, for example, was one of the greatest struggles for social justice in the history of the human race, but no more than a few thousand Americans know that it occurred. Whereas the educated American is familiar with the works of Ibsen, Bergson, Balzac, Goethe, Schiller, Renan, Voltaire, Verdi, Wagner, Tolstoi, Dostoevski, and Cervantes, their knowledge of Asiatic authors is limited probably to Hu Shih, Lin Yutang, and Tagore. As for any acquaintanceship with the great ideological conflicts—there is none. Even in the case of a world figure such as Chiang Kai-shek, we are apt to be either ignorant or misinformed. We have never had occasion to deal with a tough-minded Chinese who knew exactly what he wanted and was fully qualified to hold out for his position.

Suddenly we are discovering that the old Mandarin scholar with his long fingernails, his disarming affability, his affected humility, and his silent introspection is a man of the past. The Chinese with whom we must deal during the next twenty-five years are shrewd, independent, determined, proud, astute, thoroughly informed, and case-hardened individuals entirely capable of taking care of themselves in any diplomatic, political, or personal encounter. They cannot be awed, frightened, bulldozed, or laughed out of court.

Whereas the average American citizen of 1938 had some knowledge of the life and career of Adolf Hitler and had read at least some part of *Mein Kampf*, the American of 1962 who knows anything about the dramatic career of Mao Tse-tung and his meteoric rise to the position where he is one of the three most commanding figures of the time—is extremely rare. It is improbable that as many as 10,000 Americans have ever read his *New Democracy* or *On People's Democratic Dictatorship* in any English translation. Yet among almost one fourth of the world's population those two works take rank alongside *Das Kapital* as theoretical masterpieces, and in the opinion of trained military men, his pamphlet on guerrilla warfare is the classic of its kind for all time.

Inside China, Mao

has become more of a myth than a public figure. No one is sure where he lives, and he is seldom seen except at the most important functions in Peking. Yet everyone is made acutely aware that his is the guiding hand for China under Communist rule. His picture adorns every home and every room in public buildings. His name is invoked by people of every profession as the all-knowing leader in their field. Young children chant poems and songs dedicated to him. . . . Mao's writings are studied exhaustively and committed to memory. In many ways Mao has come to fill the symbolic position of the emperors of old who were not only heads of state but were also regarded as the first scholars of the land, the leaders in all matters affecting Chinese society, and the symbolic representatives of the unity of the people.[1]

The national song of China is in his praise:

> The East shines red,
> The sun arises,
> Mao Tse-tung appears in China,
> Toiling for the happiness of the people,
> The savior of the people! [2]

Mao Tse-tung was born of peasant parentage in Shao-shan Village, Hsiangtan County in Hunan Province. His father was a small merchant who operated a little flour mill, and the tiny house in which the boy was born has been converted into a shrine. His education began in the village school. He then went on to the Provincial First Normal School in Changsa and eventually arrived at Pekin University, where he was employed in the library as a clerk at a salary of eight dollars per month. It was there that he first came into contact with elementary Marxism, which in its Chi-

[1] Richard L. Walker, *China Under Communism* (New Haven, Conn.: Yale University Press, 1955), pp. 180-81. Used by permission.
[2] *Ibid.*, p. 181.

nese form was heavily impregnated with Leninism. The spirit of revolution was in the air due to the activities of Sun Yat-sen, and in July, 1921, at a school in the French Concession in Shanghai, the Communist Party of China was founded with twelve members, Mao being one. Before the secret organization meeting concluded the police broke it up, and the tiny group of Communist fledglings fled to Shaosing, Chekiang, where they continued their deliberations on a little boat on Lake Niepu.

Toward the close of World War I Mao went to Peking to enlist students in "work and learn" battalions for the French. The plan was that they were to be taken to Paris, where they would spend half their time in a work camp and the other half in school. Mao's interest in the project stemmed from the fact that the plan could be manipulated so that the students could get training in socialism, anarchism, and revolution. By the end of 1920 about 2,000 had gone to France, among them Chou En-lai, the present-day foreign minister of Red China. As soon as they arrived in France the French Communists took the young men in tow and proceeded to indoctrinate them in Marxism. In 1921, about the time that the Communist party was being organized in Shanghai, Chou En-lai led in the organization of the Chinese branch of the French Communist party. During the next five years he was active as an organizer in Berlin, London, and Marseilles. Sometime during this period he met Stalin, who seems to have been deeply impressed by his unusual abilities and adroit manner.

During the years following World War I the situation in China was tailored perfectly for some kind of revolutionary movement. The Peking government was decadent and ineffective. Sun Yat-sen was an inspiring agitator but less convincing as a revolutionist. In the National University at Peking Hu Shih was leading a literary and cultural revolution that bade fare to become a Chinese renaissance. At the same time another professor—Li Ta-chao, the librarian of the university—was piloting a group of students, among whom was Mao, through the mazes of *Das Kapital*. According to an estimate published in the *Chinese Recorder* in 1927, at least 75 per cent of the 250,000 college and university students of the nation were either atheists—including Mao Tse-tung—or agnostics, and no more than 10 per cent of them could have been said to have religious convictions of any kind. Japan's twenty-one demands on

China, the arbitrary transfer at Versailles of Germany's concessions in Shantung to Japan, and other affronts offered by the European powers were having the effect of rousing the youth of the nation as they had not been aroused in two hundred years. Student organizations which demanded reforms, were developing on every campus, and demonstrations of one kind and another were a commonplace. It was a student's season!

In Peking Li Ta-chao's group took the lead in organizing a great student movement, and on May 4, 1919, 10,000 young men marched on the headquarters of the government, burned the house of the Minister of Communications, and finally compelled three pro-Japanese ministers to flee for their lives. In all this Chou En-lai was one of the leaders. The entire uprising was sponsored by the intellectuals and not by the workers, which beclouds the claim that Chinese Communism started out as a proletarian movement. In his *New Democracy* Mao Tse-tung declares that these demonstrations were the actual beginning of Chinese Communism, and even though the party was not officially organized until a little more than two years later, May 4 is observed today as the Chinese Fourth of July.

If this were a historical study of Chinese Communism a vast amount of detail would have to be inserted at this point. The serious student can get the salient facts by reading *Red Dragon Over China* by Harold Martinson.[3] Our interest is in the history that is still in the making, however.

A tide of patriotism began to develop among the college students of China, who deeply resented the treatment accorded the nation at Versailles. The Soviets, quick to capitalize on that resentment, acted with dispatch and cleverness. In a "Manifesto to the Chinese People" they abdicated all extraterritorial rights, as well as the secret treaties that had been agreed upon by the czar's government and the Chinese authorities. They renounced their claim to the Manchurian railway, restored Outer Mongolia to Chinese hands, and pledged themselves to treat China as an equal. Everywhere throughout China there was rejoicing among the intellectuals and the revolutionaries. Other results were inevitable. The gates were opened wide for an inflow of Russian agents, who within weeks were subverting the Chinese youth.

[3] Minneapolis: Augsburg Publishing House, 1936.

Russia's subversion of China's youth was snowballing. In 1925 the Sun Yat-sen University for Chinese was established in Moscow with an initial enrollment of 600 students. The overflow was accommodated in the educational institutions of Leningrad, Irktusk, and other Russian cities. Some years later two more universities for Chinese only were established in Russia.[4]

Within the space of a little more than five years—from 1921 to 1927—the Communist party grew from 50 to 35,000 junior members, 2,800,000 trade-union workers, and 9,720,000 organized peasants.

Determined to take over at all levels, the Communists infiltrated everywhere and were in the process of establishing themselves in power when they were confronted by Chiang Kai-shek, and the ensuing struggle was a devastating war. As a climax to the contest Mao led an army of 200,000 that dwindled to 20,000 in one of the most desperate marches in history. Licking his wounds, and living off the land Mao dug in to rebuild his forces.

Japan's attack on China in the middle thirties played directly into the hands of the Communists, who were loud in their demands that all parties unite in defense of the country. With the defeat of Japan in 1945, the Communists had grown strong enough again to defy the Nationalist government and in 1949 delivered a series of smashing blows that drove Chiang Kai-shek to Formosa. In achieving their victory the Communists had indebted themselves to Russia for enormous quantities of supplies so that they were no longer free.

The first Communist victories were accompanied by lavish promises of land reform, social justice, freedom, and democracy. As soon as they had solidified themselves in power, however, the pressure was applied. Literally millions of "counterrevolutionaries" were liquidated, and a thoroughgoing dictatorship was set up. Because every revolution needs a "devil," the Red regime inaugurated a "hate America" campaign. All Christian missionaries were taken into custody; missionary colleges, hospitals, orphanages, and publishing plants were expropriated; and religion of every kind was put under the ban.

From the outset a systematic program of brainwashing was intro-

[4] *Ibid.,* pp. 27-28.

duced, and within a relatively brief period of time a small army of cadres had been deployed throughout the nation.

The invasion of South Korea by North Korea, and the resistance of the United Nations forces provided Mao's regime with the exact opportunity it needed. Under the pretense of defending Chinese sovereignty an army of 500,000 "volunteers" was dispatched to the aid of the beleaguered North Koreans, and a series of brilliant victories marked their initial entrance into the conflict. Their supplies were soon exhausted, but to make matters worse their Russian allies became jealous. Just at that juncture General MacArthur was recalled, and the struggle ended in a stalemate. The impression everywhere in the Orient, however, was that a mammoth victory had been won. The Chinese had beaten the paper tiger called the United States. For propaganda purposes the Chinese had won a smashing victory.

The armistice had the effect of relieving the hard-pressed regime of a costly military adventure for which it was ill-prepared, and it was able to turn to the task of consolidating its economic and political position. Herculean efforts were made to industrialize the nation. Diplomatic recognition was won from a series of governments; educational programs were launched. Meanwhile a policy of aggression was agreed upon, with every neighbor a prospective victim. Tibet was crushed; North Korea became a satellite; India was intimidated; and Russia was defied. In 1962 China was flexing her muscles for more "liberations." Trained guerillas were dispatched to Laos, Cambodia, South Vietnam, and Thailand, where they joined forces with local revolutionaries for the purpose of disrupting all orderly social, industrial, and political organization. Everywhere the regime was meddling—fishing in troubled waters.

In 1928 there were eight great world powers; in 1945 there were four; in 1950 there were two; and in 1962 there are three. *A sun has risen in the west!*

In assessing the Chinese situation in 1962 there are sixteen facts which must be faced frankly, courageously, and with a degree of humility. Each is of the utmost concern to the architects of the New World.

1. *The man of color has forced himself into the white man's world.*

This, in itself, is a revolutionary alteration of the balance of power of the whole world. Never again will the white nations be able to divide the world up into spheres of influence, preferential markets, or areas of privilege. Never again will the white man embroil the world in war without being sure that hundreds of millions of men of color will join the conflict. The new "one world" is destined to be one in which the man of color will share the benefits as he shares the burdens. He will not accept condescension, patronizing, or domination. He will demand equality of privilege, of power, and of authority. Under such circumstances the Christian Church cannot speak equivocally if it is to maintain itself as a world movement.

2. *It must be remembered that China has arrived at her present position on her own power.*

There is no more hateful word in human speech than "colonialism," so far as the Orient is concerned. For 150 years the Chinese fought a losing battle with the European powers. Plagued by disunity, defeated by conservatism, and impoverished by exploitation, they had been reduced to near servitude by the time Sun Yat-sen began his crusade. As a people the Chinese walked in humiliation, suffered terrible wounds to their pride, and stood by helpless while their culture was ignored and despised because their government was weak and corrupt. Under Communist leadership they are, today, free from all European shackles. It is true that they suffer under a brutal and unrelenting dictatorship, but as a nation they have never known anything like true democracy. In the meantime the Communists are able to make demands upon the people because the new power status of the nation represents something that has been achieved for them through their own potential strength and does not represent a concession handed down from the colonial powers. National pride is in the ascendancy.

3. *The Red China revolution is an indigenous movement.*

It is true, of course, that the Chinese Reds have been assisted in many ways by the Russians, but the actual leadership has never been allowed to slip out of Chinese hands. There have been other cataclysmic overturns in Chinese politics, in which foreigners have invaded and been absorbed. The present revolution is an inside job. Of the fifty individuals who make up the ruling clique, more than forty are peasants who have never needed to be absorbed.

4. *This has been a peasant revolution, peasant led, peasant supported, and reflects the peasant's viewpoint.*

It is precisely at this point that it differs from every other Communist revolution thus far witnessed. Moreover, it was at this point that Mao became involved in his most serious dispute with Stalin. Because there was no proletariat in China—no organized labor movement—Mao clung determinedly to the proposition that the appeal should be made to the peasants and to the peasant districts rather than to the labor leaders and the cities. His initial successes had been won among the peasants; as a peasant he knew the peasant mind; his armies had been made up of peasants; his trusted advisors were all peasants. Whereas the Russian revolution had been an imposition of authority upon the peasants by the proletariat, the Chinese peasants imposed their revolution on whatever proletariat there was in China. They set peasants in authority over peasants and peasants as teachers of peasants. It had been Lenin's fixed theory that the revolution must spread from the cities to the rural districts, but Mao's revolution began on the farmlands and took the cities captive.

5. *The Communist revolution has impressed the Chinese expatriates favorably.*

It has been estimated—probably exaggerated—that there are as many as 40,000,000 Chinese living outside China. With rare exceptions they have remained Chinese at heart and are insoluble in the political and social life of the lands of their adoption. In Indonesia, Burma, Vietnam, Thailand, and Malaya they maintain their own schools and dominate much of the commercial life of the land in which they live. With the exception of Indonesia and Malaya, they have almost completely withdrawn from the political scene. They have been without spokesmen, social influence, or friends. If one of them became involved with the law he fought his battles alone. Because of the helplessness of their "homeland government" they have been the pawns of whatever group was in control of local affairs. With the coming of the Red regime to power they have an unaccustomed ally. In Indonesia, Burma, and even to some degree in India, the Peking government has come to their defense, with the result that they have suddenly become men of importance. Because of the stature achieved by Mao and his forces theses expatriates now walk with their heads up, their chests out, and their eyes reflecting defiance. Being expatriates they have never felt the hard hand of the regime; being Chinese they are treated with a new caution and respect in the strange lands in which they live.

6. *The new prestige of the Red regime has made the 40,000,000 expatriates the most powerful potential fifth column in history.*

In all Latin American countries there are colonies of Chinese. Because of their language, their natural secretiveness, and their extreme clannishness they make an ideal listening corps. Again and again in recent years they have played the role of an advance guard for diplomats who have arranged new trade agreements and commercial treaties. The Red regime has been willing to pay them well for their services in preferential trade agreements, commissions, and personal honors.

7. *The entrance of China into the arena of world affairs is something entirely new, and highly important.*

When the Cuban government announced that it had entered into an agreement with the Chinese Government involving a sale of 1,000,000 tons of sugar, it meant that an economic stalemate had been broken. The trade may have been made at the expense of the common people in each case, but that made the transaction none the less revolutionary. The Chinese-controlled export has been thrust out into the trade of the world to stay. Being a manipulated export it is capable of working havoc in the industrial life of any nation.

8. *China is soon to possess the atom bomb.*

The essential elements in the fabrication of an atomic bomb are no longer any great secret. Chinese scientists—a small coterie of them—are eminently capable and thoroughly modern. It is commonly known at the world's capitals that the Chinese are hard at work on a bomb project. That certainly is the cause of some tension between Russia and China, for the Soviets have almost as much to fear from a nuclear armed China as has the West. The prospect of a nation without scruples in possession of nuclear weaponry is frightful.

9. *The industrial achievements of China are of the utmost importance to the West.*

The backyard furnaces were of no great industrial significance, but they were of enormous psychological worth to the regime because they had the effect of convincing the people that they were able to industrialize China's 700,000,000. They now believe they can overtake Britain as an industrial power. This is a portent of very great importance.

Whether they are right or wrong, the Chinese people—all Orientals, in fact—have come to look upon the machine as their economic savior. The young man in Afghanistan who said, as he pointed to a great Russian-built flour mill, "When it begins operating every man in this land will have bread," was reflecting the belief of hundreds of millions of the people of Asia and Africa. That the operation of such a mill depends upon a background of education in a dozen lines is not always understood. That machines are demanding servants as well as useful friends is something the masses do not realize, for they have had no experience. There is no magic in a mill operated by untrained workers.

10. *There is no tradition in either Chinese life or religion concerning a God who exercises supreme and final moral authority over this universe.*

The Chinese religions have laid great emphasis on certain virtues, but these same virtues have had to "go it alone." Back of them there has been no basic belief in a supreme and divine authority which gave them validity. When the Hebrews developed their philosophy of history and announced their belief in one God whose divine will and purpose dominated all life—either of nations or of individuals—they put their doctrine into a graphic phrase: "Thus saith the Lord." Upon this rockbase all Judeo-Christian civilization rests. Such authority is higher than that of bombs, machines, marching hosts, or economic theories. What is right and what is wrong does not depend upon governmental decrees, majorities, or plebiscites. Kings can be wrong even though they may return from military adventures with banners flying at the head of victorious hosts. Nations may be under the condemnation of the Eternal at the very moment when they are most prosperous. Industrialism may be in defiance of the divine will just when it is most confident.

It is true that the Chinese religions have produced many admirable traits of character, but there has been no single supreme authority in the Chinese pantheon. As a consequence, Communism has been able to force itself upon the people over the opposition of the ancient faiths. Because under Communism there is promise of improvement in living conditions, the arguments of the Communists carry great weight with the people.

11. *Nowhere on earth is there an educational program so intense or so widespread.*

From one end of the country to the other, wherever as many as ten people can be gathered together, the loudspeakers blare the Marxist line day and night. Indoctrination is a part of every man's employment, relaxation, recreation, and social life. At least 3,000,- 000 cadres—the regime boasts more—are dedicating their entire lives to the task of indoctrinating 700,000,000 people with Marxism-Leninism. The program begins in the prenursery schools and continues through to the brink of the grave. Women and girls are included on an equal basis with fathers and sons. Mixed with Marxism, of course, are such subjects as reading, writing, and arithmetic.

William Benton, former United States Senator and publisher of the *Encyclopaedia Britannica*, reporting in 1961, said of Chinese education, "It is a country coming alive with learning." Basing his statements on the most careful study it has been possible to make from outside the Bamboo Curtain, he said "Schools are literally leaping from the ground." In 1949 when the Communists took over there were 350,000 schools serving 25,000,000 pupils. By 1961 these figures had grown to 1,000,000 schools serving 108,000,000 pupils. At the same time the number of colleges has grown from 227 to more than 1,000. It is estimated that perhaps as many as one half the total population of the land can now read and write. If this is true it represents a monumental achievement.

12. *The eyes of the entire color world are on India and China.*

These two governments, exercising control over more than one third of the human race, launched out on independent careers about the same time. India chose the way of democracy, but China has been taken down the way of a dictatorship. Each is faced with the problem of an exploding population. Each must industrialize in order to provide for the multiplying masses. Each has the problems of ignorance and inadequate communications to contend with. Each has minor advantages and disadvantages, but roughly speaking they started even. If the Chinese become a people better fed, better housed, better educated, and with better health, in a shorter period of time, then democracy will have suffered the greatest defeat it has ever encountered. At least that will be the judgment of the color world. If the democratic powers allow India to fail the popular tide will turn almost irresistibly in the direction of Chinese Communism among 2,000,000,000 of the world's population.

13. *The Red Chinese have convinced men of color that the white man is vulnerable.*

The performance of the Chinese "volunteers" in Korea has raised confidence in the minds of the people of all the color nations in the world. There is no more cringing in the white man's presence. Any variation of the doctrine of apartheid is doomed everywhere. The military experience of the yellow man is being translated into industrial confidence. The white man's opinions, judgments, and God are no longer the standards of the world. Men of color have much to learn about economics, science, and politics, but their confidence in themselves is one of the surest guarantees that they will learn and that a new day is dawning.

14. *Russia holds a mortgage on China that cannot be paid easily.*

Those wishful thinkers who dream of a day when Mao is to declare his independence of the Soviets will dream a long dream. It is true, of course, that there is a sharp cleavage between the two, and it is further a fact that Mao and Khrushchev hold to widely different interpretations of Marxism. For military purposes each needs the other, however, and when China is in possession of the atomic bomb the relative positions of the two will be more nearly equalized—a matter that is alarming to Russia. The Soviets can tolerate a miniscule force such as Yugoslavia and Tito, but the Kremlin cannot ignore 700,000,000 regimented men and women in Asia.

On the other hand, China needs Russia too badly to risk an open break. She needs Russian technology, Russian postgraduate schools for the training of her youth, and Russian trade. When Lenin was laying his plans for world conquest he is said to have remarked—perhaps a mistaken rumor—"The shortest route to Paris is by way of Peking." The Russians of today are not inclined to dispute the judgment.

15. *The hope of any widespread revolt against the regime can be dismissed as wishful thinking.*

I watched the trickle of refugees coming through the lines at

Hong Kong in 1960—a rivulet that became a tidal wave in 1962, until as many as eight thousand per day were crossing over into the British Crown Colony and neighboring Macao. More than a million such are reported to have fled Red China in search of food, in spite of the fact that grim barricades of barbed wire were erected to hold back the tide. But any easy optimism that promises a collapse of the Mao regime faces four very stubborn facts: (1) One million refugees is but a miniscule fraction of 700,000,000 Chinese. (2) The regime has already demonstrated its brutality, and with an army of 12,000,000 troops, it will not be inclined to be squeamish. (3) Prolonged drouths are not new experiences in China, and the returning rains will have the effect of undermining any revolt. (4) The experiences of revolting populations, such as in Hungary and Tibet, that have had no assistance from the democratic powers do not encourage any widespread resistance to the regime back of the Bamboo Curtain. Masses of unarmed men are no match for modern military equipment. The Red spy system is alert, and matters will not get out of hand as they did in Hungary.

16. *Red China has never sought membership in the United Nations.*

No application lies on file awaiting action. Others have sought membership for China, speaking and arguing in her behalf. Among the Chinese people the matter is almost never discussed, however. The Chinese tradition has been one of isolation and withdrawal from the world. Even those nations which have recognized the Red regime have never been admitted to the government's confidence. Mao and his colleagues seem quite content to go it alone. So also are the people.

There is at least one additional fact which is very difficult to evaluate, but it must not be allowed to disappear from the discussions of the Chinese question. *There is still a Christian Church and a Christian movement behind the Bamboo Curtain.* No one knows just what its strength may be or who its living martyrs are. There are those, however, who have never bowed their knees to Baal. Red terrorists have driven the Christians underground, where in other centuries such have done some of their best work.

At the moment there is little more that the Christians of the Free World can do besides pray and continue their faith in their Christian brothers. The Church can prepare to be brethren when the curtain is lifted, for those who come up out of these modern catacombs will be in dire need of understanding and fellowship.

The American people must not, and the Christian Church dare not, make the mistake of misjudging dogs.

Suggestions for Further Reading

Boyd-Orr, John, and Townsend, Peter. *What's Happening in China.* London: MacDonald & Company, 1959.

Chow, Ching-wen. *Ten Years of Storm.* New York: Holt, Rhinehart & Winston, Inc., 1960.

Clark, Gerald. *Impatient Giant: Red China Today.* New York: McKay Company, 1959.

Elegant, Robert S. *The Dragon's Seed.* New York: St. Martin's Press, 1959.

Fairbanks, John K. *The United States and China.* Revised edition. Cambridge, Mass.: Harvard University Press, 1958.

Greene, Felix. *Awakened China: The Country Americans Don't Know.* Garden City, N.Y.: Doubleday & Company, 1961.

Griffith, Samuel B., translator. *Mao Tse-tung on Guerrilla Warfare.* New York: Frederick A. Praeger, Inc., 1961.

Hu, Chang-tu, *et al. China: Its People, Its Society, Its Culture.* New York: Taplinger Publishing Company, 1949.

Hunter, Edward. *Brainwashing in Red Chian.* New York: Vanguard Press, 1953.

Martinson, Harold. *Red Dragon Over Chian.* Minneapolis: Augsburg Publishing House, 1956.

Mende, Tibor. *China and Her Shadow.* London: Thames and Hudson, Ltd., 1961.

Newman, Robert P. *Recognition of Communist China?* New York: The Macmillan Company, 1961.

Quigley, Harold S. *China's Politics in Perspective.* Minneapolis: University of Minnesota Press, 1960.

Rādhākrishnan, S. *East and West in Religion.* London: Allen & Unwin, Ltd., 1958.

Walker, Richard L. *China Under Communism.* New Haven, Conn.: Yale University Press, 1955.

————. *The Continuing Struggle: Communist China and the Free World.* New York: Bookmailer, Inc., 1958.

Ward, Barbara. *India and the West.* New York: W. W. Norton & Company, 1961.

Warner, Dennis. *Hurricane from China.* New York: The Macmillan Company, 1961.

Wollaston, Nicholas. *China in the Morning.* New York: Roy Publishers, Inc., 1960.

17

Of Dogs, of Men, and of Politics

THE MOST SINISTER FACT WITH WHICH WE HAVE TO DEAL IN ANY factual discussion of Communism is the deliberate purpose of the Communist governments to change the fundamental nature and character of man himself. A scientific process commonly called "brainwashing" has been developed and is producing shocking results.

It has been discovered that the personality of an individual—and, therefore, the basic structure of society—can be altered to suit the purposes of a manipulator, who may be either an individual or a government. Not the least diabolical aspect of the matter is that the remolding can be accomplished without the consent, or even the knowledge, of the individual. In the hands of an amoral or unscrupulous ruling clique the results can be catastrophic. The possible results are of such seriousness that God-fearing men everywhere should be informed, in order that they may stand guard over their very souls.

In 1930 Ivan Petrovich Pavlov, one of the world's great physiologists, delivered a lecture before a group of Russian scientists entitled "*The Trial Excursion of a Physiologist in the Field of Psychiatry.*" In the lecture he described a series of experiments that had engaged his attention through a period of a quarter of a century. Only the fact that the lecture was delivered in Russian behind the Iron Curtain and that its full text did not become immediately available to the outside world prevented its being hailed as a revolutionary utterance of the first order. In the years to come Pavlov's *Conditioned Reflexes and Psychiatry*, in which his findings are summarized, will probably become in the field of psychology what Darwin's *Origin of Species* has become in biology.

In 1904 Pavlov was awarded a Nobel prize for original research in the physiology of digestion. In 1917 he was saved from liquidation at the hands of the Bolsheviks by the personal interference of Lenin himself, who held his scientific skill in great respect, in spite of the fact the he was an open critic of the Communist regime. About the year 1900 he had become convinced that he could learn nothing more about the human digestive system until he had precise knowledge of the workings of the human mind. He therefore turned to psychology and initiated a series of experiments in which he used dogs, because of the similarity between the canine and the human digestive processes. Modern scientists, therefore, speak of "Pavlov's dogs" when referring to conditioned reflexes.

As a physiologist Pavlov had noticed that nervous tension had much to do with the secretion of the stomach solvents. He set out, therefore, to discover what mental states might have to do with digestion, and this led him into an investigation of nervous reactions and physical functions.

By subjecting his dogs to a series of artificial stimuli Pavlov discovered that their reactions followed a fixed pattern. By fastening electrodes to their legs, by displaying food before them, by ringing a bell at the same instant food was served them, and by a variety of other devices he could produce nervous states of his own choosing. Then by measuring the chemistry of the dog's saliva he determined the exact degree of tension they developed.

At this point he made his first great discovery. By maintaining the required tension he could bring any dog to a state of nervous collapse not unlike that of the nervous exhaustion human beings sometimes suffer. No animal was immune. In that condition a dog exhibited definite symptoms, and always the same. Every dog had his "point of collapse."

The second great discovery followed immediately. When a dog was in this state of collapse it was possible to implant in him an entirely new type of behavior.

The third discovery represents the frightening aspect of the entire process. So far as Ivan Pavlov was able to discover—or, for that matter, so far as any of his disciples know—there is no way in which the dog can be restored to his original character once the new type of behavior has been implanted in the collapsed mind. Further investigation may reveal some effective method, but to date none has been found. For the present, therefore, it must be said that the "brainwashed" dog cannot be wholly restored by any known psychological process. So far as medical science knows at the moment the transformation is permanent.

Upon the basis of these three principles Russia and China have developed techniques and are employing them systematically on a worldwide scale. In doing so they are twisting, altering, remaking, warping, and even destroying human personality.

During World War I members of the fighting forces exhibited a series of strange symptoms to which the medical profession gave the name "shell shock." Men who had been subjected to severe strain sometimes went into a state of collapse; some became hysterical, and others appeared to be demented. At first it was assumed that it was the weaklings who were thus affected, but this theory was quickly abandoned on the basis of records and medical examinations. After the war whole hospitals were filled with the sufferers, few of whom ever recovered.

In 1927 Joseph Stalin came to power in Russia and began his series of purges. At about the same time the world was treated to some of the most bizarre legal cases ever exhibited. Dignitaries, churchmen, and once-honored Communist leaders were put on trial and "confessed" in open court their "mistakes." In some cases they actually asked to be punished for having "betrayed the working people."

In vivid style, and often in identical terms, the accused described their "stupidities." They accepted even the sternest sentences without complaint or regret. It was all very mysterious. None bore upon his body any scars; none seemed to have suffered any violence or indignities; none complained of any physical brutalities. Except for altered manners and strange speech they seemed to be the same persons they had always been, but their behavior was radically altered.

For a time it was suspected that they had been drugged, and I remember writing an editorial on that subject, based on medical evidence which seemed, at the time, irrefutable. A study of the behavior of great characters, such as Cardinal Mindszenty, made the drug theory eventually untenable.

Almost from the start of World War II cases began coming back from the front of men who suffered from what the medical corps called "battle fatigue." Again, as in World War I, it was at first assumed that the sufferers were the weaklings, but again this theory had to be abandoned because of the evidence. The doctors hurried to the defense of the stricken men and declared that no man is immune. "Every man is susceptible to collapse. The only difference between individuals is the time lag between the first exposure and the final collapse."

Some survived no more than a few days; others might hold up for several weeks, but all came to the breaking point if the strain was sufficiently prolonged. In a few rare instances men survived the pressure for as many as fifty-five days. Pavlov had proved that "every dog has his day," and World War II proved that "every man has his point of collapse." [1]

According to the agreement reached at Yalta Russia was permitted to take over in North Korea following the defeat of the Japanese. In 1949 the United Nations required that both the Russian and the American troops be withdrawn. The United States complied, but the Russians delayed. Meanwhile they drilled and equipped the North Korean army. On June 25, 1950, the North Korean forces struck along the 38th parallel with 187,000 troops, 173 Russian tanks, and 200 planes. President Truman moved with dispatch, and soon the troops from seventeen nations were locked in combat with the Communist North Koreans. When the tide started running in favor of the allies strong reinforcements in the form of 500,000 Chinese "volunteers" appeared at the front.[2] Almost immediately prisoners began streaming back from the front lines in both directions, and at that point another mystery appeared.

Large numbers of those who had been taken prisoner began behaving in a manner hitherto unknown in warfare. They refused to eat the food their captors provided; they destroyed their bedding and their barracks; they defied the medical officers who attempted to dress their wounds; and they attacked fellow prisoners who refused to join them in their fanatical conduct. Then a little later, American prisoners refused to return to their outfits, saying they were going to stay with their captors and "fight for peace."

[1] For a brief but satisfactory explanation of this process of brainwashing see Aldous Huxley, *Brave New World Revisited* (New York: Harper & Brothers, 1958), to which this author is deeply indebted, in the matter under discussion and many others.

[2] Some estimates put the number at 1,000,000.

Other prisoners, returning, reported a strange new form of torture. They had been held in isolation through long periods of time; they had been questioned incessantly; they had not been allowed to rest. Badgered, intimidated, threatened, pressured, cajoled, accused, ridiculed, through long periods of time, they had been bullied to the point of exhaustion.

Their bodies bore no scars; they had been subjected to few vile indignities; they accused no one of physical brutalities. Their minds had been sorely wounded, however, some had barely escaped going into a state of collapse; in some instances the pressured had gone insane.

The process was known to the Chinese as *his-nao*, and to the psychologists as psychological mass coercion. Newspapermen, translating it into vivid language, called it brainwashing. Scientifically speaking it was a wholesale application of Pavlovian principles.

The most sinister aspect of the entire matter is now appearing as the reports come out of Red China concerning the application of Pavlovian principles to an entire population. A transformation quite unparalleled is being brought about among the people of the most populous nation on earth. As these pages are being written my desk is piled high with books, brochures, reports, scientific discussions, and journalistic accounts which describe the extent to which a handful of individuals—the Red masters—are transforming the character and personalities of 700,000,000 persons. The total prospect is the most terrifying threat the human race has ever encountered.

Mao Tse-tung was introduced to the techniques of brainwashing in 1930. At that time the system was clumsy and only partially developed, but his alert mind was quick to sense the possibilities of the new technique, and he mastered the major principles. With the passing of three decades and the amassing of a vast amount of experience, the Chinese have refined the process and made it diabolically effective. Although the Russians have been familiar with Pavlov's principles since 1917, the Chinese have employed them in a wholesale fashion quite without parallel. Politically Mao and Pavlov were poles apart, but the Russian scientist put into the hands of the Chinese revolutionary the weaponry which puts all Asia at his mercy. Already the techniques have been employed against the Tibetans, Laotians, Vietnamese, and occasional nations of other border states. As the Red Chinese dragon reaches out into the rest of Asia, we may expect to see the pressures of brainwashing applied on an expanding basis.

That the reader may understand the total process a little better, it is necessary to explain it in some detail.

In Communist terms a cadre is an individual who has become an undeviating member of the Party and a more or less official interpreter of the Party line. In most cases he gives his full time to the work of the Party. In the administration of civil affairs throughout China he is the local director of Party activities at the grass roots level.[3] This means that the cadres are the hard core of the Party and the local dictators of life. They combine the functions of secret police, superintendents of education, agitators, government spokesmen, and community leaders. It is of the utmost importance, therefore, that they shall be absolutely subservient to the bosses in Peking, and without an exception they have been through the brainwashing process. Their minds are hermetically sealed against any conflicting opinion, economic heresy, or contradictory argument. "At the level of creating cadres the Communists have arrived at a system of conversion and changing of thought patterns which in many ways constitutes a new dimension of power in the world today."[4]

Recruiting cadres is a simple matter. The learned individual has always been honored in Chinese society, and by offering an education to ambitious young men and women the Communists fill the lists very easily. If a brilliant youth hesitates for any reason it is always easy to bring pressure to bear.

Once he has been accepted for cadre training there is no turning back. Everything is carried out with an air of casualness, but underneath it all there is a deadly seriousness. Only in the rarest of instances is there any overt threat, but within a few days following the candidate's "enlistment" he begins to hear grisly hints of the punishment that is meted out to those who have tried to

[3] Chinese statistics are notoriously unreliable, but it appears to be true that there were about 10,000,000 cadres as of early 1962.

[4] Walker, *China Under Communism*, p. 51. For an extended discussion of the process see Walker, Chapter 3.

withdraw or escape. Insubordination or deliberate ineptitude is dealt with speedily and ruthlessly.

Almost from the first day the trainee finds himself a member of a small group of twelve persons who are soon withdrawn from all social contacts. Inside each group there is a member of the Party who acts as a spy on all the others. The identity of this person is carefully concealed, and though the initiates may know there is one among them they never know who he—or she—is. Therefore, each one learns never to confide in any of the others.

The first work assignment is something repulsive, loathsome, or revolting. At the same time the trainee is immersed in propaganda concerning the proletariat, the duties of the working class, the honor of labor, and the necessity of undeviating loyalty to "the people"—which means the ruling clique. It is deliberately planned that this period of training shall be completely exhausting, both physically and mentally. The hours are long, the work is hateful, and the total experience is disillusioning. Meanwhile the candidate is encouraged to surrender to disgust and self-loathing. In simple terms, the aim is to bring on the state of collapse.

A period is set aside each day during which the leader of the group persuades everyone to analyze their backgrounds, family relationships, early idealism, friendships, and ambitions. This is always done in the presence of the group, and everyone is urged to assist by criticizing the confessor and pointing out his "mistakes." Anyone reluctant to criticize others falls under the same suspicion that one does who refuses to bare his inner soul. No effort is made to build up any spirit of comradeship within the group, for this would defeat the purpose of the training. Instead each individual is made to feel that every other person is his unsparing and unsympathetic critic. Meanwhile the living conditions are difficult, the assigned work is repulsive, and rest is forever being interrupted. Gradually the spirits of the group begin to disintegrate, which is the deliberate purpose of the entire procedure.

The continual spying produces a terrible fear; the confinement results in frustration; the bad food and arduous labors undermine all physical stamina; the unceasing criticism destroys the last remnant of morale. It is commonly reported that thousands of the youth of China have gone stark mad at this point.

When the trainees reach their lowest spiritual level there occurs a crisis, and at that point the indoctrination begins. The physical labors are lightened, the quality of the food improves, and long periods of time are given over to "study." Unconsciously the student discovers that his training in Marxism is attended by better living conditions, and he associates the better times with progress in Marxian understanding and acceptance.

About this time the student is required to write an autobiography in which he is expected to put down in detail his innermost thinking—including his sex fantasies, his desires, and habits. All his motives, fears, hopes, instinctive reactions, and ideals are laid out to be analyzed and graded. Under the guidance of a veteran cadre abetted by the constant criticism of the group, the trainee is persuaded to view all his early training as having been "feudal" and, therefore, evil. By this time his very soul has become public property, for each member of the group has free access to what he has written. Meanwhile his autobiography is filed away for future use in the event that the Party ever needs it for blackmail purposes.

Just when tempers are frayed, consciences are in revolt, fears are in command, and emotions are out of control, the serious indoctrination begins. The student is given big dosages of Marxism, Marxian philosophy, and Marxian economics. As his living conditions improve he receives an occasional word of commendation from his cadre and begins to experience a sense of relief from his fears. Almost unconsciously he associates this with his newly accepted ideas. He is like the person who has become depressed through a sense of guilt and experiences a sense of "forgiveness from sin." The whole is just a little like an old-fashioned camp meeting conversion.

Now he is encouraged by his cadre and shown some small honors. Life seems to clear up for him; his mental and spiritual health improves. Then he is sent out among his friends and neighbors to assist them in achieving the peace of mind that has come to him. If he shows sufficient skill he is assigned to various drives, projects, and programs and receives honors and credits proportionately.

Cadres who have become sufficiently hardened become the shock troops of the towns and villages. They are expected to lead study groups and to perfect the organization at the grass roots level. As they develop skills they are promoted. In time they become molded to the Communist pattern from which it becomes impossible to deviate. They are reborn persons, and according to Pavlov's theories they can never be restored to their original mind.

In Red China we are witnessing an effort to transform the personality of a nation of 700,000,000 persons. The mighty efforts of great conquerors pale into insignificance in comparison. Literally hundreds of millions of peasants, farmers, women, students, housewives, mothers, intellectuals, and illiterates are being subjected to the process wholesale.

Hundreds of thousands of Chinese are being organized into small groups and, so far as possible, removed from all normal social contact. They are being reduced to nervous wrecks deliberately, in order that they may be indoctrinated with Marxian dogma. They are being taught to hate the United States with a bitterness never known before. Little children are being taught to spy on their parents; young people are alienated from their homes and loved ones by every possible device; friends are set against friends. There is a common saying among them that "no man has a friend."

There have been other times when nations have risen in revolt against military or economic overlords and have shaken off their chains, but there has never been an instance in history in which the leaders of such a revolt have undertaken to remold the basic nature and personality of the race. "Red China's Mao Tse-tung has embarked on the most terrifying experiment in modern history—the mobilization and brainwashing of nearly one-quarter of the human race." [5] It must be remembered that the attack on the old Chinese customs, standards, ideals, and life is not being made by foreign conquerors. *Instead it is by native-born Chinese peasants indoctrinated in Marxian Communism adulterated with Leninism.*

Age-old customs of the most profound sanctity are being uprooted; new standards of values are being implanted in brainwashed minds; the institution of the family is in the process of being destroyed; and the spiritual powers of a great race are being appropriated by an alien ideology. Even the sex instinct is being subjugated to serve the political designs of the Party.

Under the pressure of the new industrialism the people are worked excessively and bombarded hour after hour with Com-

[5] Robert S. Elegant, and Calvin Tomkins, "Experiment—a Master Race," *Newsweek Magazine* (December 1, 1958), p. 43.

munist doctrine. Those who surrender their souls to their Communist masters discover that the harsh conditions are somewhat relieved, and this has the effect of cementing them to the regime. Surrounded by spies, living in constant fear of the police, going every day aware of the fact that no man has any constitutional rights, never sure of what the law is, the public becomes frustrated and defenseless.

Perhaps the most effective agency employed in brainwashing the Chinese is the new system of colleges and universities that have come into existence since 1949. When the Japanese struck at Shanghai in 1937 the land was dotted with honored institutions of learning of excellent academic standing, the majority of them being of missionary origins. Under the Nationalist government a beginning had been made in the establishment of high-grade government schools which might have taken rank with the best scientific institutions of the world. Since 1949, however, these have all been destroyed and their campuses occupied by public institutions of one kind and another. In their places new schools designed according to a Communist pattern have been set up, every effort being made to erase from the minds of the people all memories of or ties with their former colleges. The instruction bears little resemblance to the instruction once offered. There is much discussion, but no spirit of free inquiry. History is falsified in favor of Communist ends; economics are strictly Marxian; philosophy is strongly tinctured with Leninism and Maoism; science is restricted to those branches endorsed by the government; and social studies are limited to propaganda. Hundreds of thousands of books, among them copies of the old classics, have been burned. In other upheavals the invaders have destroyed the culture of the lands invaded, but in the case of Communist China a deliberate effort is being made to completely alter the culture to conform to Communist standards and purposes.

There is a certain impartiality about Pavlovianism. It operates inside the mentalities of one race as it does inside the minds of another. In crushing Tibet the process of brainwashing has been imposed on the Tibetan people, beginning with their young. Once the dragon has enveloped Laos the story there will be the same.

It is impossible to follow through on any careful study of brainwashing without being made aware of the fact that Pavlov's

179

principles are being applied to the East-West struggle. Ever since 1945, when Joseph Stalin took leave of the conference in Teheran, it has been standard practice for the Communist powers to take advantage of every situation to create tension. The weaving and twisting of Communist diplomacy has the effect of creating uncertainty, fears, confusion, frustration, and tension in the Free World. Every concession leads to new demands. Every pressure is designed to create anxiety; every move on the part of the free world is labeled "aggression"; in every situation the West is put on the defensive. Viewed from a psychologist's angle, it is an employment of Pavlovian principles.

The performances of Khrushchev at the United Nations in New York, in India, in Vienna, and in the famous "kitchen debate" with Vice-President Nixon ran true to Pavlovian principles. Anything that can create tension, self-criticism, uncertainty, and disunity makes a contribution to Communist effectiveness. The greater the reaction to the induced strains, the more advantageous the situation becomes, according to Communist reasoning.

It should be pointed out at this stage of the study that the psychologists are agreed that the best defense against the process of brainwashing, on the part of either a nation or an individual, is a vital religious faith. Major William E. Mayer, an Army psychiatrist, made an extended study of the behavior of American prisoners of war who had fallen into the hands of Communist captors. As a result of his investigation, made under strict scientific controls, he became convinced that young men who held to strong religious convictions—whose faith was firmly rooted and well reasoned—were best able to withstand the brainwashing techniques. Official reports from other sources—British as well as American—support the findings of Major Mayer in all respects.

The basic principle underlying Major Mayer's findings relative to individuals in their resistance to Communist pressures is equally operative in the case of the public mind. Any nation with a virile religious faith is forearmed; the nation that allows its faith to disintegrate has exposed itself to the deadly attack of the enemy.

Suggestions for Further Reading

Hunter, Edward. *Brainwashing in Red China.* New York: Vanguard Press, 1953.

Huxley, Aldous. *Brave New World Revisited.* New York: Harper & Brothers, 1958.

Meyer, Frank E. *The Moulding of Communists.* New York: Harcourt, Brace & World, Inc., 1961.

Rostow, W. W. *The Prospects for Communist China.* New York: John Wiley & Sons, Inc., 1954.

Sargent, William W. *The Battle for the Mind.* Garden City, N.Y.: Doubleday & Company, 1957.

Schein, Edgar H., et al. *Coercive Persuasion.* New York: W. W. Norton & Company, 1961.

Walker, Richard L. *China Under Communism.* New Haven, Conn.: Yale University Press, 1955.

18

Communism as a Competitive Religion

WHAT WE ARE WITNESSING IN OUR WORLD IS A WAR TO THE DEATH between two interpretations of the universe, two systems of values, two estimates of the worth of the individual, two concepts of honor, two theological systems, two philosophies, two economic systems, two estimates of the meaning of life.

Up to a certain point Christianity can take a neutral position in the case of a conflict between two economic theories. Certainly in many partisan political contests it can, and must, be neutral. When the individual is being weighed for worth, however, when the measure of justice is being estimated, when spiritual and moral freedom are in jeopardy, then the duty of religion and the religious man becomes clear and inescapable. In the deadly situation in which we find ourselves today it is the religious aspect of Communism which requires that all believers in God and in man shall accept the challenge and defend the spiritual interpretation of life.

Beginning with Marx and Engels, the Communists were quick to realize that the most massive block standing in their way was the multifaceted thing called religion. Lunarcharsky, while serving as the Russian Commissioner of Education, stated the case bluntly: "We hate Christianity and Christians. Even the best of them must be considered our worst enemies. Christian love is an obstacle to the development of the Revolution. Down with love for one's neighbors! What we want is hate . . . only then can we conquer the universe." [1] Lenin declared, "The fight against religion must not be limited or reduced to abstract, ideological preaching. The struggle must be linked up with the concrete practical class movement; its aim must be to eliminate the social roots of religion." Stalin said, "It is impossible to conquer an

[1] Quoted in the *U.S. Congressional Record*, 77, 1539-40.

enemy without having learned to hate him with all one's soul." [3]
The Leningrad radio in an official broadcast on August 27, 1950,
warned its Russian listeners that "the struggle against the Gospel
and the Christian legend must be conducted ruthlessly and with
all the means at the disposal of Communism."

It is hard to think of Communism in religious terms. In fact
there are those who experience a sense of outrage when it is suggested that Communists are actuated by something like religious
zeal. But the Communist who aligns himself with Marx's scientific
principles of history is in some way akin to the Christian who declares he is "in Christ." It is as a spiritual heresy that Communism
becomes dangerously anti-Christian.

Communism in actual fact is the foe of every form of religion and
especially of Christianity, not as a social system but as a religion. It wants
to be a religion itself, to take the place of Christianity. It professes to
answer the religious questions of the human soul and to give a meaning
to life. Communism is integrated; it embraces the whole of life; its relations are no special section of it. On this account its conflict with other
religious faiths is inevitable. Intolerance and fanaticism always have a
religious origin. No scientific, purely intellectual theory can be so intolerant and fanatical, and communism is as exclusive as a religious faith is.[4]

In spite of the fact that Communism and Christianity stand
at opposite poles in the matter of faith there is an amazing cor-
respondence between them. It will repay us to examine a few of
their characteristics and identify some of their similarities.

1. *Both have set for themselves the goal of world mastery.*

This issue was fought out inside the Christian Church in the
first century when the apostle Paul pried Christianity loose from
its Jewish moorings. At the Jerusalem Conference in A.D. 49 it was
decided that the privilege of membership in the Church should
be accorded to all men and that the objective of the movement
should be the conversion of the world.[5]

Over and over, like some haunting refrain, Communist spokesmen have declared that Communism was destined to rule the

[2] Lenin, *Religion*, pp. 3-6.
[3] Stalin, *The Patriotic War of the Soviet Union* (Moscow, 1946), p. 55.
[4] Berdyaev, *The Origin of Russian Communism*, p. 158.
[5] See Acts 15:1-29 and Gal. 2:1-10.

world. In June, 1957, Nikita Khrushchev, in the course of an interview in New York City before a nation-wide television audience, said, "I can prophesy that your grandchildren in America will live under socialism. . . . Your grandchildren will . . . not understand how their grandparents did not understand the progressive nature of a socialist society." [6] Communists do not propose to remodel the governments of the world; they propose to destroy them. This is not a charge leveled at them; it is their own frank avowal of purpose.

2. *Both Christianity and Communism have their inspired writings.*

Just as the Holy Bible is the rock base of Christian faith and practice, so *Das Kapital* is the final authority for orthodox Communists. No genuine Marxist ever expresses any doubt as to *Marx's infallibility.*

At least two heresies have appeared in the ranks of Communism, and others may develop. Tito of Yugoslavia has declared he is a true Marxist, but he does not acknowledge the authority of the Kremlin. Albania avows its Communism in the strongest of terms but acts independently of either Moscow or Peiping. There are evident differences between China and Russia, but in all the heretical states there is an intense loyalty to Marx and Lenin.

3. *Both Christianity and Communism have issued manifestos.*

In 1848 Karl Marx and Friedrich Engels prepared the platform for the Communist League, an international revolutionary organization. This was the famous Communist Manifesto, which became the blueprint for all orthodox Communists thereafter. The modern Communist, after more than a century during which the Manifesto has been attacked, analyzed, interpreted and denounced, still says, "This I most steadfastly believe."

Somewhere toward the end of the first Christian century a great Christian teacher undertook to fortify the souls of the Christians who were about to suffer terrible persecutions at the hands of the Roman Empire. Inside official circles they were viewed as revolutionaries, and in the belief that they were in need of a plain statement of the teachings of the Christian faith, this teacher put

[6] Hoover, *Masters of Deciet*, p. 3.

them down in a book which has come to be called "The Gospel According to Saint Matthew." Three chapters (5-7), popularly known as the Sermon on the Mount, serve as a Christian manifesto to this day. The dedicated Christian, reading this immortal document, says, "This I most steadfastly believe."

4. *Christianity and Communism began in obscurity.*

A search of the London papers of the period fails to reveal any mention of Marx's name during the years 1849-57, though it is known that he gave occasional lectures and served in a small way as the British correspondent for the *New York Tribune.* His book did not become available in English until after his death and was never reviewed by any publication of standing during his lifetime.

There is some small suggestion of similarity between the stacks of the British Museum Library and the manger of Bethlehem. There was a musty smell about both, and a certain anonymity surrounded those who occupied both—Karl Marx and the Nazareth family. Both were aliens and had taken refuge in strange places. At his death Jesus of Nazareth could number his followers only in tens, and the official Roman records nowhere contain any mention of his name. When the Church finally burst upon the world it took the Roman Empire completely by surprise.

5. *Both Christianity and Communism rest their faith on an infallible Creator.*

Marx assigned to his scientific principles of history all the qualities of a creator except those of personality. In spite of the fact that he lacked many of the qualities of a scientist, he succeeded in investing himself with the aura of science, and this in turn contributed to the belief among his disciples that his explanations of history were infallible.

The Christian faith rests its case on the cornerstone of Judaism, expressed in the first line of Genesis, "In the beginning God." For the orthodox Christian this is the one dependable explanation of the creation and continuance of the universe. He sets out to live in a world that has moral meaning, in which ethical principles are the final authority—principles originating in the Creator, whom he calls God.

Every attempt the Communists have made to establish their type of justice has been associated with violence, crime, cruelty, falsehood, betrayals, repression, denials of rights, and the suppression of individual liberty.

6. *Christianity and Communism believe in a savior who is the world's redeemer.*

The Christian believes in God and in Jesus Christ who was God's personal representative on this earth for the period of one lifetime. The Communist puts his trust in Karl Marx. In proving his principles of history Marx has become the world's redeemer, according to Marxian philosophy.

7. *Christianity and Communism both point to a Holy Land.*

Karl Marx learned the Russian language in order to understand the controversies that raged among the revolutionaries of Russia, but he always held the Russian in contempt and expected no effective help of any kind from Russia. Jesus wept over the city of Jerusalem and reminded it that it had always stoned the prophets who had come to deliver it.

With the unexpected development of the October Revolution, Russia became the holy land of the Communists of all the earth. Just as Palestine serves as a magnet for the affections of the Jews, Christians, and Moslems, so Moscow is the beacon that attracts the sentiments and affections of the Communists.

8. *The hopes of Christianity and Communism revolve about a chosen people.*

All the great prophets of the Old Testament believed they saw in the experiences of the Hebrews the working out of a divine plan in history in which the Hebrews were to play the stellar role. When the Christian Church broke away from its Jewish moorings it appropriated the doctrine of the chosen people and claimed for itself the prophetic promises made by the great Jewish spiritual leaders.

Communism sets out to establish the claim of the proletariat to all the privileges and benefits due to a chosen people. Whereas Jesus said the meek would inherit the earth, Marx said the workers would inherit the earth.

Every careful historian of the Russian people has called attention to the fact that among the Russians down through the centuries there has been a strong spirit of messianism—a belief that they, as a people, were destined to play a stellar role in the redemption of humanity. In the days of the czars when the Russian Orthodox Church was the custodian of the spiritual life of the people this messianic impulse was the heart and core of their religion. Under the Communists the same belief in destiny persists, but Marxism has now become the gospel.

9. *The Christian trinity is matched by a Communist trio.*

Karl Marx was the theoretician upon whose scientific principles of history the superstructure of Communist doctrine and belief has been erected. Lenin was the revolutionary statesman who provided the carriage in which Marxism might ride to triumph. Joseph Stalin created the Communist empire ringed about by satellite states. In spite of his downgrading at the hands of Khrushchev the political structure he devised is the visible form of Communism.

10. *Both Christianity and Communism created a social institution.*

Even Christians are in danger of identifying the Church with Christianity, but there is a vast body of Christian idealism outside the Church. At the heart of Christianity, however, there is the hard core called the Church, from which all this idealism is eventually derived.

At the heart of Communism stands the Party, membership therein being esteemed by Communists as a higher privilege than any other allegiance to which a man can give himself. At the top of the list of priorities of any Communist there stands his responsibility to the Party. Lenin did not coin the sentence "to the revolutionary everything is moral which serves the revolution," but he made it the basic condition of membership.

11. *Both Communism and Christianity hold to the doctrine of the Judgment Day.*

Prominent in the theology of the Jews was a doctrine called "the end of the age." This belief came over into Christianity in the form of an expectation of a final judgment when all men should stand in the presence of God to be judged for the lives they have lived. This doctrine, in part, has been taken over by Christianity in the form of a belief in the second coming of Jesus Christ.

Communist theology declares there is to be a violent overthrow of capitalism, and Nikita Khrushchev, in addressing the great Congress of Communists in October, 1961, declared that the year 1980 would see this triumph.

187

12. Both Christianity and Communism believe in the fact and reality of sin.

The Christian believes that sin is any rebellion against the will of God or any defiance of the moral order of the universe. Communists believe that private property is the sum of all villainies. Christianity labels the rebellious as sinners, and Communism calls them counter-revolutionaries.

13. Both Christianity and Communism are driven by a missionary passion, and the difference in the progress of the two rivals is the difference in the loyalties of their adherents.

The Communist wages war for the possession of the world because he believes in economic determinism. The Christian is persuaded to support the missionary program of the Church because of his loyalty to his Lord. The call of the Party or the call of the Church becomes a charge against the dedication and commitment of the individual. Generally speaking, it may be said that the next world belongs to the most dedicated—to those most willing to sacrifice. No Communist has ever been heard to say, "I do not believe in foreign missions; we have enough to do right here at home."

14. Both Christianity and Communism propose to change the nature of man.

The apostle Paul believed his very nature had been changed as a result of his contact with Jesus Christ, and this has been the basic teaching of the Church down through the centuries.

Marxism promises to the novitiate a solution of all economical, political, social, and personal problems. It proposes to make new creatures out of old believers, imposing upon them the will of the Party, for which they have been prepared by a thorough course in official brainwashing.

15. There are certain parallels between the life of Jesus and the life of Marx.

Both were Jews; both were born into good families; both enjoyed the privileges that come to a youth of the middle class in their respective generations. Neither was ever quite understood by his family; each began his serious work at about the age of thirty; neither ever knew anything of luxurious living; and neither ever seems to have regretted that condition. Jesus is said to have nowhere to lay his head, and Marx was never able to pay his rent. Neither had a great burial; the funeral of each was provided out of the generosity of friends. Jesus was buried in a borrowed tomb, and Marx was laid away in a coffin which was the gift of a friend. Marx's rites were attended by six persons, and Jesus died in the midst of a mob that included no more than six friends. Each has been succeeded by a hierarchy that has often misinterpreted him and more frequently misrepresented him.

16. *Further parallels briefly may be stated.*

Both Christianity and Communism offer themselves as philosophies of life; both promise a salvation; both conceive of a destiny for man. Each has its orthodoxy and its heresies. Both have much to say about another world, and both emphasize both faith and works. Christianity makes a sacrament out of a last supper, and Marxism embalms Lenin's body and exposes it to the worship of the people. In recent years a ceremony not entirely unlike that of baptism for children has been devised, whereby Communist parents dedicate their little ones to the cause of Communism.

Upon the outcome of the contest between these two great interpretations of life will depend the destiny of the human race for the next five hundred years.

Suggestions for Further Reading

Anderson, Gerald H., editor. *The Theology of the Christian Mission.* McGraw-Hill Book Company, 1961.

Bainton, Roland H. *Christian Attitudes Toward War and Peace.* Nashville: Abingdon Press, 1960.

Bennett, John C. *Christianity and Communism Today.* New York: Association Press, 1960.

Branscomb, B. Harvie. *The Message of Jesus.* Revised edition. Nashville: Abingdon Press, 1960.

Crossman, Richard, editor. *The God That Failed.* New York: Harper & Brothers, 1950.

Davies, A. Powell. *The First Christian: A Study of St. Paul and Christian Origins.* New York: New American Library of World Literature, 1959.

Djilas, Milovan. *Anatomy of a Moral.* New York: Frederick A. Praeger, Inc., 1959.

Gilbert, Rodney. *Competitive Coexistence.* New York: Bookmailer, Inc., 1956.

Johnson, F. Ernest. *A Vital Encounter: Christianity and Communism.* Nashville: Abingdon Press, 1962.

Lewis, John. *Marxism and the Open Mind.* London: Routledge and Kegan Paul, Ltd. 1957.

Lowry, Charles W. *Communism and Christ*. New York: Morehouse-Gorham, 1953.

Price, Frank Wilson. *Marx Meets Christ*. Philadelphia: The Westminster Press, 1957.

Sargent, William W. *The Battle for the Mind*. Garden City, N.Y.: Doubleday & Company, 1957.

Sheed, Francis J. *Communism and Man*. New York: Sheed & Ward, Inc., 1938.

Strausz-Hupé, Robert, *et al. Protracted Conflict*. New York: Harper & Brothers, 1959.

Teaching about Communism: A Resource Book for Teachers. Edited by Dean E. Triggs, Supt. Ventura County (Calif.) schools, 1962.

Ward, Dudley. *The Social Creed of The Methodist Church*. Nashville: Abingdon Press, 1961.

19

The Cold War Is a Real War

THE BLOODY FIGHTING ON THE STREETS OF LENINGRAD DURING OC-
tober, 1917, launched the Communist government of Russia,
and it also initiated an entirely new type of war which is, in
spite of its strange tactics and unprecedented weaponry, neverthe-
less a war.

It was one of Marx's most profound convictions that his scientific
principles of history would sometime lay final seige to the capitalist
society and destroy it. This he believed to be the inevitable result
of the operation of certain historic forces. Whether or not the
triumph was to come as a result of a conventional war or as the
consequence of an induced economic collapse of capitalism was
immaterial so far as his thinking was concerned. In either case
the result would be the same. It was not that he shrank from
violence, for he did not. It was only that he believed that violence
would in any case be a by-product of the operation of economic
law and historic principles.

It is quite probable that Marx would be one of the first to recognize the economic struggles and the political conflicts of our time
as an actual war were he to be a witness to the facts and circumstances with which we are confronted. Certainly the Communists
themselves recognize the time as being what it is—wartime. Their
every political gesture and economic move is calculated in terms
of the corrosive and destructive effect it may have upon the
capitalist system and the democratic philosophy of life.

There is a very great danger that we shall be deceived by Communist double-talk into thinking that we are dealing with an
antagonist who would be content with political and military peace,
that he is talking the same language we are talking because he
uses so many of the same words, and that he is really willing to
co-exist with us. It is, however, of the utmost urgency that we
shall understand that "peace" has one meaning to the Communist

191

spokesmen and an entirely different meaning to the democracies. Whenever the word appears in a Communist document or official statement it means—to the Communist at least—the kind of peace the canary has made with the cat. There is but one kind of peace that will ever satisfy the Communists. That is the peace of the tyrant who has crushed all his opposition under his iron heel.

Just as peace has one meaning to the Communists and another to the democracies, so the word "people" has a double meaning. To an American, for example, it means all the persons, individuals, or citizens in a country. To a Communist it means only those individuals who have been fortunate enough to establish themselves as members of the Party. The Kulaks of Russia and the landlords of China were never considered to be people. In the event of a Communist take-over in the United States the only ones who could hope to rate as "people" would be the card-carrying members of the Party. No others would have either hopes or rights.

Seven indisputable facts of our generation characterize our time as being wartime. The Marxist doctrine of the revolution and the Leninist doctrine of the Party leave no doubt in the mind of anyone who is familiar with the facts.

1. A war is on between two ideologies in which every human being has a stake.

If Communism should win it would mean enforced submission to Communist authority on the part of every living person. It would mean a complete revamping of life and all social institutions. It would mean the enslavement of every individual to the state. There can be no compromise. This world will go all Communist or all democratic. As long as there is even one small island of resistance neither interpretation of life is secure. There are no noncombatants, no neutral zones, no gray tones. Every person in all the earth is in the front lines.

2. Throughout the world a process of indoctrination is going on.

Dedicated Communists everywhere are seizing every opportunity to present their case. They are prepared to exploit any situation in favor of Communism. College campuses, labor union meetings, industrial groups, religious bodies, social organizations—everything is their prey, to be infiltrated wherever possible. When a sufficient number of people have been seduced they are organized into "discussion groups" where only one opinion is allowed to be expressed. No free inquiry is permitted. The art of the soft sell has been developed to the superlative degree, with the result that dupes are confused. This program is under the immediate direction of somewhat more than eighty officially recognized Communist parties organized along national lines. In some nations the war is going on under cover, and in others it is above ground. In every nation in the world the indoctrination is going on, with millions being recruited.

3. *This is an all-out war in which other than military weapons are being used.*

Wherever there are class rivalries, racial animosities, flagrant abuses, social discontent, or economic trouble spots the Communists can be depended upon to fan the flames. They gather about any social sore like blow flies, corrupting and infecting the situation and then exploiting it to their own advantage. Every device that can be made to contribute to disorder is exploited to the limit. Experienced mobsters compare notes, explain techniques, and train operators to defy law-enforcement officers and in disturbance of the peace. If a case in the courts can be exploited in their advantage, if a criminal case can be inflated with emotionalism, if a housing project can be rendered suspect, or if a visiting foreign official can be harassed, the Communists can be relied upon to make hay for the revolution. Attorney-general Robert Kennedy can offer convincing testimony at this point. Wherever it is possible to create unrest, develop violence, provoke the police, interfere with public order, or inflame the people against the authorities, Communist agents can be depended upon to be somewhere in the immediate background.

4. *Communism has developed an entirely new weaponry.*

By depriving the people of Russia and China of actual necessities, the Communists have been able to offer loans to new governments "with no strings attached." The recipients soon discover, however, that in accepting the aid they have become vassals, and sooner or later they find they have become a part of the new colonialism. Russian promises have been used to buy Egyptian cotton which has been sold subsequently in Burma at a loss, thus disrupting an ancient market for the Egyptians and weakening the economic position of Burma. By trading Czechoslovakian armaments to Cuba for sugar the Russians have been able to get it far below the price it would otherwise cost. By commercial bribes and threats the commerce of Indonesia can be manipulated in favor of Russian or Chinese preferences. By creating tensions, crises, alarms, false hopes of peace, and by the thaws in the cold war—by demands and conciliations—the Communist states in the United Nations are able to retain the diplomatic initiative and keep the Free World off-balance. No nuclear firings are necessary to the advancement of Communist plans if the psychological war continues to win the victories. By rushing arms to troubled areas, by posing as the ally of new nations struggling to be born, by shoutings for justice, and by posing as the peacemaker, the Soviets have ingratiated themselves into the good graces of the ignorant and the inexperienced nations of the world which have just begun to dream of places in the sun. In the meantime, technicians badly needed at home are being exported, industrial planning is offered, and trained agitators whip up national frenzies. Thus one small nation after another drifts into the Communist orbit.

Communist colonialism is a product of deception, manipulation, mob violence, pretense, and political inexperience. It is a very real colonialism as Hungary and Tibet can testify. No army ever marches across a border intent on conquest. Instead, guerilla bands for which no one is willing to act as sponsor infiltrate, create disturbances, incite riots, destroy public confidence, and finally take over, and the Communists then proceed to "liberate" the invaded land by making it a satellite.

Meanwhile, thousands of students from all over the color world have been provided with scholarships in Russian—and now a beginning in Chinese—universities. Along with their solid training in science, mathematics, and psychology they are indoctrinated with Marxism-Leninism and returned to their homelands as agitators.

George F. Kennan, one of the best-informed authorities on the subject of modern Russia, tells of the utterly unscrupulous way in which Russians have rewritten history, omitting all non-Russian names from crucial events, ascribing victories to Russian arms which were actually won by non-Russian armies, and crediting Russian strategists with successful campaigns that were never fought, all for the purpose of making Russian forces appear invincible.

Copies of these falsified histories are being sold and distributed literally by the millions throughout three continents.[1]

5. *Communist industrial achievements are making a profound impression on the underdeveloped countries.*

The fact that the Russian people were destitute only forty years ago, and the further fact that they are now enjoying the highest standard of living they have ever known, seems to promise that if Asia and Africa will adopt Communism they too will be able to lift themselves out of the economic mire.

Prodigious efforts are being made to export automobiles, locomotives, cranes, earth-moving machinery, hoisting devices, and other tools from China to other Asiatic and African nations as proof that Communism has freed 1,000,000,000 people from economic bondage to the "imperialistic" powers. One crude Chinese car on the streets of Bangkok, Rangoon, Mandalay, Singapore, or Djakarta creates a hundred times as much interest as a street full of cars from the United States, Germany, or Great Britain. Because the Chinese were destitute a decade ago any success they may achieve under Communism assumes an importance out of all proportion to the statistics.

6. *An entirely new type of colonialism has arrived, and the underdeveloped countries seem to be unaware of the fact that it is colonialism.*

It was a fiction invented by Russia that Poland, Hungary, Czechoslovakia, Roumania, and Albania have come to be accepted by the United Nations as independent states. In the meantime North Korea, North Vietnam, and an uncertain number of new African states have fallen into line. Their colonial status is as onerous and as burdensome as anything ever devised by the great European colonial powers. The announcement of the economic ties into which Cuba has entered with Russia and China is a grim announcement that Communist colonialism has actually arrived at our front door.

7. *The Communist man is a new creature, made in the Soviet image.*

Milovan Djilas, one-time vice-president of Yugoslavia under the Tito regime, has provided the English-speaking world with the

---

[1] See Kennan, *Russia and the West Under Lenin and Stalin* (Boston: Little, Brown & Company, 1961), Preface.

195

most realistic and shocking portrait of the Communist man thus far available. The card-carrying Communists around the world have become a new elite. Molded by the brainwashing process into the form of a new creature with a mind stamped by Marxist-Leninist dies and geared to a machine that admits of no deviation, the Communist man inside the Communist world is as much a member of a new nobility as any of the lords, counts, and barons of the old order ever were. He is a member of a new aristocracy and a slave of the same dictator who is in control of the Communist party of the world.

This, then, is the world and these are the men with whom the Christian Church must match wits, integrity, dedication, vision, and character. It is with the missionary passion of such people that the Christian Church must match devotion and stewardship.

In many lands and in many areas the white man's religion has come to be looked upon as being a part of the white man's politics, economics, and exploitation. The rising tide of nationalism, which is an accompaniment of the rising tide of Communism, is witnessing an upsurge of tribal, racial, and national gods. The position of the Christian Church—both Catholic and Protestant—has become extremely difficult and delicate. Drawing the line between the political and the religious calls for an integrity, an independence, and a Christian singleness of purpose of the highest order.

"Behold, all things are become new."

Suggestions for Further Reading

First of all, see the bibliography for Chapter 18. There is considerable overlapping of source material.

Dubois, Jules. *Freedom Is My Beat*. Indianapolis, Ind.: The Bobbs-Merrill Company, 1959.

Gunther, John. *Inside Russia Today*. New York: Harper & Brothers, 1958.

Harriman, William Averell. *Peace With Russia*. New York: Simon and Schuster, Inc., 1959.

Kissinger, Henry A. *The Necessity for Choice*. New York: Harper & Brothers, 1961.

Salisbury, Harrison E. *To Moscow and Beyond, a Reporter's Narrative*. New York: Harper & Brothers, 1960.

Salvadori, Massino. *The Economics of Freedom*. Garden City, N. Y.: Doubleday & Company, 1959.

Stevenson, Adlai. *Friends and Enemies*. New York: Harper & Brothers, 1959.

Sulzberger, C. L. *What's Wrong with U. S. Foreign Policy?* New York: Harcourt, Brace & World, Inc., 1959.

20

Who Is the Captain of Our Souls?

HAVING MADE A BRIEF EXCURSION INTO THE RATHER BAFFLING SUB-
ject of brainwashing, let us inquire concerning the manipulation
of the American mind.

The tempo of the times, the tensions with which we are beset,
the anxieties that crowd in upon us; the natural fears induced by
the prospect of nuclear warfare; the moral, social, and economic
problems that have developed since the dropping of the bomb;
the cold war; the almost daily precipitation of crises—all these have
an effect upon the mind of the nation not unlike the effect produced on the mind of the individual who is threatened with shell
shock. The growing use of sleeping pills, tranquilizers, narcotics,
and sedatives indicates that the American people are becoming
highly vulnerable to mind manipulation.

A lengthening list of techniques is ready at hand for the agitator,
the dictator, and the propagandist who set out to promote hysteria
or their own particular brand of social and political reform. The
John Birch Society, organized on fascist principles, is a natural
reaction to the pressures under which plain citizens live and against
which all citizens must stand constant guard. Never since the
signers of the Declaration of Independence affixed their names to
that immortal document has it been so necessary for the individual
citizen to stand guard over its own soul and mind. The temptation
to defend the American way with Communist weaponry is forever
with us.

A wave of near hysteria is sweeping across the nation under the
intriguing name of "anti-Communism." Under the guise of telling
the truth about Communism "schools" have been organized with
thousands in attendance; forums have been addressed by politicians,
journalists, world travelers, clergymen, public officials, and professional lecturers; literature has been distributed in carload lots; emo-

tions have been roused and passions have been fanned.

That a large measure of good has been accomplished goes without saying. A certain amount of good solid instruction has been given. Much reliable information has been disseminated. A sense of alarm has been spread through the nation, and a certain shallow liberalism has been rebuked.

At the same time serious damage has been inflicted upon the American public. Inspired by suspicion, otherwise good men have gone about raising suspicions concerning the loyalty of other good men. Churches have been divided; the schools have been rendered supersensitive; honest and qualified labor leaders have been made victims of witch hunters; corrupt public officials have been provided with bombproof political shelters; university presidents of unquestioned loyalty have been harassed; the spirit of disunity has been encouraged at the very moment that every effort should be made to promote the unity of righteous, honorable, and decent forces in the defense of the American nation and the American way.

There is something very ominous about the way the voice of criticism has been silenced among us. Conscientious and faithful schoolteachers have been terrified; clergymen daring to speak out against the evils they have seen in modern society have been subjected to vicious attacks by the zealous and ill informed; the spirit of free inquiry in our colleges and universities has been put under fire; and a frank, free, and courageous fronting of evils in some communities has become almost impossible.

All this is a complete contradiction of the genuine American way that came up out of the New England town meetings, the chautauquas, the village lyceums, and the national political campaigns where no punches were pulled. The democratic way of life can never survive the stifling of opinion, the silencing of honest voices, the elimination of protest, and the punishment of the nonconformist for his nonconformity.

The best anti-Communism consists of a loud shouting of the things we believe, the things we are for, and the doctrines that have made us great as a nation. What we are for is vastly more important that what we are against.

One of the things for which the democratic way stands is the right and the duty of self-criticism. It is far better, for example, for the American people to be warned of their sins and their dangers by democratic friends, than that they should be set upon by enemies who have discovered their weaknesses. It was Thomas Jefferson who thrust into the American concept of democracy the doctrine that the people can be trusted to arrive at moral and intelligent judgments if they can have the facts. His brand of democracy made room for the self-criticism that has saved the nation on occasions innumerable.

About the turn of the century an Austrian neurologist named Poetzel began experimenting with an instrument to which he had given the rather formidable name "tachistoscope." It consisted of a viewing box and a projector equipped with a high speed shutter which made it possible for him to throw images on a screen faster than the human eye and the conscious mind could register them. The moving picture shown in today's theater consists of sixteen images projected within the space of one second, giving the impression of a continuous image. Poetzel's projector speeded up the projection to the point that each image was just one sixty-fourth of a second instead of the conventional one sixteenth in duration.

It was Poetzel's belief that the subconscious mind registers impressions that escape the conscious mind, and that these subconscious impressions have much to do with human behavior. It was with the hope that his machine would enable him to bypass the conscious and make a direct appeal to the subconscious that he began his studies. By a series of carefully controlled experiments inside his laboratory he convinced himself that his theory was correct and soon thereafter undertook a practical application of it.

A tachistoscope was eventually set up in a British moving-picture theater in conjunction with the standard projector and was synchronized in such a way that at regular intervals of every few seconds a projection lasting just one sixty-fourth of a second was imposed on the picture that was being shown. Because of the short duration of the projection the viewer was quite unaware of the fact that he had "seen" it. At intermission, however, there was abundant proof that it had been seen and was effective. The projection had consisted of four short words, "Go buy ice cream." The audience responded by doubling the business at the ice-cream vendor's in the lobby.

A few years ago the experiment was performed again in a New Jersey theater, with the words "Go buy popcorn" superimposed repeatedly on the feature film. No viewer was aware of the fact that he had "seen" anything except the picture that had been advertised, but at the intermission the crowds swarmed out into the lobby and almost doubled the normal popcorn business.

Late in 1959 an advertisement began appearing in certain trade journals on the West Coast announcing the availability of tachistoscope advertising facilities. For a specified rate an enterprising businessman could project his message to the theater crowd, superimposing it on the feature film without anyone's being aware of the fact that he was being subjected to the appeal. An alert legislator, quick to sense the danger, introduced a bill which was enacted into law by the California legislature making it a criminal offense to use the device outside a scientific laboratory. Similar legislation is being proposed in other state legislatures. So far as is known the device is not being used anywhere but it is available, legal in most states, and effective.

Here is a technique tailor-made for the agitator, the dictator, or the propagandist. In the hands of the Ku Klux Klan, the John Birch Society, a politician, or an agitator it could be made extremely effective in swaying public opinion. Wherever there is a captive audience the tachistoscope stands ready to perform its function.

The effectiveness of the tachistoscope is heightened by a series of circumstances. The viewer is unconscious of the fact that his thinking is being influenced; he is unaware of the fact that his mind is being manipulated by an outside force. Because the subconscious mind never argues but always proceeds with absolute logic on the basis of any suggestion furnished it, the appeal to the subconscious arouses no antagonism. Unaware of the attack on his thinking, the viewer offers no defense, and because the exhortation is repeated over and over in the course of the showing of a film it achieves a type of authority that is almost absolute.

It calls for no extraordinary gift of imagination to conjure up the possibilities of this technique in the hands of a demagogue. Applied to the television shows it could be an attack on the sanity of a nation. When one considers the capability of such a machine in undermining morals, changing political opinions, shattering public confidence, promoting causes, creating hysteria, breeding hatred and disunity, it is nothing less than terrifying.

Aldous Huxley tells the story of the Tulare County (California) Road Camp prisoners who volunteered to act as guinea pigs in one of the most unusual experiments ever conducted by an American governmental unit.[1] At the solicitation of the authorities they agreed to allow their pillows to be equipped with miniature loudspeakers connected with a transmitter in the warden's office. From time to time during the night they "heard" inspirational whispers consisting of brief homilies on the subject of good behavior. An improvement in the conduct of the members of the group was observable almost immediately. The experiment was above criticism; no man participated except by his own consent; and the object was altogether praiseworthy. The technique holds sinister possibilities, however. A revolutionary organization, a student body, a concentration camp, or a group of isolated workers could be manipulated with great effectiveness.

It has been all but proved that it is possible to educate a person during sleep. Publications of unquestioned probity treat the matter with great respect. Already phonograph records are available to those who are interested in increasing their efficiency, charm, or personal effectiveness. The field has not yet been evaluated scientifically, but the evidence thus far is impressive.

What the actualities may be in this field in 1985 no one can guess, but that it will be possible to brainwash individuals in a massive program cannot be successfully denied.

The one sure defense thus far authenticated is a deep-seated religious conviction. This, incidentally, is one of the reasons the Chinese—and Russians—have made determined efforts to root out all religious activities, institutions, and memories. Scientific studies of hypnotism are in almost universal agreement in saying that while under the hypnotic spell no one can be directed to act in contradiction to a moral conviction strongly held while in the normal state of mind. A young man, for example, who has strict and stern principles on the subject of honesty cannot be persuaded to commit a theft which he *knows* to be a theft, while in a hypnotic spell. Nor can a young woman thoroughly committed to chastity

[1] *Brave New World Revisited*, pp. 105 ff.

be persuaded to indulge in unchaste activities while hypnotized. Moral convictions that are rooted in religious beliefs constitute a solid rock wall of defense.

The same built-in security applies in the case of the tachistoscope, the midnight whisper, and the "inspirational record." Once more the importance—the vital necessity—of systematic religious and moral training becomes evident.

Whatever the future may be for sleep therapy, the tachistoscope, or the midnight exhortation, we are already under the spell of depth psychology and motivational analysis. Tens of millions of individuals are being influenced and persuaded in their buying, reading, thinking, personal habits, and even moral decisions. A relatively small group of advertising experts, commonly referred to as "Madison Avenue," is exercising an influence over the American mind of inestimable importance and of which the average citizen is quite unaware.

The close of World War II found the American people equipped with an industrial machine capable of delivering prodigious quantities of consumer goods. No cities lay in ruins; no public works had to be restored; no great bridges had to be rebuilt; no river courses had to be cleared of debris left over from bombardments. The entire productivity of the greatest industrial machine of all time had to be consumed by the American public, minus whatever could be exported to a poverty-stricken world engaged in the business of rebuilding. This made it necessary to persuade the public to buy in unprecedented quantities. This, in turn, called for a vast expansion of credit. Installment buying opened the floodgates, and the advertising fraternity moved into the vacuum.

Just as science had gone to the assistance of the war machine, so the psychologists and psychoanalysts entered into an alliance with and became the advisors of salesmen. A multimillion dollar industry has grown up on the basis of designs of persuasion.[2] The new science is impressing new patterns of life upon all America— from the nightclubs of New York to remote desert settlements. Modern salesmanship designed by motivational analysis is working

[2] For an extended discussion of this theme see Vance Packard, *The Hidden Persuaders* (New York: David McKay Company, 1957). The book has been attacked from a variety of quarters, but none of the facts presented have been seriously disputed.

a transformation in our day-to-day experience. Mothers by the hundreds of thousands have left their homes to take employment in factories and offices, and the children come home from school to empty and silent houses. Packaged food stuffs have taken the place of "pies like mother used to make," and baby-sitting has become a profession.

"Something new . . . appears to be entering the pattern of . . . life with the growing power of our persuaders." [8] Our day-to-day behavior is being analyzed for the purpose of finding handles by which our minds can be manipulated in favor of the goods the advertisers have been employed to market, of the ideas to which they have leased their scientific skills, of the manners for which their clients are prepared to furnish the accoutrements, and of the entertainment they are paid to purvey.

Only a few years ago one of the leading department stores of the nation inaugurated the first appeal to teen-agers in an attempt to persuade them to open charge accounts, described as "the modern method of merchandising." The youngsters who went in debt were described as being "smart," "sophisticated," or those who "live by modern concepts." Within less than a year scores of merchants across the nation were exploiting the plan. Then, late in 1959 the idea was expanded to include young people in the junior-high schools, the result being that the storekeepers were recruiting thousands of new customers. In the meantime, the Sunday-school and public schoolteachers who were exhorting the youngsters to "live within their income" were being shrugged off as being "out of date." Debt was glorified, and it became a matter of pride on some school grounds when the youngster could boast of his charge accounts at six stores. Meanwhile the total of the private debts of the nation soared to stratospheric levels. Even the philosophy of thrift was used to persuade indebtedness, as some advertised "you save money by going in debt."

"Motivational analysis" is a technical term used to describe the study of those motives which cause people to buy. It is designed to reach the subconscious and to persuade people to buy without really knowing why they bought. It is said that the buyer buys emotionally, not reasonably, and that therefore the emotions are to be exploited.

[8] *Ibid.,* p. 6.

In support of the theory that reason does not prevail in purchasing, the fact is cited that women do not buy soap for its cleansing qualities, but because they have been persuaded that a particular brand increases their "charm." Liquor and cigarettes are portrayed as symbols of virility and masculinity. By this line of reasoning the public is appealed to on the basis of egotism, self-consciousness, self-righteousness, triviality, and pretense.

Following up this line of reasoning the manufacturer is advised to make his market, not to find it. The public is maneuvered into buying because of inner urges it does not understand but cannot resist. As one newspaper columnist advised parents, "Put an aerial up on your house, even if you cannot afford a TV set. It will save your children from an inferiority complex."

In some cases the advertiser undertakes to implant a deep fear in the mind of the prospective purchaser. We are warned against appearing at a disadvantage, against seeming to be living in the "horse and buggy days," of being "conservative," or of lacking in the spirit of adventure. Wants are portrayed as necessities; thrift is dismissed with condescension; sex is glamorized; and passion is commended. Meanwhile tensions develop, fears harass, and anxiety takes a dreadful toll of the nation's vitality. The hospitals report that despondency is the most common mental disease, and the psychiatrists' waiting rooms are crowded with well-dressed patients. A state of near collapse threatens millions, and the soul of the nation is despoiled. To stand guard under such circumstances is one of the most demanding duties of the times, and that is the first responsibility of the Church and the clergy.

According to the *Wall Street Journal* no less than $13,000,000,000 was spent in 1960 on cellophane, tinfoil, ribbons, packaging, and other devices which aim to induce the buyer to buy. No less than 3,000 firms are engaged in manufacturing packaging accessories. Meanwhile downright dishonesty struts unashamed in the supermarkets in the form of elaborate packages only a little more than half filled with actual merchandise.

Any product that promises relief from anxiety finds a ready market, partly because it raises the fears it professes to allay. The specter of fear is raised everywhere in the advertising columns. We are warned against "tired blood," "that sense of weariness," "that first sign of decay," "the sense of fatigue," the "first symptoms," "that aching back," et cetera. The strategy is simple. Make the buyer uneasy, prey upon his fears, and sell him the pills. Meanwhile the shadowy figure of Ivan Pavlov looks on in astonishment.

As long ago as 1946 Professor Clyde Miller of Columbia University, in *The Process of Persuasion*, called the American manufacturers' attention to the importance of the children's market. "If you expect to be in business for any length of time," he said, "think of what it can mean to your firm in profits if you can condition a million to ten million children who will grow up into adults trained to buy your products as soldiers are trained to advance when they hear the trigger words 'forward march!' " [4] An advertiser in *Printer's Ink*, a trade magazine, suggested:

Eager minds can be molded to want your products! In the grade schools throughout America are nearly 23,000,000 young girls and boys. These children eat food, wear out clothes, and use soap. They are consumers today and will be the buyers of tomorrow. Here is a vast market for your products. Sell these children on your brand name and they will insist that their parents buy no other.

With much of this no moral fault can be found, but the facts suggest the power of the modern advertiser to manipulate the mind of the nation.

The television screen, with its almost irresistible appeal to children, offers a mass medium made to order for those who have merchandising reasons for conditioning the minds of children. The liquor and tobacco industries have exploited this opportunity adroitly, with the result that millions of toddlers are more conversant with beer commercials than they are with the story of the birth of Jesus. Alcohol is associated with conviviality, success, distinction, and glamor. Meanwhile the costs of alcoholism are spiraling, and the problem of alcohol is appearing at lower and lower age limits. There have been cases of children twelve years of age being adjudged chronic alcoholics.

By playing on one set of fears the advertiser is able to produce another set of anxieties—the fear of being unacceptable, unscientific, retarded, conditioned, inhibited, mentally immature, emo-

[4] New York: Crown Publishing Company, p. 217. This book is now out of print but obtainable at many public and at most college libraries.

tionally unstable, unsophisticated, unprogressive, or anti-social. The publisher of a particularly vicious piece of pornographic literature advertised to his youthful readers that his publication would help them rid themselves of their inhibitions, which was a thin disguise for an abandonment of all moral restraints. By appealing to subliminal desires and hidden motives we are manipulated into voting, acting, believing, spending, and affiliating according to the standards of the propagandists. Someone has calculated that the average American is solicited to buy no less than 1,500 times during the course of the average day, including Sundays, and urged to save less than 100 times. It is not surprising, therefore, that the nation's total private indebtedness exceeded $770,000,000,000 on January 1, 1959.

An all out war is being waged on the individual. On every hand the demand is made that we conform to mass judgments. We are warned that we must surrender to the crowd, repudiate our individualism, abandon our independent opinions, and let the majority decide for us. Once this has been accomplished, the way is wide open for the demagogue and the dictator. Many of these same results have been achieved by Communism and we abhor that philosophy and all its works. When the same works come disguised as "modern concepts of living," however, we accept them with alacrity.

Never before, as now, has it been necessary for the Christian Church to insist upon the sanctity of the individual, the dignity of personal convictions, the importance of the private conscience, the supremacy of the spiritual, and the responsibility of the plain citizen as he decides for himself.

A major theme for the modern Christian pulpit might well be "I am the captain of my soul!"

Suggestions for Further Reading

Black, Hillel. *Buy Now Pay Later.* New York: William Morrow & Company, 1961.

Chase, Stuart. *Some Things Worth Knowing.* New York: Harper & Brothers, 1958.

Ginzberg, Eli. *Human Resources: The Wealth of a Nation.* New York: Simon and Schuster, Inc., 1958.

Grove, Gene. *Inside the John Birch Society.* New York: Gold Medal Books, 1961.

Hoffer, Eric. *The True Believer.* New York: New American Library of World Literature, 1958.

Hough, Lynn Harold. *The Dignity of Man.* Nashville: Abingdon Press, 1950.

Hunter, Allan. *Christians in the Arena.* Nyack, N. Y.: Fellowship Publications, 1958.

Huxley, Aldous. *Brave New World Revisited.* New York: Harper & Brothers, 1958.

Kinnear, Willis H. *The Creative Power of Mind.* Englewood Cliffs, N. J.: Prentice-Hall, Inc., 1957.

La Piere, Richard. *The Freudian Ethic, an Analysis of the Subversion of American Character.* New York: Duell, Sloan, & Pearce, Inc., 1959.

Marney, Carlyle. *Structures of Prejudice.* Nashville: Abingdon Press, 1961.

Medina, Harold R. *The Anatomy of Freedom.* New York: Holt, Rinehart & Winston, Inc., 1959.

Meyer, Karl E. *The New America.* New York: Basic Books, Inc., 1961.

Miller, Samuel H. *The Life of the Soul.* New York: Harper & Brothers, 1951.

Niebuhr, Reinhold. *The Structure of Nations and Empires.* New York: Charles Scribner's Sons, 1959.

Packard, Vance. *The Hidden Persuaders.* New York: David McKay Company, 1957.

————.*The Status Seekers.* New York: David McKay Company, 1959.

Salvadori, Massimo. *The Economics of Freedom.* Garden City, N. Y.: Doubleday & Company, 1959.

Trueblood, Elton. *Declaration of Freedom.* New York: Harper & Brothers, 1955.

Turner, Ernest S. *The Shocking History of Advertising.* New York: E. P. Dutton & Company 1953.

Weaver, Henry Grady. *The Mainspring of Human Progress.* Irving-on-Hudson, N. Y.: The Foundation for Economic Education, Inc., 1958.

21

No Nation Can Be Ignorant and Free

IN THE COURSE OF A TRIP ACROSS THE PACIFIC I FELL INTO CONVERsation with a young Japanese athlete who was scanning the sea from the vantage point of the prow of the ship. He was returning to Japan as a member of an athletic team that had just completed a highly successful tour of American colleges and universities.

"You have had a splendid chance to observe our American young people," I said. "Would you be willing to tell me what your impressions are?"

After a bit of prodding he replied, "As hosts they are delightful. As friends they are fascinating. As competitors they are fair. But one thing puzzles me. Do they not know that they arc in competition with the youth of the world, and is no one telling them that the things they are learning at taverns, nightclubs, and beach carnivals will be worth nothing to them when the going gets really tough?"

That reply deserves the most careful attention the nation can give. There is no more serious question before the American public than the one to which the young athlete referred. Modern science is the great leveler, and the issue of survival is at stake. Today's youth face the sternest competition of all time.

The fact that the United States detonated the first hydrogen bomb had the effect of confirming us in our conceits. It was so easy to believe we were the intellectual elite of the world. In our exultation we did not stop to discover that a large part of the skills that had produced the bomb had been imported in the persons of Fermi, Szilard, Teller, and Oppenheimer. These men had spent their time in laboratories instead of nightclubs, with the result that they were almost entirely unknown.

The launching of the Russian sputnik on October 4, 1957, had the effect of jolting us out of our complacency. For two decades we had read with amusement the bizarre claims of the Russians to priority in the matter of certain inventions. It was so easy to believe that all Russians were illiterate. We had read the works of Tolstoy, Pushkin, Dostoyevsky, Chekov, and Turgenev, but practically no one outside the most select scientific circles knew even the names of Lobachevsky, one of the creators of non-Euclidean geometry, Mendeleev, the formulator of the periodic table of elements; or Metchnikov, discoverer of phagocytes.

The launching of the sputniks created a tremendous shock. "How did the Russians get ahead of us?" the people asked. "What's wrong with our scientists?" "What's the matter with our schools?" As if in answer to such frightened demands, reporters began returning from Russia with excited reports of armies of engineers graduating from Russian universities, of millions of youthful scholars enrolled in Russian middle schools, of advanced courses of study, and of widespread learning. About the same time a series of horrible examples of American schools was publicized, which left the impression that our public-school education was a sorry mess.

In view of the fact there are deficiencies in the American educational system, we will be well advised if we take a careful look at the whole situation. The words of Thomas Jefferson are very modern: "If a nation expects to be ignorant and free, in a state of civilization, it expects what never was and never will be."

The Soviet government has made a persistent effort to convince the world that the level of Russian education under the czars was deplorably low, and there is an element of truth in the charge. The Soviet regime inherited a tradition of true scholarship from the czarist days, however, and about the turn of the century there was a ferment which resulted in the beginning of reforms. Except for the outbreak of World War I, it is now estimated that one half of the Russian children of school age would have had some kind of formal education.

In 1913 Lenin wrote, "There was no other country left in Europe where the masses were deprived of education, light, and knowledge, to the same extent as in Russia." [1] It was commonly believed at all the royal courts of the continent that an educated class was a revolutionary class, for every revolutionary movement between 1800 and 1900 originated in some university. Marx's father had removed

[1] *Education in the U.S.S.R*, (U.S. Dept. of Health, Education, and Welfare, Bulletin No. 14, 1957), p. 6.

him from the University of Bonn to the University of Berlin, in the hope that he would get into a more conservative atmosphere.

The Bolshevik Revolution of 1917 washed the slate clean and cleared the way for an overhauling of the school system. One of the first announcements the Communist party made was its intention to provide an educational opportunity for all children. The philosophy of freedom was in the air, and following the leadership of Pestalozzi in Switzerland and John Dewey in the United States, a "democratic order" was established in the schoolroom. The rooms were run by student committees as the factories were run by workers. Communist youth leaders were vested with the authority to countermand any orders handed down by the teachers; examinations were abolished; discipline was discarded; grades were done away with on the theory that they were "reactionary." Homework was prohibited.

In 1920, however, it was charged that the new order was diluting the quality of work done. In 1924 Lenin died, and immediately the tide of criticism mounted until in 1931 the Central Committee took the matter in hand. Under Stalin's leadership the whole of Russian life was upgraded. Rank was again established in the army, the official attitude toward free love was revised, and some of the leading educators were liquidated. The permissive schools had sealed their own doom because the graduates were unable to deal with the fundamentals of science and letters.

On December 9, 1931, the Commissar of Public Education ordered the establishment of strict discipline at all levels. Teachers were given full powers to maintain order; written examinations were restored; the use of authorized textbooks was re-established; and courses in mathematics, history, and geography were raised to places of honor.

In May, 1956, Dorothy Thompson wrote:

Secondary education is growing with immense strides. Every youth who completes it will have extended courses in basic higher mathematics —four years each of algebra and geometry—and five of a modern language. . . . There is, so far as I know, not one high school in America, where an ambitious student could get such preparation in science and mathematics.

210

The total result is that as of 1961 it can be said that some form of education is available to practically all Russian children. Official forecasts declare that the full ten-year school—which corresponds roughly to our American high school—will be available to all qualified students who seek to enroll by 1965.

Any serious study of Russian education must begin with the fact that it is deliberately Marxist. This is to say that every citizen, of whatever age, is the property of the state, to be deployed in the interest of the state exactly as any other property is deployed. The will of the state takes preference over all personal desires. The youth of Russia are not educated that they may become more splendid persons, but that they may become more useful to the government. It becomes the duty of the schools to provide whatever trained personnel may be required. Only in the narrowest sense does the individual have any choice in the matter. All Russian students live under a perpetual draft, obligated to assume any task assigned them. Because Communist doctrine makes no difference between the sexes, this principle applies to young women as well as young men. If, for example, the Central Committee should decide that 150,000 engineers are needed by 1975 the school authorities would be warned that they must have 150,000 candidates for engineering courses ready to begin their studies in 1971—and it would be done.

In 1958 an accredited group of professors from American engineering schools found that one third of the students enrolled in corresponding Russian schools were young women. In Moscow University they found 51 per cent of the undergraduates in mathematics and mechanics to be young women, and in the technical laboratories young women were working at all academic levels.

Officially, the Russian philosophy of education sounds very impressive, but it must always be interpreted in terms of the Russian state and its doctrine of the Communist man. Outside the state educational system there are no schools. A woman's study club dedicated to the study of Shakespeare could not exist without government sponsorship. There are no independent universities or research laboratories.

Prior to 1917 kindergartens were practically unknown in Russia, there being no more than 273 institutions in all the land for children under school age. Soviet leadership was quick to see the opportunity such institutions could put into the hands of the Party, and between 1919 and 1940 more than 24,000 such schools for infants were established, in which 1,171,507 children were enrolled, each one being conditioned for "collective activity."

The indoctrination begun in the kindergarten is continued throughout the entire period of education. Marxist doctrine is made a basic subject, and the material is deftly adapted to the varying age groups. Any youth's chance to go on to the University depends in large part upon the standing he establishes as a Marxist.

Critics of the American public schools have made much out of the fact that graduates of the Russian ten-year schools have been well grounded in mathematics, geography, science, and modern languages. That calls for explanation. A close watch is kept over all pupils from the first time they are enrolled until they have arrived at an age for rugged academic schedule. Those who fail to show the proper aptitudes, are drained off into labor pools, reserve schools, polytechnic institutes, or other organizations that combine vocational skills with mental training. The top 35 per cent are sent on to college, and neither they nor the "discards" have any choice in the matter.

Perhaps it should be said that all European schools follow something of the same procedure, on the theory that no more than about 25 per cent of youth are intellectually capable of doing serious intellectual work. The American system, on the other hand, proceeds upon the principle that every child is entitled to the same opportunity. In most of the American states all young people are expected to finish high school, and attendance is made compulsory up to the sixteenth year. It is not possible, therefore, to draw strict comparisons between the Russian ten-year school and the American high school.

The same strictness that prevails in the armed forces prevails in the Russian schools. In an effort to achieve the exacting goals an intense spirit of competition is everywhere encouraged. Grades earned are publicly posted; pictures of successful students are given wide publicity; gifted students are pressured to achieve exceptional results. The speeding up process, so severely criticized in American industry, is standard practice in the Russian schoolroom.

Whereas in American universities there are fully accredited schools of business administration, which train a wide variety of specialists, there is no such need under Communism. Young men who might become sales managers, executives, or advertising experts are shunted off into some type of engineering. Colleges have no graduates in public relations, management, or the promotional arts—nor are there any considerable number of lawyers. If the Commissar of Public Health decides that a certain number of physicians, surgeons, public health nurses, pharmacists, and technicians are to be needed only a comparable number are permitted to enter for such training.

In this connection it should be noted that Russia has downgraded medical research in favor of heavy industry. The diseases of men are getting less attention than the behavior of metals and molecules. The magazines reporting medical research done in any country go into the files of the Russian medical schools, which means that the Soviets are letting the rest of the world pay the costs of research and they are reaping the benefits.

From all the foregoing it must be evident that it is very difficult —and dangerous—to compare Russian with American education. It is a little like trying to compare tangerines and gasolines. It is necessary, however, that we evaluate the American philosophy of education in the light of the demands the post-sputnik age will lay upon us.

In 1637, just seventeen years following the arrival of the Pilgrims in Massachusetts, the colony required that all towns provide a school for the children. In 1847 attendance was made compulsory.

It was out of industrialization—combined with the Jeffersonian idea of an educated populace—that the public schools emerged during the second half of the nineteenth century. With the rise of the labor movement—led in its beginning by men such as Samuel Gompers, who were social reformers as much as they were trade unionists—came clear-cut demands that all children, regardless of class or wealth, be given an equal educational opportunity. Just as the czars in the old Russian society (or the gentry in early American days) had been aware of the power of education if retained as a monopoly in their hands, so the leaders of the labor movement knew that the promise of true equality, with all the prestige and power needed by an "equal" block within the pattern of society, could not be achieved without an educated rank and file.[2]

[2] From The Big Red Schoolhouse by Fred M. Hechinger, pp. 65-66. Copyright © 1959 by Fred Hechinger. Reprinted by permission of Doubleday & Company, Inc.

Many years before the demand for a public school system became general the Protestant churches founded colleges. Harvard university, the first institution of higher learning in America, was founded by the Congregational Church. The Methodists founded Cokesbury College—which was destroyed by fire—before their total American membership had reached 4,000. The first educational institutions of college level in state after state originated with some church or religious society. At least half of the state universities of the nation had their inception in the home of some clergyman or in a church building. Most Protestant schools were originally founded for the purpose of educating the clergy, but within a short space of time the educational base was broadened and liberal education was offered.

The modern concept of "every boy and girl a high-school graduate" is of relatively recent development. In 1900, when the population of the United States was almost exactly 100,000,000, the young people enrolled in the nation's high schools numbered 700,-000. In 1960, with the population at 180,000,000, the high school enrollment has risen to 8,000,000. In the same period the expenditures have risen from $147,000,000 to $17,000,000,000; this is a per-pupil increase of from $40.25 to $268.58.

At least one explanation for the ascending rates of enrollment and expenditure has been the developing industrialization of the country. The operation of power machinery depends upon the availability of skilled workers. The tardiness of industrialization in the underdeveloped lands is accounted for, in large part, by the fact that skilled workers are not available. With the development of complicated mechanical equipment during and since World War II, it has become increasingly necessary for young men and women to get specialized training if they are to find employment. The percentage of unskilled labor in the American labor force has declined yearly since 1918.

For at least five hundred years the great universities of Europe were designed to train the clergy, and a large number of scientists such as Copernicus, Galileo, and Malthus were actually clergymen. Because the schools were very selective in admitting students, literally millions of commoners found the doors closed to them. In opening their doors to all who could show a high-school diploma, the American universities represented a great innovation.

Throughout Europe the secondary schools took their cue from the universities and undertook to prepare youth for classical pursuits. This had the effect of raising a bar against all but the gifted. The American system made all young people of the appropriate age eligible. When compulsory attendance became the law of the land the schools found themselves burdened with a large number of slow learners. At the same time it became necessary to expand the curriculum to accommodate those who had no interest in or capability for becoming students in the classical sense. This had the effect of developing the vocational school.

When the breakthrough occurred the schools discovered they were confronted with an entirely new problem. Whereas in former times they had dealt with classes composed of those who "went" to school, now they had to deal with those who were "sent." The result was inevitable: The slower retarded the gifted, and education slowed down to the lowest common denominator. Lessons within the capabilities of the slow learners encouraged the gifted ones to laziness.

At this critical juncture a new philosophy of education developed, which has become the source of much controversy. John Dewey of the influential Teachers College of Columbia University proposed that the "whole child" should be educated. It was his theory that the student should be trained to do everything that needed to be done if he were to be described as "well educated."

The focal point of the storm that arose was Dr. Dewey's principle of "learning by doing." In other words, the child was not to be instructed, but he was to discover the facts and meanings of life as a result of his own explorations. Competition between individuals was to be eliminated; no grades were to be given; each child was expected to compete with himself. Report cards went into the discord. The teacher, meanwhile, became a standby with reduced authority.

As a result of the Dewey philosophy there came an elective system and a proliferation of "courses." Young people began graduating without having accumulated the skills and disciplines that come with mathematics, science, foreign languages, geography, and philosophy. Then the universities found it necessary to establish courses in remedial English for freshmen who arrived incapable of reading and writing simple prose. As a corollary there developed the idea

215

that teachers must know *how* to teach, whether or not they knew *what* to teach. There was the case, for example, of the young man who was accredited—with a PhD—to teach teachers to teach science, who had himself never taken even one course in any natural science. There was that teacher of "photography" who gave his advanced class an examination in which it was necessary to use simple arithmetic in calculating exposures, and every member of the class failed because of complete ignorance of the simple principles of eighth-grade arithmetic!

American educators at the high-school level are ready to defend the American high school against the charge of triviality, and it is doubtless true that the "horrible examples" are not characteristic of the whole system. Lest we be guilty of unfair criticism, let us point out that the American public gets just about what it wants, and the easygoing standards of the public schools have been what we have been satisfied with.

Compulsory attendance means that some children are in school who ought not be there. There are those others who steel themselves against any learning. About 70 per cent are unable to keep pace with the gifted students. In the European and Russian systems these are weeded out. In a few cases local boards of education are able to provide courses for all levels of ability, but according to Dr. James B. Conant, unless the school has an annual area of graduation of at least a hundred, it is impractical—if not impossible—to finance the more abundant offerings, except at extravagant costs. Across the nation about 30 per cent of the twelfth-grade students attend high schools too small to do an adequate job. In Russia the slow learners have been drained off by the time they are fourteen. About 20 per cent finally get to the universities. Literally millions never even hope to go to college.

The American high school labors under a unique requirement which makes it difficult to establish any fair comparison with any other school on earth. It is expected to provide (1) a general education for all citizens, (2) training in productive skills which enable the individual to earn a comfortable living, and (3) an economic program for those who aspire to enroll in a university for academic pursuits. In addition, it is expected to challenge the gifted student, discover the genius, sidetrack the incapable, maintain democracy among the millions who were never born equal, and

216

provide the nation with the material out of which nuclear scientists, geophysicists, chemists, engineers, architects, biochemists, dramatists, artists, journalists, theologians, historians, mathematicians, biologists, and statesmen can be developed who will take first rank throughout the world. -

By general agreement the engineer is the man of the future. The Russian success in the matter of space traffic has aroused in the mind of the average taxpayer an enormous interest in the production of engineers capable of meeting the Russian competition. Obviously the beginning of the solution lies in the high school. The teacher of mathematics, English, history, or language must be more than a person who knows the subject himself. Unless he is afire in his field he will kindle no flames. Novices do not produce the spirit of academic integrity, and unless there is such integrity there will be no great scholarship or leadership.

Just as man cannot live by bread alone, so also the nation cannot live by engineers alone. There are vast areas of life which are as essential to survival as relativity, nuclear reactions, or atomic weights. The maintenance of a great little symphony orchestra may be as important in the life of the community as the acquisition of a new industry. Providing ideas and ideals is as necessary to survival as any training in any science. It is at this point that the responsibility of the Church appears.

The expenses that may be incurred in providing adequate schools may be expected to spiral. This means that the Church must take its stand alongside the schools—especially when bond issues are being voted upon—and preach its doctrine of stewardship with all its might. There was a leading layman in a certain community who fought the school bonds tooth and toenail for no better reason than that he had no children in school. If he had denied the deity of Jesus it would have resulted in a congregational war of the first order, but when he fought the school bonds no one thought it strange. He would have resented the charge that he was an immoral man. He was orthodox as a churchman, but he was a liability as a citizen, and his pastor owed him some stern counseling. He did not need "peace of mind." He needed Christian vision!

The Church must take a stand with its youth, insisting that they discharge their citizenship duties as students. The impression must be made upon youngsters associated with the Church that they

217

must be better in their classrooms, laboratories, and libraries. Pastors should be interested in and know something about the classroom work of every youth under his spiritual care. The pastor should charge them with their duties as young churchmen—they are the ones upon whom tomorrow's nation will depend. This means that the finest minds of the community must be directed to the teaching profession, as well as toward the ministry.

The essential base of education is spiritual. The teacher, like the preacher, lives by faith. He holds certain ideals dear and entertains a persistent faith in their ultimate vindication. In the face of the erosion which attacks his idealism on all sides, in the face of the secularism and materialism with which he is beset, the educator is in dire need of the assurances a stable faith provides. If any man ought to feel at home in the Sunday-morning worship service, the educator is that one. The preacher, in his study, who does not prepare to speak to the mind as well as to the heart of the schoolman is failing in his duty to the community. No church owes a greater obligation to any soul, in any community, than it owes to those who train the young.

Suggestions for Further Reading

Bereday, George Z. F. et al. *The Changing Soviet School.* Boston: Houghton Mifflin Company, 1960.

Bereday, George Z. F., and Pennar, Jaan, editors. *The Politics of Soviet Education.* New York: Frederick A. Praeger, Inc., 1960.

Conant, James B. *The American High School Today.* New York: McGraw-Hill Book Company, 1959.

De Witt, Nicholas. *Soviet Professional Manpower.* National Science Foundation, Washington, 1955.

Education in the U.S.S.R. U.S. Dept. of Health, Education, and Welfare, 1958.

Freeman, Roger A. *School Needs in the Decade Ahead.* Washington Institute for Social Science Research, 1958.

Hechinger, Fred M. *The Big Red Schoolhouse.* Garden City, N.Y.: Doubleday & Company 1959.

Holmes, Brian. *American Criticism of American Education.* Columbus, Ohio: Ohio State University Press, 1957.

Knapp, Robert H. and Greenbaum, Joseph J. *The Younger American Scholar.* Chicago: University of Chicago Press, 1953.

Knapp, Robert H, and Goodrich, H. B. *Origins of American Scientists* Chicago: University of Chicago Press, 1953.

Liddell Hart, B. H. *The Red Army.* New York: Harcourt, Brace & World Inc., 1956.

Lynd, Albert. *Quackery in the Public Schools.* New York: Grosset & Dunlap, Inc., 1956.

Mayer, Martin. *The Schools.* New York: Harper & Brothers, 1961.

Miller, John D. *Financing Higher Education in America.* New York: Columbia University Press, 1952.

Rickover, Hyman G. *Education and Freedom.* New York: E. P. Dutton & Company, 1959.

Rudd, Augustin G. *Bending the Twig.* New York: Bookmailer, Inc., 1957.

Trace, Arthur S., Jr. *What Ivan Knows That Johnny Doesn't.* New York: Random House, 1961.

22

Seven Imperatives of Survival

THE PROBLEMS THAT HAVE BEEN DESCRIBED IN THE FOREGOING chapters constitute a moral and spiritual obligation to the future that is quite without precedent or parallel. Other generations have inherited crises, wars, revolutions, and social upheavals in which profound spiritual changes have been involved. This generation, however, has become responsible for preserving the political, moral, economic, and cultural progress of the centuries. The citizens of the world a hundred years from now will live as slaves or as free men, depending upon the fidelity, devotion, and discernment of the American people and their government during the next twenty-five years. To ignore or to underestimate even one can be fatal.

1. It is absolutely imperative that we shall recognize the issue with which we are confronted as being that of the survival of our Christian civilization—nothing less!

Two well-known American citizens visited Russia during the summer of 1959, and upon their return each was invited to report their experiences and offer their observations. They had not traveled together; they were unknown to each other; there was no collusion between them. Yet both speakers opened their addresses with a series of almost identical statements: "I have returned from a very moving experience, and in simple honesty I must tell you that we are in a war to the finish. *And we can lose!*"

It is well-nigh impossible for the average American to think in terms of defeat. Since 1776 the American tradition has been that of victory. We have lost battles, but never a war. With the exception of a single instance—Washington, D.C., in the War of 1812 —no American city has ever suffered damage at the hands of any foreign invader. No nation in history has ever been so delivered from war's desolation. I hold as a grim treasure a splinter from a shell which exploded in an oil field along the California coast in 1942, only a few weeks following Pearl Harbor. It was fired from a

Japanese submarine a mile or two offshore and fell among the oil wells without doing any damage. That shell and four others from the same salvo are the only enemy projectiles ever to have fallen on the Pacific coast of the United States mainland.

The time has come, however, when necessity compels us to face the facts, no matter how dire they may be. We are not dealing with fiction or fancy. We are confronted by an implacable foe who has worked out all his logistical problems, planned his strategy, commandeered his resources, calculated all the risks, and has his commanders on the field. All this he has done without the slightest semblance of stealth, subterfuge, or ambiguity. The only uncertainty is his timetable.

His program has been announced quite frankly, and since 1919 it has been published repeatedly. In that year Stalin announced, "The world has split into two irreconcilable camps: the camp of imperialism and the camp of socialism." [1] In 1947 Andrei Zhdanov, the Russian cultural commissar spoke for the Soviets, saying that the "imperialist camp" was led by the United States and that the "anti-imperialist camp" was led by the U.S.S.R. and "the countries of the new democracy" and that between the two there could be no reconciliation. [2] In 1959 the Communist Party of the Soviet Union announced that "there are two world systems: capitalism, which is breathing its last, and socialism, which is brimming over with a growing vital force and enjoys the support of the working people of all countries." [3] In 1957 Khrushchev, in explaining his doctrine of peaceful coexistence to a Soviet audience, told them that we cannot coexist eternally. Upon his return from the summit conference in Vienna, June, 1961, President Kennedy reported that the Russian Premier "believes the world will move his way without resort to force." In tens of thousands of public schools in both Russia and China little children hear it said day after day that the imperialists are doomed and that according to the scientific principles of history they are destined to disappear and to be supplanted by the Communist state. This doctrine is accepted by every Communist party in the world and by every card-carrying Communist no matter what his race or color may be.

[1] Stalin, *Works* (Moscow: Foreign Languages Publishing House, 1953), IV, 243.
[2] "On the International Situation," *Political Affairs* (December, 1947).
[3] Resolution of the twenty-first Congress of the Communist Party of the U.S.S.R.

In two terrible situations—shocking beyond all the powers of any historian to describe—the Communist world has served brutal notice on the Free World as to what may be expected. In Hungary and in Tibet we have had previews of precisely what Nikita Khrushchev meant when he said, "We must push them into their graves."

What Stalin concealed behind a cryptic smile; what Lenin, before him, spelled out mostly for Communist consumption, Khrushchev has broadcast to the world. We can no longer avoid knowing the score. He has told it in words and revealed it in actions. His words, to be sure, are still designed to confuse; but his actions speak louder—and more unmistakably—than words. We can no longer doubt Communist intentions.[4]

There has been a vast reluctance on the part of the Free World to accept the plain statements of the Communist spokesmen. To continue to shut our eyes and stop our ears is to seal the doom of our Christian civilization!

2. *It is absolutely imperative that we recognize the fact that we are already at war.*

Marching hosts, waving flags, thundering cannon, and the stench of high explosives in the air have so long served as identifications of war that it is difficult for the peace-loving man or nation to recognize the incriminating possibilities of the modern conflict. War has taken on a whole new series of characteristics before our very eyes. Vast struggles are going on, upon the issues of which the fate of millions hangs, and all the while there is the danger that the justice-loving individual may be utterly unaware of the deadly seriousness of the contest or of the real issues involved. A whole new strategy is being employed, as a result of which sweeping victories are being chalked up by the Communist forces. Government after government has been destroyed and state after state has come under the dominance of Communist powers without one army going into battle. Economic, pedagogical, psychological, philosophical, and propaganda weapons are producing results just as spectacular as any that could be produced with intercontinental ballistic missiles.

[4] Harry and Bonaro Overstreet, *The War Called Peace* (New York: W. W. Norton & Company, 1961), p. 7.

Trade agreements, foreign aid, financial credit, selected markets, dumping of surpluses, infiltrations, guerrilla wars, racial prejudices, perferential tariffs, tourism, contrived demonstrations, social discontent, university scholarships, synthetics, student revels—these and other means just as offensive and effective have become accredited weapons in national arsenals. A student mob on a beach may be as serious a defeat as the sinking of a submarine. The clearance of an accused lyncher by an all-white jury can have the effect of driving 200,000 men of color into the arms of the Communists in Asia or Africa.

I recall with grave concern the profoundly disturbing effect I saw produced inside the highest echelon of an Asiatic government by a resolution adopted by less than half a hundred students relative to the admission of Red China to the United Nations. Only the wisdom of the American ambassador and the calm counsel of two trusted American citizens prevented the matter from becoming an "incident." In another instance a resolution adopted by twelve people meeting as a committee in a small church committee room was announced in a screaming headline in a great Asiatic city.

A sentry who allows an enemy to slip through the lines under cover of darkness may do his country less damage than a thoughtless dozen citizens with a series of half-baked resolutions. Living in a fishbowl world lays a heavy obligation upon even the humblest and most inconspicuous of us. The war in which we are engaged has thrust every citizen and every organization into the front lines of the nation's defenses.

3. It is absolutely imperative that we recognize the science of brainwashing as the diabolical thing it is and that we resist it with all the intelligence with which we are endowed.

In spite of the fact that Pavlov was determinedly opposed to the Communist philosophy, that he was introduced into Russian affairs by Nikolai Lenin, and that he stood at one time in grave danger of being liquidated because of his criticism of the regime, his scientific findings have provided the practical base for the most monstrous assault ever made on the mind and soul of the race.

It cannot be stressed too strongly that there is a contrived program just underneath the recurrent crises with which we have had had to deal. By arousing fears, threatening nuclear attacks, continuing testings, stirring up discontent, propagandizing U2 incidents, scuttling summit conferences, stimulating riots and demonstrations, demanding revisions of United Nations procedures, attacking the secretary general, threatening peace treaties with East Germany, meddling in trouble spots, fishing in muddy waters, and dispatching arms to guerrilla bands Khrushchev had succeeded in keeping the world distraught and the Free World forces off balance. The Berlin issue, the shelling of Matsu and Quemoy, disorderly demonstrations in the United Nations Assembly, walkouts of satellites, and intermittent threats of intervention in behalf of "oppressed peoples" are all calculated to create anxiety and uncertainty among the peoples of the Free World; these in turn being expected to result in concessions, disunity, dissension, and further retreats. Negotiations, conferences, and diplomatic missions are all calculated in terms of the tensions they can provoke and the weariness they can induce.

The process being applied to the world is identical in its psychological structure with the studied techniques of the brainwashers who set out to bring individuals to the state of "nervous collapse." The global results can be much the same.

It will be of great advantage, therefore, if we study the procedures of the psychiatrists who have ministered to the brainwashed in the prison camps. In this connection it is profoundly interesting to discover that almost without exception, they regard religious convictions and spiritual disciplines as being among their most valuable allies. It is as if there were an ally inside the personality of the deeply religious man which serves as a solid wall of defense against brainwashing.

No church will ever render a greater service to its members than when it strengthens and deepens the Christian faith of the people. No preacher in his pulpit will render his people any greater service than when he assists them to "believe" and to venture out on their own faith. With the world threatened as it is, to preach on a petty theme is to betray one's self, one's people, and one's faith. Economic and political survival are dependent upon a victorious religious faith.

During the thirties and the early forties the Communist Party of the United States—at the instigation of Moscow—made a sustained and determined effort to infiltrate the churches and the ranks of the clergy. Moscow had long understood, quite correctly, the diametrical opposition of the Christian philosophy to Marx's scientific principles of history, and the practical politicians among the Soviets were well aware of the pivotal position of religion in the life of the American people. In Communist councils it was agreed that some dent must be made upon the churches or the task of building a strong Party would be doubly difficult. With the exception of an occasional individual and a few who were quickly discredited, however, no impression was made.[5] The whole was an open confession that a convinced Christian and a dedicated church represent an impassable barrier in the way of any effort to popularize Communism.

The Christian Church will make its greatest contribution to the Free World's survival when it is most effective in deepening the moral convictions and strengthening the religious faith of the people. A vital religious faith has no competitor as a life preserver in the presence of Communism, but we must forever deal with the real fundamentals.

4. *It is absolutely imperative that parliamentary and constitutional government shall be maintained on the earth.*

It is regrettable that the attention of the American people is not called more frequently to the thrilling scene enacted on board the "Mayflower" the night prior to the landing of the Pilgrims on the rocky shore of New England. There it was that the institution of parliamentary government was launched on the North American continent as seventy-four courageous individuals stepped forward to sign the Mayflower Compact. In doing so they agreed (1) that they would enact just laws by which they would be governed, and (2) that they bound themselves in the most solemn fashion to obey those laws which they, themselves, enacted. In these two pledges there are all the germs of democratic government.

With the institution of parliamentary government gone every individual would be at the mercy of the state. No man would be allowed to become a member of any organization of any kind except by the permission of the Party. His lunch club, his sports committee, his cultural society, his religious group, or his educational

[5] For a thoroughly documented report on this whole matter, see Ralph Lord Roy, *Communism in the Churches* (New York: Harcourt, Brace & World, Inc., 1960).

association would be subject to the most searching scrutiny at the hands of the government, and every such grouping would be so infiltrated that there would be no independence of movement or of judgment.

5. *It is absolutely imperative that democratic principles shall be employed in the defense of democracy.*

During the period that I served as editor of a religious magazine I received a manuscript from a well-known professor entitled "Hitler Is Where Hitlerism Is." The thesis of the article was that even a democracy is in danger of becoming fascist when it stoops to the use of fascist methods to achieve democratic ends. It is not the personality of a dictator that makes a dictatorship. A dictatorial administrator is capable of manipulating democratic processes in fascist fashion. The techniques of the police state seem to offer short cuts in maintaining law and order, but fascist methods remain fascist—even though they are employed by officers of a democratic state.

The doctrine that every prisoner is presumed to be innocent until he has been proved guilty is a basic part of our philosophy of jurisprudence. There is no more important rule of law within the knowledge of man. The Napoleonic code presumes a man to be guilty and lays the burden of proof of innocence upon the accused. In setting up the Constitution of the United States the Founding Fathers repudiated the latter and built upon the former theory of justice, thereby making an outlaw of the whole doctrine of guilt by association.

Equality before the law, the right of trial by jury, the protection of the rights of the accused, and the sanctity of the legal process—these are the priceless possessions of the humblest and the poorest among us. To ignore or to evade the implication of these principles is to undermine the American way. Failure to respect such fundamentals has brought down upon the heads of Congressional committees, commissions, police chiefs, and even the minor courts the wrath of just men and rebukes at the hands of the United States Supreme Court. If democracy is to be preserved it must be respected by its hired servants. It is the responsibility of all godly men to join their voices in the demand that it be so.

Extremists, whether they be rightists or leftists, are capable of doing the cause of democracy great harm. Whatever their protestations of loyalty may be, those who propose to take out of the hands of the constituted authorities the responsibility for passing judgment and enforcing the law are sinners against democracy. Whenever any group of individuals, whosever they are or whatever their reasons, undertakes to apply sanctions against those with whom they disagree the cause of democracy has been turned back toward the jungle.

We have not, on the whole, achieved justice between classes, economic groups, races, or minorities. To deny any man access to employment, food, medical care, burial privileges, education, opportunity or any of the rights guaranteed by the Constitution because of race, color, religion, or social status is to fail the sacred cause of democracy.

If the Christian Church is charged with the responsibility of preaching justice in the spirit and with the courage of the Old Testament prophets, then its duty in the case of any of the exploited and the oppressed is clear. Any man exercising his democratic rights under the Constitution of the United States has a right to expect the friendly support of all those who call themselves Christian. For the Church to fail in this regard is as serious as if it were guilty of a gross theological heresy. Jesus of Nazareth once identified himself with the poor, the hungry, and the defrauded, and that identification has never been rescinded.

6. *It is absolutely imperative that the Free World continue strong.*

The war in which we find ourselves engaged puts every citizen into the front lines. The mechanic at his lathe, the engineer at his drafting board, the nurse on duty at the hospital, the trucker on the highway, the pharmacist compounding behind his screen at the prescription counter, the farmer on his tractor, the clergyman visiting the forgotten and the forlorn, the teacher standing before a room full of little ones, and the student in the library or the laboratory—we are all a vital part of the nation's defenses.

To delay the testing of a missile by the practice of featherbedding or to defraud the public by a deceitful war contract is to serve Communism more effectively than taking to the soapboxes and haranguing the passing throng. To do less than one's best among the testtubes is to fail as an American as surely as if one were to prove a

coward in a foxhole. To pick snap courses in college, to skimp one's
work at the cannery, to gouge one's neighbor behind the counter
at the grocery store, to preach disunity and suspicion from the pulpit, to indulge in any type of bigotry, to array one group of honest
men against another group of honest men, to sell one's vote on election day, to vote for a proposal just because it is good for you, to
destroy public property, to participate in any way in any bribetaking
—to be guilty of any such things is to play into the hands of the
Communists.

The responsibility for the moral and spiritual training of the
young has never rested more heavily upon the Christian Church
than it does today in the midst of "this war called peace." The
crumbling walls of the American home impose a burden upon the
public and the church-school teacher he has never known before.
What shall it profit a child if he is able to recite the names of the
kings and prophets of Judah and Israel if he cannot keep his fingers
off other people's property?

The obligation that rests upon the local congregation to provide
adequate facilities and equipment for effective scientific education
has never been heavier. Money saved on educational equipment
may have to be spent on juvenile courts and schools of correction.

7. *It is absolutely imperative that good religion shall be an active
ally of democratic government.*

Democracy is a bold adventure of the spiritual into the realm of
the political. It can be a success only in those lands and among
those people who are devoted to the proposition that man has been
made in the image of God and that the individual is the supreme
unit of value in our civilization.

It is not enough that a congregation shall be instructed in sound
doctrine. It is one of the first duties of the Church to thrust into
the life of the nation and the community a body of citizens who
are socially sensitive, politically moral, individually dependable, and
of unimpeachable integrity.

If the Christian Church retreats from this world, threatened as it
is by Communism and totalitarianism, and takes refuge in theology
it will deserve the terrible fate that is certain to descend upon it.
If, on the other hand, it is able to supply the motives, the inspira-
tion, the inner power, and the convictions that fortify men's souls

in the face of the impending struggle it will have earned its own immortality.

Suggestions for Further Reading

For further reading in the fields suggested by the foregoing text the reader is referred to the bibliography indicated at the close of Chapters 12, 18, 20, and 23, for all these fields overlap. In addition to the suggestions made in connection with previous chapters, however, the following books are listed because of their general interest and their relatedness to the theme of this chapter.

Buckley, William F., Jr. *The Committee and It's Critics; a Calm Review of the House Committee on Un-American Activities.* New York: G. P. Putnam's Sons, 1962.

Conant, James B. *Slums and Suburbs.* New York: McGraw-Hill Book Company, Inc., 1961.

James, Daniel. *Cuba; the First Soviet Satellite in the Americas.* New York: Avon Book Division of the Hearst Corporation, 1961.

Kraft, Joseph. *The Struggle for Algeria.* Garden City, N.Y.: Doubleday & Company, Inc., 1961.

Rivero, Nicolas. *Castro's Cuba: An American Dilemma.* Washington, D.C.: Robert B. Luce, Inc., 1962.

Smith, Robert F. *The United States and Cuba.* New York: Twayne Publishers, Inc., 1960.

Wise, David and Ross, Thomas B. *The U-2 Affair.* New York: Random House, 1960.

23

If the Communists Take Over
in the United States

LET IT BE SAID AT THE OUTSET THAT THE QUESTION RAISED IN THE title of this chapter is no literary figure of speech. We are not dealing with any purely academic issue. Instead, we are looking at a series of deliberate statements by Communist leaders in which they have stated their ultimate objectives in the clearest possible terms. It is the goal toward which every Communist strategy is aimed—the take-over of the entire world.

In November, 1956, at a public reception in Moscow for Prime Minister Wladyslaw Gomulka of Poland, which was attended by scores of diplomats and high ranking officials representing Western governments, Nikita Khrushchev announced, "History is on our side. We will bury you!" Approximately one year later, in 1957, in the course of a lengthy address to a huge gathering of Soviet officials and plain people, Khrushchev stated the case in language that is unmistakably clear. Said he: "We cannot coexist eternally. One of us must go to his grave. We do not want to go to the grave. They don't want to go to their graves either. So what must be done? We must push them to their graves." [1]

In these two statements we have perfect examples of the highly dramatic and graphic speech of a peasant, but the figures represent a deadly seriousness. They are as exact as if they had been phrased in strict legal or scholastic terms. The ultimate goal of Communism is the destruction of democracy. Let us look, then, at the inescapable implications of these two blunt and brutal announcements.

Khrushchev was reasserting Marx's unalterable belief in the scientific principles of history. This means that humanity is helpless in

[1] Quoted by General John E. Hull (Ret.), "Trade with Soviet Russia," *Soviet Economic Challenge: Proceedings of the Fifth National Military-Industrial Conference* (Chicago: The Institute for American Strategy, 1959), p. 19.

the face of the oncoming of Communism—that to oppose it is as stupid as trying to outwit the law of gravity. Exactly as the Christian believes in the ultimate triumph of the will of God the Communist believes in the ultimate supremacy of the scientific principles. At the same time Khrushchev was notifying the world that if it became necessary to "push" democracy to its grave the Communists were prepared to do that very thing. That means war to the death! In addition, it should be noted that "the grave" in Communist terms means "the end." To the Communist, at least, the matter is perfectly plain. Either Communism or democracy must be destroyed, and the Communists have boldly declared their purpose to "bury" democracy. If they should win, what then might we expect should happen to the United States, for example?

1. *The free press would be destroyed.*

This is not a matter of frenzied prediction. It has been a matter of common observation. In every land where there has been a Communist take-over the first object of attack has been the media of communications. Within thirty minutes after Fidel Castro arrived in Havana the radio stations were all in his possession. Within a matter of days he had taken over the newspapers. From that moment on the Cuban people heard nothing except that which the dictator chose to tell them. No opinion has been expressed publicly which was in any way in disagreement with the policies or the pronouncements of Castro.

The first objective of any Communist take-over is the mind of the nation that is being taken over. To control the thinking of a nation one must control the media by which ideas get through to the minds of the people. Within a matter of minutes—or at most hours—every radio, television, and newspaper would be in the hands of the Communists. This would extend to all house organs, parish papers, denominational publications, Sunday-school literature, magazines, scientific periodicals, and trade journals. In those papers that might be published by the Communist government every headline, feature, cartoon, and illustration would be dictated by official government authorities. The free press is one of the bulwarks of democracy. Communism cannot endure it!

2. *All freedom of assembly would be ended.*

No public meetings of any kind would be permitted without official approval. This rule would apply to every type of gathering—

religious, professional, social, political, scientific, or recreational. This would mean the end of all fraternal orders, lunch clubs, women's clubs, garden clubs, or any other type of organization where programs are presented or issues are discussed. If any group wanted to meet for any reason it would be necessary to get official permission, to submit to the authorities a description of the program that was to be presented, and to consent to the injection of a period of indoctrination into the program, this to be furnished by and supervised by the government. Even a dinner party consisting of as many as ten guests would be investigated and might be subject to suppression.

On the other hand, tens of thousands of meetings would be scheduled by the Party, attendance upon which would be compulsory. The programs of such meetings would be long harangues on the subject of Marxism, from which there could be no possible escape.

3. All forms of constitutional government would be outlawed.

Any constitution represents an agreement between the government and the people in which the rights of all are described and the duties outlined. Under a Communist regime no individual has any rights. Therefore a constitution which recognized rights would be null and void. The American Bill of Rights, for example, consists of a series of prohibitions imposed on the government in the interests of the people. Each one proposes to protect the people *against* their government. Such a concept would be intolerable in the case of a Communist take-over.

From the very moment, then, that the Communists came to power the Constitution of the United States, the constitutions of the various states, and even city charters would become null and void. All business that had to be transacted for the public would be handled by the Communist committee in charge, in the selection of which the ordinary citizens would have no voice whatever.

4. The right of trial by jury would be liquidated.

According to the Napoleonic code, under which Russia has conducted her criminal trials for almost a hundred years, the accused is assumed to be guilty until he can prove that he is innocent. Under the code which is the instrument of government in American and British trials the accused is assumed to be innocent until the prosecution proves him guilty. Under the Russian Communist code the case is decided in the privacy of the Party committee room, and the judge executes the orders. There are no juries consisting of a man's "peers." Even his defense attorney is not permitted to cross-examine the witnesses produced by the prosecution, and it sometimes happens that he does not know what the law is under which his client is being tried until the court opens and the charge is made.

5. *All rights of private property are to be repudiated.*

Karl Marx assigned all the evils and injustices of this world to the "crime of private property." It is, in the Communist's vocabulary, the sum of all villainies. Therefore, liberation of any people means the appropriation of their private property by the political authorities.

This would mean that all securities would immediately become valueless. Insurance policies, deeds of trust, mortgages, and titles to property would all become scraps of paper. No individual or corporation would be allowed to collect any outstanding debt. Corporations, estates, foundations, endowments, and trusts would be liquidated in favor of the state. Communism has not come as long as there are any vestiges of private property remaining.

6. *There would be no free elections.*

One of the first promises Fidel Castro made to the Cuban people was that "free elections" were to be held as soon as practicable. Two years following his take-over, he announced that none are necessary, and therefore none are to be held. Theoretically, there can be no free election under a Communist regime, for the simple reason that the regime is always right—that is, it has followed the Marxist line—and according to Communist logic any popular election would be no better than a waste of time. No matter how such an election might go it would in no way change the pattern or the program of the government.

7. *There could be no independent organizations.*

No group of citizens would be allowed to organize for any purpose without the consent of the government, and in giving that consent the government would require that the officers chosen would be acceptable, the programs approved, and the objectives satisfactory to the state. All such groups as the Y.M.C.A., Y.W.C.A., Boy Scouts, Girl Scouts, Camp Fire Girls, lunch clubs, fraternal orders, charitable organizations, recreational clubs, social organizations, college fraternities and sororities, labor unions, trade associations, professional societies, voluntary health associations, farmers' granges, and co-operatives would be required to disband or conform to the government regulations as to officers and programs. There could not be even so much as a motor cycle club, a ski club, or a little-league baseball organization that was not Communist approved.

8. No independent opinion could be tolerated.

In every land in which a Communist take-over has occurred there is an official Party "line." This represents the last word in finance, political purpose, economic administration, education, and social philosophy. Just as it is impossible to add to the octave or the spectrum, so it is impossible for the private citizen to deviate from the official line in either his private conduct or conversation. The one true interpretation of life has been provided by Marx, according to Communist reasoning, and therefore the one scientific attitude possible is to conform.

9. Free choice of profession by individuals would be outlawed.

No youth would be allowed to decide what profession he would follow, for that would be decided for him by the Party on the basis of the anticipated national needs. He would not even be allowed to decide whether or not he would attend the university. If he happened to be in the top 25 per cent in the schools up until the time he was 14 he would automatically go into the group that was destined for the university. If he were in the lower 75 per cent he would be assigned to the labor battalions on the basis of the current needs for workers. Similarly, adults would be assigned to their industrial responsibilities as soldiers are assigned to their military duties.

10. All free inquiry would come under the ban.

There could be no local "studies" of social or moral conditions permitted. There could be nowhere any free discussion of matters of state, government, health, education, economics, or politics. In every case the Party would decide the matter, and "discussions" would consist of a description and a memorizing of the official decisions. The Communist state does not permit itself to be questioned or analyzed.

11. We would be subjected to a program of twenty-four-hour-a-day brainwashing.

We would never be allowed to free ourselves from slogans, loudspeakers, official indoctrination, discussions, and fear. We would live under a government of terror in an atmosphere of frightened suspicion. The whole purpose of the government would be to remold us in the pattern of the Marxist man.

12. Absolute freedom of worship could not be permitted.

Worship services might be permitted, but the matters with which the church could concern itself would be strictly limited. There could be no Sunday schools, religious education, church training classes, spiritual instruction, or evangelism of any form. No church gatherings of any kind, except for worship approved by the government, would be permitted. There could be no "fellowship" dinners, "coffee socials" following the morning service, or men's clubs' dinners. There could be no women's societies which aimed at missionary work, social service, political studies, or discussions.

13. All education would be taken over by the state.

No parent would have any choice in the matter of what schooling his child was to have, what studies he was to pursue, what texts were to be consulted, or what routines were to be followed. From the moment the child entered the door of the schoolhouse until he returned to the home fireside he would be completely beyond the reach of the parents, who would have no choice other than submission.

14. Every man's economic interests would be subject to the dictates of the government.

Any man would be limited in the matter of what he could or could not buy, he would be compelled to accept the goods that were offered and not the goods he might prefer or seek. He would be spied upon, threatened on occasion and forever reminded that he was the property of the state. Only within certain narrow limits would he be permitted to save for his old age; in everything he would be regimented and regularized.

15. The members of the Communist party would become the new elite.

The only ones in the community who might seek or expect any special favors would be those members of the Party whose credentials were above reproach. There is no caste system anywhere in the world so hard or so closely guarded as that which exists in every land in which the Communists have taken over. It is almost true that a card-carrying Communist is the only man in any Communist country who has any "rights" which protect him in any aspect of his life or activities.

Let any reader compare the foregoing description with the conditions now existing in his hometown and he will understand at least in some small part what a Communist take-over would imply for him.

These harsh certainties are not the product of an overactive imagination. The reader is invited to compare the items enumerated with the observable facts in Cuba, Tibet, Hungary, or today's China. The stern realities immediately become evident.

24

What Does the Church Have to Say?

HENRY WARD BEECHER WAS FOND OF TELLING THE STORY OF A LITTLE dog that accompanied him when he made his pastoral rounds in a rural community in Indiana during his first years in the ministry. One afternoon it came upon a chipmunk exploring among some bushes at the side of the road and chased it for some distance along a stone wall. The chipmunk was not actually worried, for its fat little pursuer never really threatened it, and besides, the wild thing knew where there was a hole in the fence.

When the small dog finally reached the hole through which the chipmunk had slipped he found his way completely barred. The nimble little creature was out of danger and already exploring on the other side of the fence, quite without concern. Meanwhile the dog was reduced to the necessity of barking futilely at the hole.

The interesting thing about the whole affair, according to Dr. Beecher, was the fact that every time they passed that way during the weeks that followed the dog took up the chase again when he came in sight of the wall. With all the excitement he would have invested in a new adventure he chased the chipmunk, now long gone, exactly as he had the first time.

One of the first duties of the Christian Church is to be contemporaneous. If it is to be a saving agent in any generation it must be immersed in the problems of that generation. Unfortunately, as in the case of the dog that chased the chipmunk, the modern Church is spending altogether too much time and money fighting battles that do not need to be refought. As one keen observer commented, "The Church is spending too much time talking to itself, and the psychologists say that the individual who does that is on his way to a mental ward." The first responsibility of the Church, therefore, is to speak to a world that is in the midst of the problems and confusion that go with the dawn of the Atomic Age.

It is quite possible that we have imputed to the Christians of the first Christian century virtues and piety beyond their actual deserts. It has been easy to idealize them, although the New Testament makes it perfectly plain that they were in many ways imperfect. They have, however, won the acclaim of succeeding centuries because they confronted the issues, problems, and terrors of their own century and discharged their obligations with honor in spite of the price they were compelled to pay. As Dr. Halford E. Luccock said on one occasion, "It is impossible to read the Acts of the Apostles without getting the impression that those early Christians were fighting for something."

One of the colorful identifications of the apostolic Church was the fact that it never hesitated if it became necessary to walk right up to trouble and face it. Those first-century Christians never seemed to worry about whether or not they were making a good impression on the newspapers, the chamber of commerce, the labor federations, the philosophy departments at the universities, or the secret service of the Roman government. As Alan Walker, the Australian evangelist puts it, "They often seemed to be out of step with their times, but that was because they were listening to the drum beats of another drummer."

It was because the Christians attacked the evils of their times that they made a difference in their generations. They wasted little time on the chipmunks that were a generation gone, nor did they fritter away their time waiting for the chipmunks that were expected to put in an appearance a generation after they were gone. Instead, they laid siege to the evils of their own times with all the vigor and conviction of which they were capable.

A second characteristic of the Christians of the first Christian century was the fact that they proposed to lay siege to the whole world. As John Wesley said, some seventeen hundred years later, "The world is my parish," so those first-century Christians took their Lord at his word and laid their plans for capturing the whole world.

It is a little difficult for certain segments of the modern Church to understand the responsibility of the Church for speaking to the whole world. There are still those among us who have "no interest in foreign missions; we have enough to do right here at home." It is so easy to think the obligations of the Church are confined to one's own neighborhood.

Jesus of Nazareth settled that issue, however, long before he went to Calvary. The word "world" was forever on his lips—"ye are the light of the world," "woe unto the world," "the end of the world," shall be preached "in all the world," "go ye into all the world and preach," "all the kingdoms of the world," "I am the light of the world," "light is come into the world."

To the Jerusalem Sadducees—3,000 of them, all living inside Jerusalem—the world ended at the walls of the city. To the Pharisees, the world was bounded on the east by the Jordan River, on the north by Capernaum, on the west by the Mediterranean, and on the south by the desert. Inside the land there was an enclave of about 75,000 Samaritans—into whose territory no Jew ever entered except under dire necessity—who were even more foreign than the Romans themselves. They were in no sense a part of the Pharisees' world. For Jesus, however, the world extended as far east as the sunlight, as far north as the unknown, as far west as the setting sun, and as far south as the heat of the desert, and it included everything in between—even the Samaritans. The message he came to deliver to the world was for all men, including those his fellow Jews despised. The Church that stops short of Jesus' boundaries is one that has not followed its Lord all the way.

This issue of "all the world" arose inside the Church before it was fifty years old. The Jewish wing of Christendom, living in Jerusalem, was determined to keep the movement inside Judaism. It was insisted that all converts to Christ must, first of all, become Jews via circumcision, before they could be considered eligible for membership in the Church. The apostle Paul led the forces favoring emancipation, and after a vigorous debate, they carried the day. Thereafter the Church had to be considered a world institution and Christianity a world religion. As William Booth, the founder of the Salvation Army, put it hundreds of years later, the Christians were to "go after the last man." If those orders were valid for the first century they are likewise valid for our generation. They have never been rescinded.

An additional difficulty with which the Church is beset is its responsibility for speaking truthfully, bravely, and hopefully to the age in which it finds itself. It is not a question of merely living at peace with one's surroundings. The Church is dedicated to the proposition that if there is anything evil in those surroundings it must be changed and that the Church has been delegated of God to demand the change.

Strangely enough, it is precisely at this point that the most threatening fissure appears in the structure of the modern Church. There are those, for example, whose chief concern is the second coming of their Lord. This is an event, for them, still in the future. A revivified Jesus is to appear and sit in judgment upon this world. Those who have been saved—that is, those who have experienced a certain standard type of conversion—are to be the elite and the elect, favored ones who are to share in the triumph that is to be supernaturally achieved.

Then there are those who, bewildered by the complexities of the times, plead for a return to the "simple gospel of the simple age." They seem to hope that by shutting their eyes to the problems of the day they may escape all responsibility for helping solve them. Theirs is a faith that holds aloof, that requires no "blood, sweat, and tears." To be saved means to be preserved.

Among the popular slogans of the day inside certain religious circles is the exhortation "back to the Bible." Of course the scriptures are the fountainhead of our gospel, but if we return to the scriptures with any real understanding of the text we will discover that the scriptural greats were in every case men who preached to their own generations. Isaiah dealt with a series of political problems that developed during the half century he was God's accredited representative in Jerusalem. Amos was speaking neither to Moses nor to Augustine when he cried out, "Let justice flow down like a mighty stream." Instead he was speaking to Amaziah, the high priest of the Bethel shrine, and to the reigning king then on the throne. He was preaching to a land-grabbing, liquor-drinking, labor-oppressing, woman-despoiling, peasant-robbing, secular generation which believed it could bribe God to forget its rapacity and paganism by piling the altars high with lambs, sheep, goats, and oxen to be burned by the holy fires. It was the generation of which he was a part that was the target for Amos' indictment. He neither raked over the cold ashes of a burned out fire nor muddled through green wood that would not burn until next winter. He was called to preach to his own generation, and he condemned the sins that came under his own eyes.

It is to this generation—the first of the Atomic Age—that the Church of this generation is to preach. That preaching must deal with the question of raped land, hungry millions, exploited races, diseased multitudes, wretched masses, delinquent youth, truant parents, ignorant nations, oppressed minorities, and all those others in whom the image of God is blurred. The self-righteous and the self-centered must be called to judgment. Even some highly moral people will have to be condemned for keeping silent in the presence of popular immoralities. The priests and the Levites who pass by on the other side of the road must be identified as to what they really are—sinners in the sight of God. The bomb testers must be summoned to stand trial before the judgments of the Eternal. So also must the racists, the hatemongers, and the defilers of the public mind.

Such a message at such a time as ours calls for spiritual statesmanship of the highest order and courage unmatched and unprecedented. Likewise, it calls for a theology that is rooted and grounded in human experience.

To begin with, the Church of the living God *must believe that God has some opinions concerning this world.* It must believe that God has been outraged by our wastage of life and resources. Surely the Most High cannot be indifferent to the fact that the great scientific achievement of all time—the greatest secret God has ever allowed to be revealed to the minds and hands of men—has been dedicated to the frightful business of dealing death! That which is capable of lifting loads off the backs of men, restoring health to broken bodies, and clearing the way to health and plenty dedicated to the black art of killing! Can any honest man believe that a God who would come to this world, take on the disguise of a village carpenter, and be known as Jesus of Nazareth would have no concern for a world that has just come into possession of atomic energy and is about to do itself to death?

Does the Church really believe God has a word of admonition, guidance, and hope for such a generation as ours? It may hold steadfastly to the belief that the faith was once delivered to the saints, but does it really believe that this same faith is being delivered to the modern saints? If so, who are the saints to whom the faith has been delivered during the period of the last ninety days? It is to those who are sure they can pass a theological examination with flying colors, thus proving their "orthodoxy"? Is it to those who have exhausted themselves in "much serving" in the Lord's kitchen at the Church? Is it to those who put theological jigsaw puzzles together behind the doors of libraries and psychological conferences?

Suppose, for example, that all the kings, prime ministers, presidents, dictators, and rulers of the earth could be convened in one vast convocation. And suppose the Church were given the privilege of addressing them for one hour. What would it say? If it repeated last Sunday's sermons, how impressive would that be? What difference would it make in the minds of the rulers? With what authority could the Church claim to speak?

Suppose in the second instance, that not one sermon were to be preached from any pulpit in the land next Sunday. How much of a loser would the first Atomic Age generation be?

Who among us is prepared to go before the world with the desperation of Amos, saying, "The Lord said to me, 'Go, preach to my people'?" Who of us is sure his preachments are of God? Who of us is completely assured that the Lord God is standing beside him, endorsing his words as he preaches? Who of us is so firmly rooted in our confidence in God that we are prepared to speak truth to the great, wisdom to the sophisticated, humility to the learned, and judgment to the self-righteous?

The average sanctuary is apt to be a safe retreat behind stained glass. The clerical robe suggests detachment and otherworldliness— a certain ancient splendor unrelated to the struggles and agonies of the hungry and the hardpressed. The worshipers come to be comforted. As a young man from India remarked after visiting a series of American churches, "I was greatly impressed by the fact that the pews were all cushioned. There seemed even to be cushions in the sermons." Charles Ray Goff, for many years the pastor of the famous Chicago Temple, said: "There is very grave danger that the shepherd of the flock shall become the petted lamb."

The modern preacher is forever tempted to comfort those who are not afflicted, to forgive the impenitent, to chastise sinners with the same fervor one would display in applying the lash to a good customer, and to keep out of politics and economics when the politicians are guilty of gross sins against the people. One leading layman in a certain congregation expressed it rather neatly when he said, "I don't want to hear about the troubles of the world when I go to church. Hell! I want something spiritual."

The issue then which confronts the Church in this first generation of the Atomic Age can be stated very easily. Are we to allow the global struggle for human rights, social justice, and world peace to intrude upon the calm and the confidence of our sanctuaries?

The facts that have been presented in the foregoing chapters must have made it plain that we are living in the midst of a crisis, when all the hard-won gains of the centuries stand in jeopardy. For the Church and the clergy to hold aloof from the grim and grimy task of saving eternal values is to forfeit all our claims on the loyalty of truly righteous men. The Church will have no right to claim any divine commission if, in this hour of destiny, it withdraws behind Gothic windows and makes of its pulpit a bombproof shelter.

There are many facets of the faith upon which godly men of all shades of political and theological opinion can agree. The supreme moral authority of God, to which all governments are subject; the spiritual interpretation of life; the divinity and dignity of man; the sanctity of the individual; human rights as against property rights, love against hate; the justice and judgments of God; the Christian concept of democracy, the responsibility of the strong for the weak; the purposes of God and the duties of man; the freedom of the human spirit upon which the state dare not intrude—these are the common heritage of all mankind, and these represent ideals to which all democratic governments are pledged in defense. To preserve them the Church is called of God.

Throughout vast areas of the earth these holy things are being trampled under the feet of regimented and brainwashed millions. The plight of Hungary and Tibet summons righteous men everywhere to the defense of human liberties. So also does the fate of twenty-three little boys, all under the age of nine, whose names appear on a plaque in a coal-mining village near Manchester, England, followed by this frightful sentence: "In the year 1932 the Lord terribly visited the colliery of Robert Clark and the above named were called to meet their Maker."

The message of the Church for this present generation is extremely simple, in spite of the confusion with which it is sometimes presented. "*The Eternal God is sitting in judgment upon the ways of men and the prevailing mood of our society.*"

If it is the duty of the Christian churches to preach the gospel to all the world then the Church is obliged to take a sympathetic attitude toward young nations struggling to be born. Just as patience is needed in dealing with teen-agers inside our families, so patience is needed in dealing with political infants inside the family of nations.

The Christian Church is assigned to the task of preaching a gospel of love to a world saturated with hate. One does not travel far in either Asia, Africa, or South America without being made aware of the violent antipathies everywhere in evidence. The United Nations is working through at least twenty great agencies in behalf of goodwill around the earth, but the bitterness of the races and nations is running ahead of judgment and discretion. In spite of all the collective efforts in the direction of goodwill the world continues to bleed profusely from wounds newly inflicted by hatred. Never has a healing ministry—spiritual as well as physical—been so badly needed. Christian evangelism must take on an entirely new coloration. It is not sufficient for several hundred students in a mission college to raise their hands in a public meeting, thus indicating their willingness to be "followers of Christ." A matured and seasoned Christian is produced only by a protracted process of education and training. This means a measured and disciplined spiritual experience.

The brainwashing applied to the millions by Russia and China is designed to produce a remolded individual, fitted to meet the demands a Communist world will lay upon him. Is the Church prepared to remold the lives of men and refashion them in the likeness of God? Can it persuade itself that it is doing the will of God if it is not remolding the lives of its worshipers?

These, then, are questions the Christian Church must answer as it enters the Atomic Age. These are inescapable issues with which it is confronted.

Does the Church really believe that God is trying to speak to this world?

Does the Church know what he is trying to say?

Has the Church failed to understand the will of God because it has been listening too attentively to competitive voices?

Is what the Church is saying in any way similar to what God is trying to say?

Is the preacher, as he stands in the pulpit on the sabbath day, in any way sure that he is saying the things Jesus would say to this generation if he had the privilege of the preacher's pulpit?

Is the Christian pulpit furnishing any real guidance in interpreting the mind of God for this Atomic Age generation?

Is it possible to believe that the word the Church is delivering to the world will make any difference in the future that is upon us?

It was a beautiful spring morning in Minnesota as I pulled up to the curb in front of my office door at the church. Our custodian, a man of rare piety and a shrewd observer of the passing scene, was leaning against the building beside the door absorbing the crisp air and ingratiating sunshine, with remnants of the winter's snow scattered all about.

As I greeted the old man, of whom I was very fond, he responded cheerily, and then, with a twinkle in his eye, he asked, "Any late news from God this morning?"

That, if you please, is the question that is being directed at the Church today from every quarter. The Church that is sure it has such a word, need have no fear for its future.

Index